The Highest Good in the *Nicomachean Ethics* and the *Bhagavad Gītā*

Also available from Bloomsbury:

Chinese and Buddhist Philosophy in Early Twentieth-Century German Thought, by Eric S. Nelson

Comparative Philosophy without Borders, edited by Arindam Chakrabarti and Ralph Weber

Cultivating a Good Life in Early Chinese and Ancient Greek Philosophy, edited by Karyn Lai, Rick Benitez, and Hyun Jin Kim

Indian and Intercultural Philosophy, by Douglas Berger

Material Objects in Confucian and Aristotelian Metaphysics, by James Dominic Rooney

The Highest Good in the *Nicomachean Ethics* and the *Bhagavad Gītā*

Knowledge, Happiness, and Freedom

Roopen Majithia

BLOOMSBURY ACADEMIC
LONDON • NEW YORK • OXFORD • NEW DELHI • SYDNEY

BLOOMSBURY ACADEMIC
Bloomsbury Publishing Plc, 50 Bedford Square, London, WC1B 3DP, UK
Bloomsbury Publishing Inc, 1359 Broadway, 12th Floor, New York, NY 10018, USA
Bloomsbury Publishing Ireland, 29 Earlsfort Terrace, Dublin 2, D02 AY28, Ireland

BLOOMSBURY, BLOOMSBURY ACADEMIC and the Diana logo are trademarks of Bloomsbury Publishing Plc

First published in Great Britain 2024
This paperback edition published 2025

A catalogue record for this book is available from the British Library.

ISBN: HB: 978-1-3502-1509-2
PB: 978-1-3502-1513-9
ePDF: 978-1-3502-1510-8
eBook: 978-1-3502-1511-5

Typeset by Integra Software Services Pvt. Ltd.

To find out more about our authors and books visit www.bloomsbury.com and sign up for our newsletters.

In memory of my parents

Contents

Acknowledgements viii
Abbreviations ix

1 Introduction 1
2 Ethical Intentionality in the *Nicomachean Ethics* 13
3 Character, Personality, and Agency in Aristotle 35
4 The Nature of Moral Intentionality in the *Bhagavad Gītā* 59
5 Personhood in the *Bhagavad Gītā* 77
Coda 1 (to Chapters 2–5) 99
6 Ethical Content in the *Nicomachean Ethics* 105
7 Ethical Content in the *Bhagavad Gītā* 127
Coda 2 (to Chapters 6–7) 147
8 *Karma* and *Sanyāsa Yoga* in the *Bhagavad Gītā* 155
9 Active and Contemplative Lives in the *Nicomachean Ethics* 179
10 Conclusion 207

Appendix 1 219
Appendix 2 224
Bibliography 232
Index 245

Acknowledgements

I am grateful for sabbatical support from Mount Allison University in general and the department of Philosophy in particular, without which this project would not have been possible. Financial support for conference and sabbatical travel and open access funding was made possible by Mount Allison's Marjorie Young Bell fund, the Baxter fund, and the Hart-Massey-Almerrin fund, for which I am very thankful.

I am also grateful for the feedback I have received at various fora over the years including, but not limited to, the Mount Allison Philosophy's Phoenix Colloquium, The Society for Ancient Greek Philosophy's annual conference, and The Society for Asian and Comparative Philosophy's annual conference.

Finally, I would like to thank my family and especially my spouse, Pronoti, for their patience and support over the years which was crucial in bringing this project to fruition.

Abbreviations

BG	*Bhagavad Gītā*
BGB	Śankara's commentary on the *Gītā*
DA	*De Anima*
EE	*Eudemian Ethics*
MS	*Manusmṛiti*
NE	*Nicomachean Ethics*
RGB	Rāmānuja's commentary on the *Gītā*

1

Introduction

1.0 Introduction

This effort attempts to bring the *Nicomachean Ethics* and the *Bhagavad Gītā* into a cross-cultural conversation with each other on the issues of ethics, agency, and the good life. Both texts are enormously influential in and even across their respective traditions so that examining them will offer insight into their tradition's framing considerations and trajectories. We will see that despite their substantive differences, both seem to be interested in similar concerns (such as the relation of the form and content of ethical action, the nature of ethical agency, and the relation of the practical and contemplative lives in the pursuit of the highest good). Yet the focus on the priority of the individual (in Aristotle) and of the social (in the *Gītā*) shapes their responses so that they are at once irreducible yet insightful, as I hope to show.

1.1 Why These Texts?

When we think of the names of ancient ethical texts in either tradition, it is not unusual to have the *Ethics* and the *Gītā* come up. This is at least in part because of their use in universities to introduce Greek ethical ideas in particular or to introduce Brahmanism more broadly. Such use indicates not just how representative but also how formative they are of their respective traditions. Aristotle's *Ethics* is powerfully influenced by Plato and Socrates and seems to consider their ethical ideas systematically; but it is also enormously influential on the Hellenistic tradition that follows, and on later Christianity. Thinkers in early modernity seem to move away from Aristotle's model of character-driven ethics to ones that are rule-driven,[1] even if this move eventually sparks a twentieth-century revival of neo-Aristotelian virtue ethics that in turn spawns a whole range of variants.[2] The *Gītā* seems to represent a moment of synthesis in the philosophical discussions in the subcontinent between orthodox Brahmanism and various competing views; a moment that sees it gather all available resources from within the orthodoxy and bring them to bear on the practical life where it faces stiff challenges especially from early Buddhism. The ensuing syncretism—which does not seem to hesitate to borrow from competing views—has a profound impact on orthodox strains of thinking in general and on the practical front in particular. Moving forward, the text's views on the practical front seem to form the backbone of all the orthodox schools/*darśana*s even if their respective positions on other matters shape the details differently. The commentarial tradition on the *Gītā*—of which Śaṇkara's from the ninth century CE is the earliest we have even if it is not the earliest written—is healthy and from it over two hundred Sanskrit commentaries from the medieval age onwards are extant. The first translation of the work into a European language in 1785 was supported to help understand and administer the natives of the British colony better, even if it is received with more enthusiasm in Europe and especially in Germany. In the twentieth century, the text is at the center of a rallying cry for freedom from colonial rule from traditional quarters as well as from western educated ones such as Gandhi and Aurobindo.[3] Thus both these texts seem to have a profound impact on originating (at least in part by synthesizing past views) and shaping the trajectories of their respective traditions.

Moreover, while the influential nature of our texts on their respective traditions may not be in doubt, they both discuss issues (among others) that have long been of interest to me. The first concerns the nature of ethical action, broadly construed. While it is easy enough to simply focus on the action itself as many do, our texts seem to agree that the nature of what we do is shaped and even changed by why it is done. The consideration of why an action is undertaken takes us to the very heart of the nature of ethical agency and character in both our texts, even though they end up in very different places by the end of the discussion. The issue of the content of ethical action (or its "what") on the other hand, is concerned with assessing the consistency that is the advantage of rule-governed ethics like the *Gītā*'s and the flexibility often associated with character-based ethics like Aristotle's. Surprisingly, despite differences in the locus of perspective, both texts seem to reach a convergence when it comes to balancing considerations of consistency and flexibility in ethical action. Finally, I consider the relation between the practical and contemplative lives in the context of what it means to live well in both texts. While their skewed relationship ends up making the good life in the *Ethics* less accessible, the *Gītā*'s revolutionary suggestion of bringing a contemplative dimension to action makes the good life universally available.

The focus of this exercise is on a cluster of issues that we might therefore broadly call ethical, though the *Gītā* (unlike the *Ethics*) considers much more than that. It is a work of great poetic beauty that encompasses epistemic and metaphysical issues in syncretic fashion. This will mean we will need to elucidate and interpret these non-ethical views in order to better understand its ethical position, which is not without its challenges given the poetic nature of the text. To maintain balance, we will take recourse to texts beyond the *Ethics*, especially since in keeping with its title, Aristotle's text has a much more restricted scope than the *Gītā*.

1.2 Methodology

The language of "cross-cultural conversation" attempts to continue the philosophical dialogue between traditions initiated early in the twentieth century as comparative philosophy.[4] The focus on "conversation" is meant to emphasize several things:

(1) That each side in the conversation will get to take its time to make its position clear. This means there has been an attempt to minimize possible objections from, and comparisons with, the other side to ensure that reasonably original interpretations of the texts on both sides are developed without distraction. It is hoped that a smoother narrative is more consistent with the notion of a conversation (as opposed to, say, a debate) and also makes for easier reading. At various points in the development of the views, there will be an attempt to have the positions come to a head, so to speak, in the codas and in the final chapter. This directed speaking to each other from time to time and the ensuing braiding of issues, it is hoped, will ensure that the conversation stays focused and on track.

(2) That a considered and considerate approach to each side of the conversation allows for a careful approach to the purported common problems that concern us here. So the focus is very much on common problems (even if it is not on a common solution) which require us not so much to level the playing field but to navigate the complexities of difference that shape the articulation of the problem.[5] Thus a cross-cultural conversation attempts to balance the emphasis on careful development of context that is so important to traditional comparative philosophy, with a focus on common problems which is at the heart of fusion

philosophy—but with a difference. A conversation—which is different from a dialectical enterprise that focuses on a destination-solution—is concerned to show how the problems are shaped by overarching priorities and commitments of the conversationalists. In our exercise, therefore, we will see how the problems and hence solutions we are concerned with are shaped by the emphasis on the individual or the social.

(3) That it is a possible consequence that our conversation is inconclusive for a variety of reasons—because conversations by their nature can be (3.i) interminable, or (3.ii) because conversation as a mode of philosophy cannot easily be construed to be concerned with the truth, or (3.iii) because the positions of the conversationalists are incommensurable.

(3.i) Spoken conversations can be interminable in turn because they get stuck in a rut and hence become repetitive. But hopefully a conversation like ours which is written down can avoid the pitfall of repetition simply because it is more considered, in ways that spoken conversations—especially heated ones—are sometimes not. Yet we might find ourselves usefully repeating aspects of the conversation since it is not always possible to discuss every aspect of a response to a problem at the same time; for sometimes the narrative thread of the argument in one text may not always match that of the other.

(3.ii) If the conversationalists' views are shaped by their commitments, say, to the individual or the social and likely to other framing considerations of their respective traditions (even if it is as founding members or as upstarts), then perhaps we can speak of the truth in terms of such frames of reference. That is, we can consider how a conversationalist's view is consistent with the framing considerations of their tradition, even as the position innovates and moves the tradition forward in ways that are still true to it. But influential texts often innovate not just in reference to the framing considerations but often about them as well, which complicates the task. Such complications will help us address the problem of incommensurability that may arise in such cross-cultural conversations.

(3.iii) The problem of incommensurability arises in a cross-cultural conversation perhaps because the conversationalists are speaking past each other, and this might be at least in part because of the incommensurability of their respective framing considerations and hence of the truth.[6] Thus, for instance, we might wonder how a world-view that takes its central task to be the development and flourishing of the self (as in the *Ethics*) can speak in a meaningful way with one that seems to take its cornerstone to be the undermining of it (as in the *Gītā*). While the difference is in fact more nuanced, as we will see, it seems to me that two broad kinds of response are possible:

(3.iii.a) First, we should be clear that if in fact there is this kind of incommensurability, that it is not primarily because the conversation is across cultures. After all, we can see that similar if not the same positions are taken across cultures even if they might not have the same priority within cultures.[7] Thus, for instance, Plotinus and Spinoza and perhaps even the Stoics, can be seen to have similar predilections to *Gītā* on the self, and the hedonistic Charvāka on the priority of the self-in-world with Aristotle (even if how this priority is conceived is very different). In fact, one could see how Spinoza's monism is in reaction to, and in conversation with, Descartes' pluralism, so that their differences arise out of common concerns such as the nature of substance, the relation of mental to the physical, etc.

(3.iii.b) Second, that while positions taken therefore may seem at odds, they are united by a set of common, human concerns. While these common concerns are easier to see when the differences arise in a conversation within a tradition (as between Descartes and Spinoza), they may need uncovering to allow for a conversation across traditions (as is the case between the *Ethics* and the *Gītā*). Thus, if I am right in thinking that the question concerning the nature of ethical agency—mentioned above and detailed below—is of common concern to both texts, then the question itself unites what may seem like very different responses; for the seeming incommensurability of response should not be conflated with an incommensurability of concern. Moreover, tracing what seems like different responses to the same concern might help us identify factors that drive the direction of the answers: whether these be differences in framing considerations (whose importance is thus highlighted), or how the response relates to other responses of related concern, etc. In the process of assessing a response, we can see how the framing considerations themselves might have shifted, sometimes seismically, in ways that affect the trajectory of a tradition. Hence the importance of Descartes' *Cogito* is that while such an argument had been articulated before, it is taken to be the epistemological dimension of the tradition's shift of focus back on humanism in general and to the individual in particular.

Even if, therefore, we can speak of truth in relation to framing considerations, the fact that these considerations can shift speaks to how conversations across traditions (as much as within them) can affect seemingly incommensurable positions. For it is possible to reconsider a position even if it means the framing considerations have a to take a "walk-about" the periphery defined by the problems of common concern. Hence to segregate the truth in terms of a tradition's framing considerations may be misleading. Of course, this possible shift in framing considerations is difficult if the framing considerations are deeply and historically entrenched; or are a part of a larger, retrenching exercise (as with renaissance humanism, which might explain Spinoza's failure to shift the discourse away from the individual in Descartes). If nothing else, therefore, the contrasting light provided by a conversation might help us appreciate such entrenched commitments more clearly. But it may also be that conversations between influential texts can help readers from one or both traditions reflect on ways that they might reconsider their commitments in the always ongoing exercise of an examined life.[8] Thus even if our thesis is concerned to show how commitments to the respective tradition's framing considerations shape responses to common problems, it may be that the exercise helps in changing our minds about our own responses to these problems.[9]

A sustained attempt will therefore be made to speak to the framing considerations of the respective texts and traditions, as part of the exercise of a cross-cultural conversation. This presents a challenge since even the use of the language of framing considerations has been developed in the western tradition and is revealing at the very least of my professional commitments and training, if nothing else.[10] But perhaps this "educational bias" can be balanced by my own personal commitments to, along with teaching and thinking about, those that many of the subcontinental philosophical traditions share: the priority of freedom/*mokṣa*, the importance of the meditative dimension in action and in reflection in the search for it, and the shaping of the individual and social life that is organized by such search. After all, we may be right in thinking that it is a myth to seek a view from nowhere since we are always grounded in a somewhere. Perhaps the best I can do—following a recent, parallel trend in contemporary literary writing by immigrants—is to speak from a somewhere that feels like a nowhere. A nowhere between old and new worlds, ideas and possibilities, and a rootlessness that is therefore rooted in both but also seems like it is in neither.[11]

1.3 Brief Introduction to the *Ethics* and the *Gītā*

The *Ethics* is centrally concerned with examining the constituents, conditions, and context of the good or happy life. Aristotle tells us that the main ingredient in such a life is activity in accordance with virtue because such activity is the only candidate that satisfies what he takes to be important conditions of virtue such as completeness, self-sufficiency, and because it allows us to fulfill our human potential. Virtue is the properly conditioned state of natural dispositions that we have and is both practical and theoretical (Book 1). On the practical front, the proper conditioning or educating of the mind gives us the state of knowledge of ethics that is actualized in the activities of the ethical life. Education involves the instruction of reason in wishing for the right kinds of ends and learning how to deliberate and choose the right means to them (Book 3). But such an education also presupposes the cultivation of the non-rational dispositions of appetitive and spirited desire responsible for bringing practical rationality to fruition in action (Book 2). Ideally, education and cultivation together give us the person of practical wisdom who navigates not just the particular circumstances of the good life, but also considers what is conducive to it in general (Book 6). In addition to practical wisdom, the text gives us extensive discussions of the practical virtues and especially the key Greek virtues of temperance, courage, and justice (Books 3, 4 and 5). The place (as opposed to the nature) of theoretical virtue in the good life is only briefly and controversially discussed, despite its importance in the completion of the good life (Book 10). A better understanding of the relation of practical and theoretical virtue will therefore require us to consider other texts in Aristotle's corpus. Finally, the *Ethics* also discusses the role of fortune (Book 1), friendship, and character (Books 8 and 9) as part of its discussion of the conditions and context of the good life, as well as the place of pleasure in it (Books 7 and 10).

The *Gītā* begins with its protagonist Arjuna, the great Pandava warrior, asking his friend and divine incarnate Krishna why he should fight a battle that will surely result in the death of his extended kin, friends, and community. Such is his despair at the thought of fighting that he considers renouncing the world for a life of asceticism. The *Gītā* itself is part of the epic *Mahābhārata* which explains how the cousinly rivalry between the Pandavas and Kauravas comes to such a head in the first place because of competing claims to the kingdom of Kurukṣetra.[12] Krishna unequivocally urges Arjuna to fight in terms of the path/*yoga* of action/*karma* by explaining how in the final analysis playing one's role in society can lead to the same goal of freedom/*mokṣa* as the path of renunciation/*dhyāna*. Krishna as the divine incarnate also explains how the path of devotion/*bhakti*—which also does not require forsaking the world—completes the triune of possible paths to freedom. Along the way, the *Gītā* discusses the empirical and psychological aspects of human nature and their relation to Nature as a whole, the relation between human and Divine nature, all while making veiled references to and responses against rival schools of its time. In doing all of this, the *Gītā* does not hesitate to rely on important strains of its own orthodox Brahmanical tradition, modify and critique the tradition's views in its ongoing defence, and borrow from rival positions.

1.4 Outline of Chapters

I conclude this chapter with a quick précis of the upcoming chapters.

Chapter 2 discusses the form rather than the content of moral action in the *Ethics*, or what is normally discussed in terms of moral intentionality. I argue that while such discussions are usually concerned with reason (and specifically with deliberative choice and wish), the non-rational desires originating in emotion and appetite have teleologies that are harnessed by the process of habituation or cultivation. Key to the education of reason and the cultivation of desire is love, which unifies and harmonizes the rational and non-rational teleologies in the virtuous person.

Chapter 3 shows how an autonomous and harmonious personality/character is unified by self-love in the *Ethics* in ways that are continuous with the role of love in virtuous action. This chapter also distinguishes the construction of character from its basis in the self of personal identity and shows how self-love or self-friendship is the basis of friendship with others. The constructed nature of character in turn will allow us to think about the life of virtue as an artifact.

Chapter 4 turns to the form (as opposed to the content) of moral action in the *Gītā*, where an initial assessment suggests that the intentional aspects are also rational (grounded in the intellect's desire for knowledge) and non-rational (sourced in sense-driven desire). Both these dimensions are unified by the notion of detached action that is therefore essentially concerned with desire, even if distinguishing the text's various discussions of selfhood from character and personality remain as yet unclear.

Chapter 5 completes the understanding of detachment in the *Gītā* by developing a contextualized analysis of the detached sage—whose actions are seamlessly in sync with Nature—as lacking in desire, passion, and agency. This assessment is undertaken by working through the implications of the text's *guṇa*/strand theory from its various discussions of selfhood, character, and personality.

Coda 1 (to chapters 2–5) initiates a conversation on the common themes of intentionality, tripartition, and personality emerging from the above discussion. Here it becomes clear that the treatment of ethical action and its grounding in desire is in the service of constructing a flourishing agent in the *Ethics*, while it seems to fulfill the opposite purpose of deconstructing such agency in the *Gītā*.

Chapter 6 shows how the standard of ethical content for Aristotle can be the virtuous person and not a rule or a law and yet find a place for rules and laws. Such a view allows us to walk a fine line between excessive ethical latitude if we just rely on the virtuous person as standard, and not enough flexibility if we rely solely on the law. Key to this view is the close relationship between practically and politically wise individuals for Aristotle in the *Ethics*, and of the importance of the state and its laws for the realization of the individual good.

Chapter 7 discusses how obligations are prescribed by scriptural/*dharm*ic injunction in the *Gītā* and yet finds place for discretion and supererogatory action by way of the sage as standard. Such a view involves an understanding of *dharma* and the principle of world welfare's relation to detachment, and the implications of this relationship for latitude in, and the evolution of, *dharma* in the wider, social context.

Coda 2 (to chapters 6–7) considers how the emphasis on the individual in the *Ethics* and the holism of the *Gītā* does not detract from their respective affirmations of the world. Even so, they take very different routes to get there: the *Ethics* by prioritizing individuals and the *Gītā* by emphasizing the social, which means that latitude in ethical action is distributed accordingly.

Chapter 8 undertakes an examination of the nature of self-knowledge that is the ground of freedom/*mokṣa* in the *Gītā*, which the text tells us is accessible to the paths/*yoga*s of knowledge/*jñāna*, action/*karma*, and devotion/*bhakti*. Such wide accessibility requires an examination of what is common to these paths as well as distinguishing the types of self-knowledge discussed in the text.

Chapter 9 explores the parallel discussion of the relation of the practical and theoretical virtues in Aristotle and the conditions that must be fulfilled if they are to be unified in a well-lived, happy life. In the process of so doing, we will consider the separate possible lives of practical virtue, theoretical virtue, and others to see how these compare to the complete happy life.

Chapter 10 synthesizes the discussions of the codas and chapters 8 and 9 and shows how substantialism and holism shape the texts' views on the nature of the highest good and the access to it even if both agree for different reasons that it is never the direct focus of action. We will conclude by reflecting some more on the influence of the texts on their respective traditions and their ways of life.

Notes

1 See J. B. Schneewind, "The Misfortunes of Virtue," *Ethics: An International Journal of Social, Political, and Legal Philosophy* 101, no. 1 (1990): 42–63.

2 For a broad sense of the lay of the land, see Rosalind Hursthouse and Glen Pettigrove, "Virtue Ethics," in *The Stanford Encyclopedia of Philosophy*, ed. Edward

N. Zalta and Uri Nodelman, Winter 2022 (Metaphysics Research Lab, Stanford University, 2022), https://plato.stanford.edu/archives/win2022/entries/ethics-virtue/.

3 For more details on the *Gītā*'s historical trajectory, see Richard H. Davis, *The Bhagavad Gita: A Biography, The Bhagavad Gita* (Princeton, NJ: Princeton University Press, 2014).

4 For more details on the origins of this term and its development as a methodology, see Wilhelm Halbfass, "India and the Comparative Method," *Philosophy East and West* 35, no. 1 (1985): 3–15. Halbfass says that the term itself became popular after P. Masson-Oursel's book *La Philosophie Comparée*, which appeared in English translation in 1926 as *Comparative Philosophy*. But he suggests that it might have originated in the Indian philosopher B. N. Seal's 1899 *Comparative Studies in Vasihnavism and Christianity*, with whose later work Masson-Oursel was familiar (see esp. pp. 4–6).

5 See Nalini Bhushan, Jay L. Garfield, and Daniel Raveh, *Contrary Thinking: Selected Essays of Daya Krishna* (New York: Oxford University Press, 2011), 66. Daya Krishna points to the challenges of attempting to level the playing field in a world dominated by western culture. Hence discussions have been bogged down, for instance, by the question of whether there is such a thing as philosophy outside the western tradition.

6 See, for instance, Alasdair C. MacIntyre, *Whose Justice? Which Rationality?* (Notre Dame, IN: University of Notre Dame Press, 1988), 166.

7 See Stephen C. Angle, "The Minimal Definition and Methodology of Comparative Philosophy: A Report from a Conference," *Comparative Philosophy* 1, no. 1 (2010): 108, who makes a similar point.

8 See Kwame Anthony Appiah, *Cosmopolitanism: Ethics in a World of Strangers* (New York: W. W. Norton and Company, 2006), ch. 6, who follows von Neumann in suggesting that we never accept new ideas outright though we eventually get used to them. But I think Socrates' language of the examined life is more useful since it is more active than passive.

9 Hence readers may find this discussion to parallel one in our time between liberalism and its alternatives, even if such a discourse is on the political front whereas ours is primarily on the personal and ethical.

10 See Bhushan et al., *Contrary Thinking*, 60–3.

11 Perhaps a better way to think about location is not a view from nowhere but a view from above, as suggested by Jessica Frazier in "'The View From Above': A Theory of Comparative Philosophy," *Religious Studies* 56, no. 1 (March 2020): 32–48. Frazier suggests that such a view from above considers a web of ideas that underlie different conceptual systems so that one can see what defines and constitutes an idea as well as what does not. In such a web, only some ideas are alive for a

particular view that one can navigate, so that others then form a backdrop of virtual possibilities the totality of which can be marvelled at as a whole. Whereas the practical nature of our exercise requires that the marvelling leads to an affirmation and perhaps even a changing of mind regarding our commitments, and therefore always lands us somewhere.

12 While the Pandavas have what seems the most immediately legitimate claim to the kingdom, the story is quite complicated because of the ways in which primogeniture has been consistently set aside in the family. See J. A. B. Buitenen, *The Bhagavadgītā in the Mahābhārata: Text and Translation* (Chicago: University of Chicago Press, 1981), 1–3, for a concise sense of the compelling considerations to support the case on both sides, and for the unfolding tragedy that paralyzes Arjuna.

2

Ethical Intentionality in the *Nicomachean Ethics*

2.0 Introduction

The eventual concern of this project is to consider in a dialogical context the nature of human agency and its highest ends in both the *Nicomachean Ethics* and the *Bhagavad Gītā*. But to do so, we begin with what seems closest to the ground: the nature of ethical action in all of its detail, which as we will see, shapes the nature of human agency in important ways and is essentially connected to its highest goals in both texts. It is convenient for our purposes to think about ethical action itself in terms of its form and its content, modifying a distinction made by Kant.[1] By "form" I mean the shape that intention gives the content of the action which significantly structures action in a variety of ways. More specifically, the form of an ethical action tells us how we can get at why an action is undertaken. Whereas the content of the ethical action—which can be based on a content generating principle such as the Golden Rule—gives us the "what" of the action or what is actually done. Now we might think that the Golden Rule can give us both: I generously spend time listening to my troubled friend because this is what I would expect from a friend. Here, the what (listening to my friend) and the why (because this is what the Golden Rule entails) are grounded in the Rule, even if they need not be. Thus, I could listen to my friend because I expect something in return, or because I want to be perceived as a good person, etc. In other words, the "why" shapes the "what" of an action in a variety of ways that are not always obvious to a bystander or for that matter to the agent herself. Another important point is that the "what" and the "why" can be spoken of in terms of intention, since I can intend to act as the Golden Rule requires as much as I can intend to do so because the Golden Rule so requires, whereas for our purposes we restrict our use of the term for the latter.[2] While both the *Ethics* and the *Gītā* have very different ways of generating the content of moral action, both are very interested in the nature of this kind of ethical intentionality that is concerned with the "why" of an action, as we shall see.

We might ask why we should be concerned with intention; after all, the action seems all-important since ethics is about what is done. Moreover, it is hard to know why the action is undertaken since intentionality is not always transparent to the agent or anyone else, whereas it is easy to see the impact of the action. Such concern perhaps betrays our contemporary apprehensiveness about judging people (in terms of their intentions) as opposed to their actions, about assessing what we can obviously perceive rather than what we might be required to infer. It is also possible that our disquiet is rooted in the enormously influential and less than savory early modern views of human nature that we are essentially self-interested creatures.[3] Such a view colors modern ethical theory so that utilitarianism, for instance, has challenges moving from the pursuit of the agent's happiness to that of others, and balancing them.[4] More importantly, it might explain why utilitarianism is focused on outcomes rather than intentions as at least one central figure articulates.[5] Even Kant, the founder of modern deontology, agrees that the focus should be on the action despite his emphasis on intentionality, and even if he disagrees with the utilitarians on most other matters. Our ancient texts are different insofar as they seem not to share this implicit pessimism about human nature. This is manifest in their interest in thinking about how intentionality of action shapes and is in turn shaped by the character, personality or person that acts; for they are convinced that there is more to goodness than can be found in actions, even if this takes them in very different directions as we will see.

Implicit in the discussion so far is the view that intention is concerned with action and essentially involves rationality. After all, the focus here is very much on why we do what we do for Aristotle such that it shapes the nature of the content. But, as I will show, seeking to understand such intentionality will require us to examine Aristotle's conception of choice and wish which are rational in nature. In addition, it will also require us to consider the nature of desire for two reasons: first because both choice and wish involve desire, either by definition (since choice is defined as deliberative desire) or by nature (since wish is rational desire). Second, because Aristotle seems to think that rational action is impossible without desire's cooperation. The story is complicated further because we will need to consider how rational (i.e., wish) and non-rational desire (i.e., desires that are based in emotion/*thumos* and appetite/*epithumia*) come together. Thus, in this chapter I will argue that Aristotle brings about such integration of desire in ways that essentially involve love, thereby setting the stage for how the rational and non-rational are harmonized in self-love in the next chapter.

2.1 Aristotle on Intention in Virtuous Action

Since our focus in this chapter is on Aristotle's views on why ethical or what he calls "virtuous" action is undertaken (i.e., the intention that grounds it), it makes sense to begin with what he means by virtuous action. We will see that the rational aspects of such action are shaped not only by why the action is undertaken but by the process of deliberative thought through which the "what" is determined, so that the resulting choice of action then involves both the "why" and the "what" in relation to the agent's end which in turn is grasped by a rational desire (wish).

Aristotle lists three conditions of virtuous action wherein his views on intentionality only become eventually obvious (*NE* 3.4 1105a30–1105b5).[6] The first and least important condition is knowledge of virtue which he says is more important in craft-knowledge than in acting ethically. This downplaying of knowledge may seem surprising in an ethical treatise, but we should note that Aristotle is not denying that knowledge (which is in part concerned with determining the "what" of ethical action) is a necessary condition of virtue. What he is saying is that knowledge by itself carries little or no weight since many people know what they should do but cannot live up to it (*NE* 3.4 1105b12–18); what Aristotle will later call incontinence or weakness-of-will broadly construed (*NE* 7.4 1148b8–14).[7] So if knowledge of virtue is not enough to ensure virtuous action, we need something else, which brings us to the second condition of virtuous action: that virtuous action is virtuous only when it originates in a firm and unchanging virtuous character. Given Aristotle's emphasis on character, this requirement is not surprising since it speaks to the kind of person who is capable not only of knowing the good but acting on it based on such unchanging character. This character, then, as we will see, is the product of the rational shaping of our non-rational desires so that the synchrony between the rational and non-rational consistently leads to virtuous action. Consistency of right action, then, is a sign of an unchanging virtuous character that separates virtuous actions from those that only appear so (as in the case of fortuitously and usually inconsistently so right actions) or just approximate them (as in the case of those who are working towards virtue).

The third condition is really two different but related conditions that finally get us to the "what" and the "why" of virtuous action. Aristotle says that virtuous action must be chosen and chosen for its own sake. So, choice marks out not only the considerations that determine what is chosen but why it is chosen, i.e., for its own sake. Since we are speaking of virtuous action here, Aristotle seems to be suggesting that the virtuous action is undertaken for its own sake, or what he takes to amount to the same thing, because it is virtuous or good (*NE* 3.2 1112a3–8).[8] To say that a virtuous action that is undertaken for its own sake is undertaken for virtue is obviously true. To say that it is undertaken as good is also plausible since it is virtuous action, even if we will have to contend with Aristotle's view that all action (virtuous or otherwise) is undertaken as good. All of this makes sense on a first approach considering what was said before: the same action can be intended in different ways which then affects the nature of the action itself so that to undertake action in this way is to undertake it because it is virtuous or good. Still, it is important to reiterate that such a requirement is concerned with the "why" or end of such action (its *telos*) which in this case is virtue, separate from the aim or outcome (or *skopos*) of the action, or that which is the product of the "what" of the action as I have called it, so that both are necessary for virtue (*EE* 1.2 1214b6–14).[9]

2.2 Choice and Deliberation and Means to Ends

While the main discussion regarding the content of virtuous action will be undertaken later in chapter 6, we will focus here on some of the formal aspects of how this content is obtained, starting with choice. Aristotle defines choice as "… the deliberate desire of things in our own power; for when we have decided as a result of deliberation, we desire in accordance with our deliberation" (*NE* 3.3 1113a9–11).

There is much in this definition that sits well with how we commonly think of choice understood as a rational exercise of picking out an action, and some aspects that do not. Hence we might say that one chooses to move one's finger to the left rather than to the right. Yet Aristotle clearly thinks that there are non-rational or desiderative aspects involved in successful choice in ways that may not be included in our usual ways of thinking about it. The rational aspects of choice for Aristotle involve what we do to pick out some of our actions since not all that we do is chosen, though it can be voluntary (like absent-minded doodling) or even involuntary (like when we are pushed). What separates a chosen action from an involuntary one is that it is picked out of at least two options (that is, either to undertake an action or not), though usually more, and is therefore thought to be in our power.[10] What separates choice from voluntary action is some kind of forethought, what Aristotle calls "deliberation."

Aristotle is among the first in the tradition to demarcate deliberation as a special kind of thinking involved in practical matters, and his views on it remain influential (*NE* 3.3 1112a18–1113a2). Our usage of the term is often in the context of legal matters, when we say, for instance, that the judge deliberated on the matter before she reached a decision. Clearly, even in our usage, deliberation is different from daydreaming, since it leads to choice and hence to action; but for Aristotle it is also different from the kind of thinking involved in theoretical matters. This is not because the two don't share an investigative approach, because they do; in fact, Aristotle's archetypical example of deliberation here is the working out a geometrical proof in which the last in the order of analysis is the first in the order of doing (*NE* 3.3 1112b15–24). Nor do the differences arise because the practical and theoretical are concerned with different objects since Aristotle says that the practical is concerned with things that happen in a certain way for the most part. That is, the practical is concerned with a world in which things happen regularly, wherein the theoretical, we could say, is concerned with just this regularity (cf. *NE* 6.7 1141a21–24; 1141b15–22).[11] This regularity would include, for instance, that the sun will rise every day, that a spear will kill if it pierces the heart, that chicken is wholesome and will nourish the body, etc.[12] The practical deliberative thinking therefore presupposes a predictable world but is focused on outcomes that are not predictable, Aristotle says, because the outcomes are obscure to us and the way to them is indeterminate.

An example can make Aristotle's views on deliberation clearer. Socrates the wily warrior might choose to attempt to save Alcibiades from certain death in battle by distracting the enemy with a diversionary tactic. Such a tactic is one among several possible options that Socrates might employ after due deliberation. Such options might concern a single syllogistic exercise which picks out one among several diversionary tactics.[13] Or the options might involve several possible ways in which Alcibiades might be saved (diversions, full-on charges, etc.), each of which involves syllogistic thinking that may seem more or less plausible to Socrates. Of course, the one that is picked is not guaranteed to succeed in saving Alcibiades despite the language of geometrical proofs or the fact that all the options rely on the world being predictable in important ways. Moreover, even if the diversionary tactic works, it may not be repeatable precisely because it is predictable. The point of course is that deliberation presupposes a world that is predictable in certain ways without which it could not get off the ground, and that this is so even though such a world still leaves us with enough uncertainty to navigate so that the outcome is not guaranteed.

If deliberation determines *what* the choice of action might be (*prohairesis*), for instance the particulars of Socrates' diversionary tactics to save Alcibiades, choice is also concerned with *why* the action is chosen (*proslaboûsa*) (*NE* 3.8 1116b31–1117a4). As we saw above, Aristotle thinks that action in accordance with virtue is chosen for its own sake, or as good. The problem is that we all undertake actions for the most part because we think they are good even if they are not. So, a thief usually conceives his actions as good even though he realizes that they are unlawful. Aristotle agrees for he says in the famous beginning of the *Ethics* that every action is thought to aim at, and is therefore undertaken as, *some* kind of good (*NE* 1.1 1094a1–3). Yet this does not mean that every action actually *is* good. This is because it really depends on how choice is related to the nature of the agent's overall ends in life. These ends, Aristotle tells us, are a function of wish which can therefore be for the real or apparent good since the thief must have them as much as a good person does (*NE* 3.4 1113a15–16).

2.3 Wish is for Ends

But now we have to think about how the good person's choice, which we saw is an end in itself, is also a means to the end set by wish (understood as being for the real rather than the apparent good), since this latter point not only seems to follow from the above but is also something that Aristotle explicitly says (*NE* 3.2 1111b26–28). We could suppose further that the good person's wish is to act well or nobly in every circumstance since this is what it would plausibly mean to be a good person. The usual solution is to see that the specific action picked out by deliberation and choice is constitutive of wish rather than separate from it.[14] So we might say that Socrates picks out the diversionary, courageous action that instantiates his wish to act well in general. Such a choice is usually contrasted with walking to the barbershop as a means to (and separate from) the end of getting a haircut. Crucially, this focus on the *skopos*/aim of choice allows us to see how the *telos*/end of the action comes into play: for to choose an action as an end itself or as good, is precisely what it means to instantiate the wish to act well in that situation.[15] This is why Aristotle uses the alternate language of nobility to capture his meaning in this context; for the noble or fine (*to kalon*) in the Greek includes within it the notion of what is not mean or shabby, but what is fitting (*to prepon*) and thereby pleasing to the eye.[16] Thus wish for the real good involves choice that is an end in itself, or is fine. But there is an additional feature of the real versus apparent good that explains why it is chosen for its own sake: the real good or the activities of virtue constitute happiness for Aristotle so that to choose virtue is to not only do what is good in that situation but what simultaneously constitutes that which is good per se and what in fact turns out to be good for the agent (i.e., their happiness or their flourishing; more on this in chapter 6). Choice and wish of virtuous action therefore come together in the good in ways that are not the case, as we see below, for the apparent good.

Apparent goods are of two kinds, Aristotle tells us: those that are pleasant and those that are useful (*NE* 2.3 1104b29–1105a1).[17] We often undertake actions for the sake of obtaining pleasure; thus we choose to pursue a passing sexual liaison because our end is the pleasure it will bring and to this extent do not act for the action itself. Now since pleasure is in fact an end in itself (since many do pursue it for its own sake), one could construe our choosing as being of the sexual activity as an end in itself. But the point of course is that the relevant, important ethical choices are often made prior to the sexual activity itself, which means that such choices are not ends in themselves but means to the end of pleasure. When an action is undertaken for the sake of utility (such as when Socrates might save Alcibiades for his own greater glory), then the action can hardly be said to be undertaken for its own sake, even if it appears to be for the good of the agent.[18] So it would seem that virtuous choice and wish are united by the real rather than the apparent good, and the fact that both seem to be in the business of relating reason and desire. For while choice is deliberative desire, wish is said to be rational desire, a rational desire for choice to be undertaken for its own sake than for the sake of pleasure or utility.

It might therefore make sense to say more about wish as we transition to the discussion of the desiderative aspects of choice. Unlike choice, though, wish does not bring reason and desire together because Aristotle says wish *is* rational desire (*DA* 3.10 433a17–26)[19]; that is, there is something about wishing that is a wanting which has a rational dimension. This makes sense since even if an agent's outlook in life is such that they wish for an apparent good like bodily pleasure, it needs to be conceived as a good whilst being desired as such so that what makes it the apparent good is that the desire does not originate in reason. One would therefore think that virtuous wish originates in reason, given that knowledge is a condition of virtue as we saw above. Yet this reasoning cannot be deliberation that culminates in choice since this would make it no different from choice, whereas wish we saw is different because it is a rational desire. In fact, Aristotle tells us that we do not deliberate and choose higher order ends[20] such as health and happiness:

> … wish relates rather to the end, choice to what contributes to the end; for instance, we wish to be healthy, but we choose the acts which make us healthy, and we wish to be happy and say we do, but we cannot well say we choose to be so; for, in general, choice seems to relate to things in our own power.
>
> (*NE* 3.2 1111b26–30)

Presumably, the point is, as in the case of virtue, we can only choose healthy acts if we are healthy, or else such choice is either incidentally healthy or helps us on our way to health. It is not in our power to suddenly be healthy since it takes time to get there so that wish here speaks not to the desire to become healthy as much as it does to what the healthy person wishes when it comes to food and exercise. In the same way, the virtuous person wishes to act well because of who they are (i.e, because they perceive the real as opposed to the apparent good). They do not have to deliberate about whether they should act well before they choose to act well; for the wish to act well (which picks out a general orientation, cf. *NE* 4.3 1124a13–20; 5.1 1129a7–10) is a given, which choice then instantiates in that situation. Not only does Aristotle therefore suggest that there is a temporal component in the development of wish, but that wish as a desire can itself be at odds with desires that pursue immediate gratification (as in the case of those who are conflicted) precisely because its rational grounding allows it to apprehend futurity (*DA* 433b5–13). This language of apprehension is appropriate since it allows us to emphasize the fact that the object of wish (whether real or otherwise) is apparent to the agent so that it separates the rationality of wish from that of choice even further (*NE* 3.4 1113a31–1113b1); for it would seem that Aristotle is speaking here of an intellectual grasping or intuiting that is quite different from the discursive reasoning that is deliberative choice. Such ends appear to the good person because of who they are, which is why Aristotle denies that we deliberate about ends. But Aristotle also thinks that such grasping occurs in moral perception that allows us to see, for instance, that a friend needs help. While such perception is itself not an action, it is the basis of action (*NE* 6.11 1143b2–3; 1139a19–20) that is the result of deliberative choice grounded in wish. Thus, a good person's response in such a situation would mean an almost immediate wish to help, determining what constitutes the best or fine kind of help in that situation, and choosing the most plausible option that might help, for its own sake, i.e, without concern for utility or pleasure. Thus "seeing" is the language that Aristotle uses to speak of ultimates in both directions when it comes to practical action so that what is deliberated upon is enclosed by intuition that stops logical regress at both ends, regress that would otherwise threaten the very possibility of action (*NE* 3.3 1112b33–1113a2). I will say more in section 2.7 on how Aristotle thinks such intuition is cultivated.[21]

So far, we have considered the rational aspects of intention, and in so doing, have examined Aristotle's conceptions of choice, deliberation, and wish. It is time now to turn our attention to the non-rational parts because we saw that choice, which plays an essential role in intentionality for Aristotle, has non-rational components as well.

2.4 Aristotle on Desire and Intention

As we have already seen, Aristotle defines choice as deliberate desire of things in our power to undertake. The rational aspects of choice thus defined are clearly teleological and work towards a wished for end or *telos* for its own sake. Deliberation ranges over possible means to such ends and terminates in a rational recognition of what needs to be done in that set of circumstances that forwards one's goal or *skopos* (which in turn is consistent with the real good that is wished). Aristotle thinks that this rational terminus is not enough for action and says:

> What affirmation and negation are to thinking, pursuit and avoidance are in desire; so that since moral virtue is a state of character concerned with choice, and choice is deliberate desire, therefore both the reasoning must be true and the desire right, if choice is to be good, and the latter must pursue what the former asserts.
>
> (*NE* 6.2 1139a20–25)

Well before David Hume, Aristotle sees that if reason is to move us to action it must be supported by desire at every level. Not only is this the case for the end that is grasped by wish conceived as a rational desire, but choice for him has a place for it. The difference, as I have suggested, is that these are non-rational desires that are not the same as the rational aspects of deliberative choice (or as those that constitute wish for that matter) but need to be brought in line with deliberative reason so that choice leads to action. Without this harmonization, we have at least one kind of failure in choice (i.e., weakness of will/incontinence broadly construed) so that we can deliberate and think we need to do something but cannot bring ourselves to action because our desires do not cooperate with our thinking (*NE* 3.2 1111b13–16; 7.9 1151a5–11). Hence it would seem that that the desire *qua* wish is not enough to obtain the right outcome in action without desire in choice cooperating. The shaping of both rational and non-rational desires interestingly enough is a rational exercise, and is what Aristotle discusses in terms of the development of dispositions or of character (*hexis*).

2.5 Desire and Character

Character, as we will see in chapter 6, is key to understanding how right action is determined. Here we will develop how character as personality for Aristotle is understood in terms of the virtues (*NE* 2.5 1106a11–12). Thus, a person can be temperate, brave, generous, and sociable and these character traits or virtues constitute her character. But we need to be careful, because the virtues here are what Aristotle calls "moral virtues" and have to do broadly with feelings/*pathē* and more specifically with emotion/*thumos* and appetite/*epithumia*, as opposed to intellectual ones such as wisdom or deliberation. Aristotle initially defines moral virtue exclusively in terms of passions or feelings/*pathē*, including what I separate out here in terms of the appetites/*epithumia* and emotion/*thumos*.[22] What Aristotle means in *NE* 2.5 is that the way in which a person feels in a particular set of circumstances tells us a great deal about her character. A temperate person will not want to overindulge at a banquet and will eat moderately. A courageous person will not feel too much fear or confidence in a dangerous situation. But it is unclear *how* what one feels or wants translates into action in accordance with virtue.

It is important to see that how one feels is not always the same as what one desires, yet there is obviously a very close connection between them (cf. *DA* 3.10 and esp. 433b.21–31). If a situation causes an agent to feel a great deal of fear, it is not unreasonable to expect her to have an aversion to the object of her fear because it appears bad to her. But the connection is even stronger in the case of our appetites; hunger, which might be characterized as a perceived lack of food, is inseparable from the desire for food as pleasurable.[23] Aversion and desire, as we have seen Aristotle say above, is the basis of action; it is no wonder, then, that Aristotle says that these should be in line with the rational aspects of choice, if the action is to be in accordance with virtue.[24]

Emotions and appetites therefore manifest their teleological orientation through or as desire. But not every such desire is appropriate, which is why Aristotle says that moral virtue has to do with the way we feel, and not just that we have the capacity to feel (*NE* 2.5 1105b25–28; 1105b35–1106a1). We are habituated to feel in sync with practical reason through a lengthy process of training (which I discuss more fully below) so that action successfully ensues. It is because we require such training that moral virtue is considered praiseworthy since it is something of an achievement. This is not to deny that emotions and appetites have inherent teleological propensities before these are shaped by habit towards virtue or vice. Aristotle initially suggests that we are born neutral when it comes to the moral virtues (*NE* 2.1 1103a19–25). Yet this suggestion has more to do with emphasizing that we can go either way in our development—and are therefore morally responsible for it—than with denying inherent teleological propensities. Hence later in the text he speaks of our natural tendency to pursue bodily pleasure that is clearly indicative of appetite's original teleology (*NE* 2.9 1109a14–15). Similarly, he acknowledges that different character types are so by nature (*NE* 6.13 1144b4–6). So, some of us are naturally capable of handling pressure in difficult situations (*NE* 3.8 1117a3–5), others are naturally inclined to be generous, and so on.

It might be worth further substantiating the claim that the non-rational aspects have their own teleological orientation, since even Aristotle sometimes seems to suggest otherwise. Hence he compares the natural version of moral virtue to a stumbling blind body, and reason as sight which then provides direction (*NE* 6.13 1144b9–12). Still, the blind body can stumble in some direction, say, driven by sound or smell, even if it ultimately proves not to be the right direction. Similarly, appetite can drive a crawling baby to attempt to eat all that he comes across, and reason is clearly not involved. That appetite and emotion can have their own teleological orientation that is at odds with reason is clearly the case from what Aristotle says about the incontinent in the proper sense (as opposed to the broad sense which includes emotional as well as appetitive incontinence), or who we might call the weak-willed person. After all, the incontinent person is someone whose deliberation or opinion requires one kind of action, but whose appetites lead her to fail to so act, or act in a contrary fashion (*NE* 7.3 1147a34–1147b3; 7.7 1150b20–25). Moreover, the human propensity to seek bodily pleasure for Aristotle confirms, at the very least, that the appetites have a natural teleology presumably because of their focus on immediate gratification in contrast with wish.

It is time now to bring together all aspects of what has been said so far, to help determine where we need to go. We have seen that the virtuous person wishes, or has a rational desire, for the real as opposed to the apparent good. Wishing is concerned with ends in Aristotle's teleologically driven action theory, whereas choice is concerned with the means to the end set by wish. Virtuous choice we saw has two dimensions, the first of which is concerned with how or why the action is undertaken, that is, for its own sake or as good. The second, the deliberative aspect of choice determines how the good that is wished for is to be instantiated in particular circumstances. But if the choice is to come to fruition in action, the desire in choice, understood as "deliberative desire," must line up with the deliberative outcomes. These desires originate in the appetites (for food and sex) and in the emotions (such as anger, jealousy, fear, etc.), and need to be cultivated to be in harmony with the deliberative outcomes that instantiate wish understood as intuited, rational desire. The next step, therefore, is to understand the framework within which one's upbringing (or what I call "cultivation") operates to obtain such synergy. Key to understanding this will be to see how the good as conceived by rational desire (or wish) is grasped by emotion and appetite in ways that will centrally involve love.

2.6 Love and Virtue

What unifies Aristotle's action theory is the notion of love, something which has not been emphasized enough in the long scholarly tradition on the *Ethics*.[25] This is partly because love as a desire is not just emotional but has rational and appetitive aspects that are only implicitly discussed, which we will therefore need to make explicit. But the lack of emphasis is also because an important passage where Aristotle suggests that love is a necessary condition for virtuous action has been neglected. The passage purportedly is about the place of pleasure in Aristotle's theory of virtue, and the connection between pleasure and virtue is made through love:

> Their [i.e., the virtuous person's] life is also in itself pleasant. For pleasure is a state of soul, and to each man that which he is said to be a lover of is pleasant; e.g. not only is a horse pleasant to the lover of horses, and a spectacle to the lover of sights, but also in the same way just acts are pleasant to the lover of justice (*philodikaiō*) and in general virtuous acts to the lover of virtue (*philaretō*) … besides what we have said, the man who does not rejoice (*chaironta*) in noble actions is not even good; since no one would call a man just who did not enjoy acting justly, nor any man liberal who did not enjoy liberal actions; and similarly in all other cases.
>
> (*NE* 1.81099a7–a20)

Love/*philia* broadly construed applies to relations to people (in friendship) as much as it can to activities and objects (virtue, knowledge, and wine), and is therefore a multifaceted desire. It seems reasonable to say that when we love what we do we usually enjoy the activity and find pleasure in it, and by implication, find painful those activities we despise. It goes without saying that not all of us love the same activities, which is why two people might take pleasure in different ones. Aristotle characterizes every virtuous person as a lover of virtue for whom action in accordance with virtue is pleasurable, rather than someone for whom virtue is a burden. Thus, if an action that appears to conform to virtue is not enjoyed, it is merely that, an appearance, and not action in accordance with virtue. This in turn means that love of virtue is a prerequisite for action in accordance with virtue since loving virtue is the basis for finding it pleasurable. Aristotle also seems to be speaking in the passage above of love in terms of persons (lovers of virtue) and their actions (i.e., just actions) and therefore implicitly of choice and wish. We will therefore attempt to work out the relation between love, choice, and wish, and begin with the relation between love and wish.

A lover of virtue is not only virtuous but wishes to act well or virtuously so that love and wish as desires must be intimately related. The connection becomes obvious when the apparent good, which we know is the object of wish, is in fact the only object of rational love for Aristotle (*NE* 9.3 1165b13–15).[26] Thus we may love honor as an end even if it is an apparent good since it is dependent on others to bestow on us, whereas the real good (i.e., virtuous activity) is not since it is something that we do (*NE* 1.5 1096a6–8; 1095b25–30). But the fact that we can make honor an end by loving it suggests that love is what makes it 'endy'; after all, to love is to desire something intrinsically, or as an end. What makes it rational is that which is loved in this way is simultaneously apprehended as good, which as we saw is a function of rational intuition.[27] We don't say we love exercise, for instance, if we only think of it as a means to health so that exercise is usually only loved as such when in fact one is healthy. As we saw, the fact that we can love bodily pleasure in this way—that is, as an object of wish which then broadly informs our outlook in life—does not take away from the fact that such a desire is rational precisely because it shapes our outlook. Thus, in the case of virtuous ends, not only must reason be the origin of the rational aspects of wish, but so must the desiderative ones in the end *qua* fine/*kalon* (*NE* 8.13 1162b34–1163a1); after all, the object of love is not without an aesthetic dimension precisely because it is fine. Whereas an excessive love of bodily pleasure originates in the body and not in reason. Thus, one way to distinguish the apparent from the real good is precisely in terms of their desiderative origins.

If wish is rational love, and choice too like wish has rational and desiderative dimensions, we can start by determining the place of love in the rational, deliberative aspects of choice. The rational aspects of choice we saw determine the "what" and the "why" of an action, where the former is specifically in the domain of deliberation that leads up to picking out the action that precedes the hoped-for outcome/*skopos*. Whereas the "why" is concerned with the end/*telos* of the action, which ideally is for the sake of the action itself (or as good), and which then is an instantiation of the wish to act well. So, it would seem that love in choice manifests in intentionality when in fact the action is chosen for its own sake since love is what makes such choice 'endy,' and in turn explains the place of love in the conditions of virtuous action. Here too its role is essentially concerned with immediacy in end-making, wherein it instantiates the love of virtue in wish that expresses the agent's outlook in life.

The non-rational dimensions of choice (understood as deliberative desire) are broadly conceived as feeling/*pathē* which is separated into emotion/*thumos* and appetite/*epithumia*, as we saw in the previous section. The place of love here is easier to determine at one level since love is usually conceived as a non-rational desire, but with a reminder that for Aristotle only the good is loved. The problem of course is that goodness is a rational concept, and we are speaking here of non-rational desire. In the case of emotion, Aristotle tells us that while it cannot conceive the good it can heed it, though it only does so indirectly (*NE* 7.6 1149a24–1149b1). Thus anger can be aroused by a perceived insult (*qua* bad) and doused by a correction of this perception (for example, by saying that it was directed at someone else), wherein both the perception and the correction involve significant rational dimensions.[28] In the virtuous, this shift in emotion is clearly guided by deliberation as it determines which avenue of response is worth pursuing as good and which is worth avoiding as bad. Anger does not itself see the deliberative outcomes as good or bad since it cannot itself reason, but rather as a visceral, aesthetic response to the fine/*kalon* and the unfine.[29] Love as an emotion in the love of virtue therefore manifests in the harmony with the virtuous, deliberative choice of an action seen as an end in itself (or as good) that instantiates rational wish for the real good. It is when the appropriate emotional dimensions of love are missing in choice that it is possible to act contrary to the rational aspects of choice and wish (as in the case of the hot-tempered, who are incontinent, broadly construed *NE* 7.4 1147b32–34; 4.5 1125b10–15); for without the appropriate emotional desire, virtuous action is not possible, even as the inappropriate forms of desire are the basis of such broadly incontinent actions. By extension, emotion can also follow rational choice that is shaped by pleasure rather than reason per se, so long as pleasure is conceived as the apparent good and thus as fine. In all these cases, the emotions' response to what appears fine, therefore, expresses their visceral affinity to the aesthetic dimensions of the good.

If love as an emotion works with a conception of the good *qua* fine even if it cannot create it, things are quite different when it comes to appetitive love. For appetite cannot pursue things as ends in terms of good or bad, but rather as pleasurable or painful (*NE* 3.1 1111a34; 3.2 1111b17). After all, we do not usually ask why one pursues pleasure, since it is obviously an end in itself. Here the role of the non-rational in providing the motive force to action becomes obvious, for we clearly pursue or avoid the things that are pleasurable or painful. Thus, we are lovers of healthy food if we enjoy it and avoid unhealthy food as distasteful at the visceral level of appetite. Since pleasure accompanies all kinds of love as we saw Aristotle say in the quote above, it needs to be said that only in the case of appetitive love is pleasure an appropriate motivator of action in the temperate. But even here, this motivation is what allows it to cooperate with reason whose focus on temperance is based on rational considerations to produce action.

2.7 On the Development of Character

It is important to consider the role of love in the development of character given the latter's essential connection to desire. Our consideration is complicated by Aristotle's distinction between the education of reason and the cultivation of the non-rational aspects of desire (*ethismos*) early in the text (*NE* 2.1 1103a15–19). But contrary to how it may seem, the process of education and cultivation constitute a deeply integrated exercise, even if Aristotle thinks that the latter stages of an education can only be completed in his classroom *qua* university. The discussion of the education of reason will be fleshed out more fully in chapter 3 and then again in chapter 6, though the education of rational desire (*qua* wish) will be undertaken here along with that of non-rational desire. What will become clear is that wish plays a bridging role between the cultivation of non-rational desire and the education of reason since it shares in the characteristics of both and is in fact itself developed on the back of the former.

Starting with the appetitive aspects of non-rational desire, we can ask how one comes to enjoy healthy food (as an aspect of the virtue of temperance). While we saw that some of us are inclined to eat well naturally, most of us need help to do so. This help ideally comes at a young age when children are encouraged to eat healthy food such as fruit and finding pleasure in its sweetness. Over time, a person comes to love healthy food based on having eaten well consistently and finding it enjoyable. Since excessively sweet things like refined sugar can be a source of ill-health and intemperance and undermine the enjoyment of naturally sweet and healthy things, their place in the diet is discouraged or minimized. (But in the case of sexual intemperance which has detrimental social consequences, for instance, the discouragement takes the form not just of disapproval but of punishment.) In the temperate adult, therefore, the easier access to refined sugar's excessively sweet nature is found to be overwhelming and eventually avoided or minimized as a matter of course (*NE* 2.3 1104b9–11). Note that the appetitive dimension of the love of healthy food is a function of the pleasure that one takes in it and is cultivated by encouraging healthy eating which in turn engenders healthy desires for more of the same. When such desire is regularly generated so that the agent consistently pursues healthy and temperate eating with pleasure (in accordance with, and amenable to, reason's contextual dictates), we might say that an aspect of the temperate disposition has been developed, and that such a person is a lover of healthy food.

There is a similar relation between actions and feelings when it comes to the non-rational *qua* emotions, even though the emotions can heed the good and come to love it as fine/*kalon*. Feeling in certain ways, we saw, causes us to pursue or avoid courses of action because of the mediation of desire; thus, fear causes aversion and hence avoidance in us. Aristotle thinks that we can be taught to learn to fear things less or more, and the way to do so is in reverse; if feeling in certain ways eventually causes us to act in certain ways, then acting in certain ways leads us to feel in certain ways (*NE* 2.1 1103a26–1103b25). Learning to stand our ground in situations that usually frighten us leads us to feel less frightened and more confident over time, and clearly this is mediated by less aversion. Part of such learning usually involves shifting the attention from the aversive aspects of the situation (that involve bodily harm, for instance) to those that are fine (such as honor) which in turn lead to feeling less fear and more confidence and thus to the increasing likelihood of standing our ground. Emotional love of the fine is therefore deeply intertwined with the balance of confidence and fear that Aristotle thinks are constituents of a courageous disposition. Even though the motivation here is not pleasure as is the case in appetitive love, the growing love of the fine is eventually and deeply pleasurable along with the feelings of confidence and fear (*qua* exhilaration), as Aristotle says must be the case in the lover of virtue (*NE* 1.8 1099a5–21). In such a person, the courageous disposition responds to reason's contextual conception of the good (in terms of deliberative choice and wish) *qua* fine by producing courageous action.

Wish or rational desire that is concerned with our global priorities develops from the bottom up, on the back of the local cultivation of virtuous action. We saw above that cultivation involves encouraging individuals to pursue and avoid actions in terms of pleasure and pain (for the appetites) or the fine or unfine (for the emotions) so that over time one is disposed to desire consistently in such ways. Such encouragement is often performative (when we encourage children to follow our lead in eating, for instance) and is accompanied with normative language ("eating fruit is healthy and good") so that the developed disposition not only finds healthy food wholesome and tasty but wishes for it as good in general (*NE* 3.4 1113a26–29). Healthy or virtuous outlooks therefore are developed because we act in healthy and virtuous ways and because we are encouraged to do so in evaluative language whose truth we come to see (i.e., apprehend) over time. We are lovers of health or virtue in this sense precisely because we come to treat health and virtue as ends in themselves; that is, when we wish them for their own sake or as good. But, as I proposed earlier, this is something that appears to the individual and not something deliberated upon; and it is apprehended or intuited *qua* wish in this fashion, I suggest, because it is available to our nature to do so when we are on our way to functioning well as human beings (as will be discussed in chapter 6 section 1). Aristotle is very careful to say that our nature does not necessitate that we apprehend virtue, since he thinks we are born dispositionally neutral and can develop well or badly (*NE* 2.1 1103a19–25); but that we come to apprehend virtue (just as we might health) as the good, as our dispositions firm up and we come to be lovers of virtue.[30] The health analogy is particularly instructive here since we come to see that health is an end in itself not only by acting in healthy ways, but because being healthy (or unhealthy) is an option that is available to our nature. Such "coming to see" on the back of cultivated action explains why Aristotle speaks of virtue making the goal or end right, since wish is developed on the back of moral virtue (*NE* 6.12 1143a32–1143b14).[31]

In closing, it might be useful to take stock of what we have so far, and how it sets us up for what is to come. We started with the intentional dimensions of virtuous action, and specifically with how this shapes its nature. While "the why" clearly involves reason as it manifests in choice and wish, the story is complicated by the fact that both choice and wish involve desire that is both non-rational and rational and whose orientation therefore impacts the nature of virtuous action. Since Aristotle suggests that love is a necessary condition for being virtuous and for virtuous action, we worked out the implications of this suggestion for the cultivation of rational and non-rational desire. It turns out that love in all of its dimensions is essential to the pursuit of an object of desire for itself (that is, as good or as pleasurable) so that love is key in the story of virtue even if it remains unclear how the three aspects of love are unified. This will require us to look at the notion of the right kind of self-love (which is the basis of friendship for Aristotle) that is found in virtuous individuals and which implicitly unifies the above discussed tri-dimensional aspects of love.

Notes

1 See Immanuel Kant, *Grounding for the Metaphysics of Morals: With On a Supposed Right to Lie Because of Philanthropic Concerns*, trans. James W. Ellington, 3rd ed. (Indianapolis, IN: Hackett Publishing Co., 1993), 2–3.

2 See G. E. M. Anscombe, *Intention*, 2nd ed. (Ithaca, NY: Cornell University Press, Blackwell, 1963), 1.

3 See J. B. Schneewind, "The Misfortunes of Virtue," *Ethics: An International Journal of Social, Political, and Legal Philosophy* 101, no. 1 (1990): 56–57.

4 Thus see MacIntyre on Sidgwick in Alasdair MacIntyre, *After Virtue: A Study in Moral Theory*, 3rd ed. (Notre Dame, IN: University of Notre Dame Press, 2007), 64–65. See also J. J. C. Smart and Bernard Williams, *Utilitarianism: For and Against* (Cambridge: Cambridge University Press, 1973), 93–100.

5 See John Stuart Mill, *Utilitarianism* (Indianapolis, IN: Hackett Publishing Co., 2001), 20.

6 Aristotle, "Nicomachean Ethics," in *The Complete Works of Aristotle: The Revised Oxford Translation*, ed. Jonathan Barnes, trans. W. D. Ross, updated by J. O. Urmson, Bollingen Series 71 (Princeton, NJ: Princeton University Press, 1984).

7 See Sarah Broadie, *Ethics with Aristotle* (New York, Toronto: Oxford University Press, 1991), 85–86.

8 But see Iakovos Vasiliou, "Aristotle, Agents, and Actions," in *Aristotle's Nicomachean Ethics: A Critical Guide*, ed. Jon Miller, Cambridge Critical Guides (Cambridge: Cambridge University Press, 2011), 170–90, who thinks there is a distinction between undertaking an action for an end, even a supreme end like virtue, and the motive for such action such as fame (see esp. 183–85). Thus, we might want to be virtuous and undertake action for its own sake but want to do so for the sake of fame so that we might pursue the former in certain situations even if the latter is not possible. But then it is hard to see how virtue is the supreme end for such an agent, especially since it is possible to explain how virtue can be an end itself and a means to fame. After all, Aristotle does say that final ends are ends in themselves and can be means to more final ends (*NE* 1.7 1097a30–36).

9 Aristotle, "Eudemian Ethics," in *The Complete Works of Aristotle*, ed. Barnes, trans. J. Solomon, Bollingen Series 71. Clearly distinguishing the *telos* and *skopos* of an action is not new, the most recent iteration of which can be found in Sukaina Hirji, "Acting Virtuously as an End in Aristotle's Nicomachean Ethics," *British Journal for the History of Philosophy* 26, no. 6 (2018): 1006–26. Hirji argues that when an agent acts virtuously by building a house for someone and thereby obtains a good for the political community (and which thereby constitutes its outcome/*skopos*), she at the same time engages in an instance of acting virtuously (i.e. she undertakes such action because it is virtuous and thereby satisfies the requirement that the action be undertaken for the appropriate end/*telos* of virtue).

10 See A. W. Price, "Choice and Action in Aristotle," *Phronesis: A Journal of Ancient Philosophy* 61, no. 4 (2016): 435–62. Price agrees that choice is a choice of one action over at least another, even if he thinks wish is just as specific in ways that I do not. More on this below.

11 See James Allen, "Practical and Theoretical Knowledge in Aristotle," in *Bridging the Gap between Aristotle's Science and Ethics | Ancient Philosophy*, ed. Devin Henry and Margarethe Nielesen (Cambridge: Cambridge University Press, 2015), 69, who rightly emphasizes that the goal of deliberation as an aspect of practical wisdom and therefore of the practical intellect is action, whereas the goal of theoretical wisdom is contemplation for Aristotle.

12 This is at least one reason to think that the practical and theoretical intellects are themselves only distinct in application, despite what Aristotle sometimes suggests. I will give more considered reasons for the unity of intellect in the next chapter. See Allen, "Practical and Theoretical Knowledge in Aristotle," 64 for a similar view, despite his emphasis on their differences, as seen in the previous footnote. An important, earlier version of this view is held by Kathleen V. Wilkes, "The Good Man and the Good for Man in Aristotle's *Nicomachean Ethics*," in *Essays on Aristotle's Ethics*, ed. Amélie Rorty, Major Thinkers Series 2 (Berkeley: University of California Press, 1980), 352–54.

13 I do not preclude the possibility, as unusual as it may be by Aristotle's lights, that there may only be a single possible tactical diversion, or that there may not be any other way in which Alcibiades can be saved. See Karen Margrethe Nielsen, "Deliberation as Inquiry: Aristotle's Alternative to the Presumption of Open Alternatives," *The Philosophical Review* 120, no. 3 (July 1, 2011): 383–421.

14 See, for instance, Aristotle, *Nicomachean Ethics*, trans. Terence Irwin, 3rd ed. (Indianapolis, IN: Hackett Publishing Co., 2019), 368–69.

15 I therefore think that a particular outcome such as "I need to help X" is not the product of wish as does Price, "Choice and Action in Aristotle," 452–54. Rather it is the increasingly specific outcome towards which we deliberate so that we determine and choose the action that constitutes such helping, such as "Lending X money to help X." This choice of action that leads to an outcome wherein X is

benefitted is one that instantiates the wish to act well. Price suggests (footnote 14, p. 442) that his view is driven by what he takes to be a difference between being healthy which is displayed in healthy action and being happy which is identical with living and acting well. But then on this view it seems possible that one need not be virtuous to act virtuously as is the case of being healthy to act in a healthy fashion, which I deny.

16 See J. O. Urmson, *Aristotle's Ethics* (Oxford: Blackwell, 1988), 114–16; Kelly Rogers, "Aristotle's Conception of Τὸ Καλόν," *Ancient Philosophy* 13, no. 2 (October 1, 1993): 355–71. I agree with Rogers in thinking that the aesthetic dimension of the fine is related to its fittingness (p. 357), though Irwin seems to think they are different. See T. H. Irwin, "Beauty and Morality in Aristotle," in *Aristotle's Nicomachean Ethics*, ed. Miller, 245.

17 The specific language here is of "three objects of choice" which I take to apply to wish as well since choice instantiates wish, and as we will see in the next chapter, because the three kinds of friendship involve just these goods that are wished upon a friend.

18 On a different but related note, this reading also helps explain how Aristotle thinks it is possible to act contrary to choice when, for instance, an agent retreats from battle instead of taking a stand even though they wish to act courageously and thinks that this entails the latter rather than the former. For it is not that they do not consciously choose to retreat, but that they do not choose such an action for its own sake (but rather do so from considerations of self-preservation, etc.).

19 Jonathan Barnes, ed., "On The Soul," in *The Complete Works of Aristotle: The Revised Oxford Translation*, by Aristotle, trans. J. A. Smith, Bollingen Series 71 (Princeton, NJ: Princeton University Press, 1984), 641–92 [hereafter *De Anima* or *DA*].

20 It is important to point out that this discussion is limited to a certain kind of wishing that is concerned with the broader outlook of an agent's life and does not include what we might wish for others, or for more intermediate ends such as wishing to win a marathon.

21 For more details, see my "Function, Intuition and Ends in Aristotle's Ethics," *Ethical Theory and Moral Practice* 9, no. 2 (April 1, 2006): 187–200. This reading is at odds with Jessica Dawn Moss, *Aristotle on the Apparent Good: Perception, Phantasia, Thought, and Desire*, Oxford Aristotle Studies (Oxford: Oxford University Press, 2012). Moss (pp. 3–16) thinks that the language of "appearance" ultimately grounds it in the imagination, whereas I think it is a form of intuition based on Aristotle's suggestion that wish is a form of rational desire. For while perception and by extension imagination are deeply intertwined with cognitive elements (as in the case of incidental perception), I do not think they are reducible to cognition.

22 Later, he even suggests that there is a rational/non-rational divide which does not mean that the non-rational itself is a hegemonic block of appetite that is at odds with reason, since the discussion of emotion/*thumos* is usually implicit

in the context. The discussion of incontinence, for instance, is broader than incontinence proper (which has to do with food and sex). Aristotle not only speaks of incontinence with regard to things that are pleasant, but also regarding courage, which is usually representative of *thumos* (*NE* 9.4 1166b5–11). Thus, Aristotle distinguishes the person who follows his passions (or emotions) from the incontinent (*NE* 1.4 1095a1–11); and in *NE* 1.13, Aristotle distinguishes the appetitive aspect as part of the desiring aspect, and the familiar examples of courage and temperance make clear that *thumos* is the remaining aspect (*NE* 1.13 1102b25–30). In what follows, therefore, I will explicitly take Aristotle to be speaking of the tripartite soul, understood as rational, emotional, and appetitive (and which will also be more fully worked out in chapter 3).

23 See Klaus Corcilius, "Aristotle's Definition of Non-Rational Pleasure and Pain and Desire," in *Aristotle's Nicomachean Ethics*, ed. Miller, 134–35. Corcilius suggests that appetite desiring is nothing other than the perceptual capacity of an animal that under certain conditions (for example of a lack of nourishment as in hunger) can initiate the process of restoring the animal's natural state. See my "Self and Soul in Aristotle," *Transcendent Philosophy* 5 (2004): 181–206, where I make a similar case for the identity of the faculties of perception and desire, even if I no longer hold with my views on selfhood discussed there.

24 See L. A. Kosman, "Being Properly Affected: Virtues and Feelings in Aristotle's Ethics," in *Essays on Aristotle's Ethics*, ed. Rorty, 103–16.

25 See Jozef Müller, "What Aristotelian Decisions Cannot Be," *Ancient Philosophy* 36, no. 1 (2016): 173–95. Müller recognizes the challenge of explaining the relation of non-rational desires in choice that are distinct from wish into a unified theory of desire that is not merely metaphorical, a task which I attempt to fulfill in terms of love below.

26 But slightly earlier (*NE* 8.2 1155b15–21), Aristotle tells us that the good, useful, and pleasant are objects of love, which may seem inconsistent but is not. For at one level, Aristotle is saying that the pleasant and useful are rationally loved because they are perceived as goods, albeit apparent ones. Whereas, as we will see, appetitive love is of pleasure and emotional love is of the good conceived by reason even when the good is pleasure. It would therefore seem that in the final analysis there are two objects of love: the good and the pleasant since the useful can be reduced to one or the other.

27 But see Anna Lännström, *Loving the Fine: Virtue and Happiness in Aristotle's Ethics* (Notre Dame, IN: Notre Dame Press, 2006), 10–11, who thinks that loving the fine is when desire aims at what is rightly conceived by reason. Whereas I think in addition that desire in wish, which determines what is aimed at, also involves love.

28 Hence I think anger is amenable to the rational rather than that anger is partly constituted by rational elements, or else it is hard to see how it is non-rational. But see Nancy Sherman, "The Habituation of Character," in *Aristotle's Ethics: Critical*

Essays, ed. Nancy Sherman, Critical Essays on the Classics (Lanham, MD: Rowman & Littlefield, 1999), 241.

29 For a different view, see Giles Pearson, "Non-Rational Desire and Aristotle's Moral Psychology," in *Aristotle's Nicomachean Ethics*, ed. Miller, 144–69; and Giles Pearson, *Aristotle on Desire*, Cambridge Classical Studies (Cambridge: Cambridge University Press, 2012), ch. 5, esp. 133–38. Pearson thinks that the emotions involve quasi-reasoning because otherwise animals who also possess emotions would be able to reason as well (p. 154). My reading avoids the problem of something appearing rational but in fact is not because it conceives the emotional response to the good and bad in aesthetic terms. Moreover, it should be noted that Aristotle does grant that animals have practical wisdom insofar as they have the " … power of foresight with regard to their own life" (*NE* 6.7 1141a28), which may assuage the concerns that Pearson raises.

30 The other option here is that we become lovers of pleasure broadly speaking, since this is also available to our nature as animals.

31 For an opposed view, see Moss, *Aristotle on the Apparent Good*, 155–62. Moss thinks that cultivation develops the imagination to have a generalized appearance of the good. But despite the cognitive elements in the imagination, it is unclear to me how such a reading allows Aristotle to say that something is up to us in our development in *NE* 3.5. For while we could imagine ourselves differently, the fact that so much hinges on imaginative rather than the essentially cognitive aspects of cultivation means how this might happen is not obvious. I will attempt to show how responsibility for one's character is possible on my reading in chapter 3 section 5.

3

Character, Personality, and Agency in Aristotle

3.0 Introduction

We turn our attention to Aristotle's discussion of self-love since this will help us unify the role of love in virtue and cement its centrality to the intentional aspects of Aristotle's ethical enterprise. Since this important discussion of self-love occurs in the context of the discussion of friendship, we will first discuss the characteristics of friendship and especially virtue friendship for Aristotle before uncovering how friendship with others is grounded in self-love or self-friendship. But the self of self-love, we will see, is not the metaphysical self of personal identity, even if it presupposes this self. Rather, the self here is the character or personality (as in "selfish" or "selfless") which is an attribute of the hylomorphic substance that is the self of personal identity for Aristotle. Such a personality, it turns out, is a construct whose rough outlines we began to draw in the previous chapter, even as our focus here is on the integration between its constituent parts of reason, emotion, and appetite. But if friendship is based on self-friendship, it may not be unreasonable to ask how important features of equity and autonomy that exist between friends apply to self-friendship. After all, not only are the parts of the soul unequal, but the discussion of cultivation of character suggests that the self is a construct in the hands of another. The implicit responses to these questions in the *Ethics*, we will see, help us understand how the self is a harmony that essentially, if only eventually, involves a self-making that unifies the making and the doing in love. But if the self is a product of making as it goes about the activities of virtue, then this has interesting implications for thinking about the life of virtue as an artifact, as opposed to just in terms of a life of virtuous activity as is usually done. For it allows us to see how much more tenuous happiness in the fullest sense might be, especially when we consider the place and pursuit of philosophy in such a life in chapter 9.

3.1 The Meaning of *Philia*

It seems reasonable therefore to begin with friendship between selves since Aristotle eventually makes the claim that friendship and especially the best friendship between good people is based on self-friendship (*NE* 9.4 1166a1–12). "Friendship" translates *philia,* but the cognate verb, *philein,* does not have an obvious parallel translation, which is why "love" is often used. This presents a minor challenge as *philia* (the noun) for Aristotle is far broader than its translation "friendship" suggests, since it covers a mother's relation with her child at one end, business relations at the other, and what we normally take to be the relations connecting friends in between.[1] But weakening the cognate verb's translation to "affection," for instance, does not capture the paradigmatic examples of the activity for Aristotle between a parent and child or between best friends. For clearly a mother usually has more than just affection for her child, for instance. Hence, we will use "love" to translate "*philein,*" which has the advantage of capturing the central activity of the paradigmatic instances of friendship. But rather than translate one's love for oneself (*philautos*) as "self-friendship," we will use the standard "self-love," which has the advantage of emphasizing the continuity of the discussion on love initiated in chapter 2.

While friendship for Aristotle is wider in one sense than it is for us, it is narrower than what can be loved; for we can love dogs and paintings but cannot be said to be friends with them. This is so because friendship, we would agree with Aristotle, involves goodwill—literally, wishing our friends the good for the friend's sake—that is reciprocated and recognized as such. If I have goodwill towards someone who does not know it, even if she has the same towards me, then this is not yet friendship, which requires the mutual recognition of the reciprocity of goodwill at the very least (*NE* 8.2 1155b32–1156a5). Even so, while there cannot be such mutually recognized goodwill with a painting, it is not obvious why a friendship is not possible with a dog. After all, there surely is mutually recognized goodwill between dog and master of some sort, yet clearly not enough for Aristotle to include it in his broad conception of friendship. Perhaps the missing component is not so much that the master cannot wish his dog well for his own sake, but that the dog cannot do so for his master. The dog may have deep affection for his master, and even attempt to save him from drowning, for instance; but Aristotle I think would say that this involves goodwill which involves rationality to be able to wish the good for the master's own sake, and to be able to make choices to instantiate such a wish. This asymmetric reciprocity between master and dog is another reason why, as we will see, that "self-love" is a better translation than "self-friendship" since it signals that the internal relations within a person are not quite the same as the relations between friends. That friendship centrally involves rationality for Aristotle is clear from his insistence that friendship is a state of character that involves choice and wish (*NE* 8.5 1157b30–33), both of which are key to rational action as we have seen in the previous chapter (and more on their role in friendship below).

If goodwill is a necessary condition of virtue and involves wishing the good for one's friend, it should follow that such a wished for good is both apparent and real as discussed in the previous chapter; and in fact, Aristotle confirms exactly this in the early part of Book 8 (*NE* 8.2 1155b15–1156a5). That is, while the real good is virtue, the apparent good is pleasure and utility so that friendships therefore are of these three sorts. The paradigmatic version of virtue friendship is the most stable and enduring because friends wish for the real good for each other, which, as suggested earlier, is also good for them; an act of generosity not only benefits one's friend but constitutes one's flourishing insofar as one acts finely. Sometimes Aristotle emphasizes the benefits of virtue for the agent's flourishing (for example, *NE* 9.8 1169a18–1169b1) but this is misleading especially when it comes to the other-regarding virtues since the real good is both good for others and for oneself precisely because it is other-regarding.[2] But this becomes a real problem in the lesser forms of friendship where the apparent good is, first and foremost, wished for *oneself*. That is, most of us who are less-than-virtuous undertake pleasure and utility friendships because we wish them to be pleasurable or useful to us first, and only by extension to the other (*NE* 8.3 1156a9–17). This is problematic for it may not be that our friends want the same from us, or want it as consistently, which means such friendships tend to be unstable and short-lived. That is, the instability arises because what is pleasurable and useful can shift easily, thereby endangering the relationship; and this is especially so when the friends want different goods from each other. But more needs to be said about stability in this context.

A friend can be conceived in terms of her wealth, position, and power as much as by her sense of humor; and this seems no more or no less transient than doing so in terms of one's character. It is true that wealth, position, and even one's sense of humor can be lost in adversity, but we know too that one's character can change in such circumstances as well. But Aristotle is not speaking here of just any character, but of the very best kind, the kind that is virtuous. It is this character that he wants to insist is stable (*NE* 8.3 1156b13), and, we saw in the previous chapter, is essentially defined as a prerequisite of virtue that is developed by cultivation. At an intuitive level, this makes sense, for a good person's character is integral to her and unlikely to change in adversity, as Aristotle confirms elsewhere (*NE* 1.10 1101a9–10). Fittingly, Aristotle says in contrast that a vicious nature is changeable for it is neither simple nor good. Even if a person consistently pursues bodily pleasure (as opposed to the weak-willed who sometimes do), Aristotle thinks the target is constantly shifting (*NE* 7.14 1154b29–30). This may be not only because more of the same is necessary to satisfy a sweet tooth, but because different things seem pleasant at different times depending, for instance, on a deteriorating state of health. Since vice is an extreme, we can imagine how the pursuit of pleasure maximized can be divisive and self-destructive. As we will see, the issue of stability and its lack will end up being a key theme of this chapter, especially when it comes to one's relation with oneself. But first we must see what else Aristotle has to say about the stability and longevity of friendship.

So, there would seem to be a strong relation between the stability and longevity of virtue friendship and the fact that virtuous individuals are stable, which becomes obvious in Aristotle's discussion of the characteristics of such friendship (*NE* 9.4 1166a1–8). He tells us that it is not enough for the virtuous agent to simply wish the good for her friend (condition 1); she must consistently make choices to instantiate such wishes for the friend's sake, which *qua* virtuous she will do. But to do so, friends must live together or spend a great deal of time together (condition 2), for while absence does not kill a friendship, an extended separation makes it inactive (*NE* 8.5 1157b11–12). Wishing the good for a friend for Aristotle includes many of the things we might include: existence (condition 3), wealth, and honor (*NE* 9.8 1169a20ff). Of course, all of these are wished for in accordance with virtue, which is the highest good. Courage requires, for instance, that the friend's life is protected even at the cost of one's own; justice, that the friend gets the external goods she deserves that are in the agent's power to procure, and so on. But since in perfect friendships both friends are virtuous, they share a common conception of the good. Hence Aristotle thinks they will not only make similar choices (condition 4) but will enjoy and despise the same things because of their common conception of the good (condition 5). All these conditions are therefore not only about (a) the fact that virtue friendships involve wishing and choosing the good for each other (conditions 1–3), but (b) that the stability comes from the similarity and consistency of what is chosen and wished *for* per se (conditions 4–5). Such stability and consistency arises because the virtuous individuals, as we saw, are so themselves. But now Aristotle says that this stability and consistency of the individual is so because the same relation of friendship that applies between friends also applies within the friend "insofar as he is two or more" (*NE* 9.4 1166a33–34), and so much so that the other-friendships are grounded in self-friendship (*NE* 9.4 1166a2).

Self-friendship or self-love/*philautos*, as Aristotle eventually calls it, of the right kind satisfies the conditions of virtue friendship in ways that the wrong kinds of self-love (or what we might call "selfishness") does not. Wishing and choosing the good for a friend is not incompatible with wishing and choosing the good for the agent herself, as we just saw. But it is also unlikely that the agent can consistently wish and choose the real good for the friend if the agent were not herself virtuous and therefore able to consistently wish the good for herself. Being able to wish and choose the real good for herself not only satisfies (a) (and hence conditions 1, 2, and 3), but it also means that since she consistently does so, she is not at odds with herself regarding the good (as is the case for those who are weak-willed), which satisfies (b) (and hence conditions 4 and 5). So, we at least have an initial sense of how friendship can be based on self-love. Aristotle does seem to think that the self-lover who wishes and chooses the apparent as opposed to the real good and which as we saw is for herself first, is also called a self-lover—albeit of the kind that we would call "selfish." Even though such a self-lover can satisfy conditions 1, 2, and 3, he thinks, for reasons that we will look at more fully below, that she is unable to satisfy conditions 4 and 5.

So now that we have the basic setup of the primacy of self-love for friendship for Aristotle, we are able to enumerate how we will assess its implications. First, it is unclear what Aristotle means by the "self" in "self-lover," which we will need to assess in the context of his views on substance and personal identity. Second, we will need to look at the suggestion that the self is partite and perhaps only bi-partite; that the partite nature of the self refers to the rational and the non-rational (broadly construed) becomes quickly obvious in the characteristics of virtue friendship that are based in self-love. For he says that good people are not at odds with themselves, and that their choices and wishes are consistently in accord with reason so that the same things are consistently enjoyed and detested. The language of pleasure reminds us that Aristotle thinks that lovers of virtue will find virtue enjoyable but does not seem to separate out the appetites (which are explicitly driven by pleasure and pain, as we saw in chapter 2) from the emotions (which can apprehend the good). This lack of clarity on tripartition is not helped by the way in which the wrong kind of self-lover is spoken of in terms of incontinence and therefore of appetite, so that these individuals are characterized as being at odds with themselves in ways in which the better kind of self-lovers are not. Third, and perhaps most interestingly, we will examine how the language of love in self-love extends the scope of love to include not just the object of virtue but its subject as well and bring about the subject's internal unity and harmony.

3.2 Aristotle on Personhood and Personality

Aristotle has a unique notion of hylomorphic substance that grounds his notion of the person or self (see Appendix 1 for details). Thus, Socrates is a combination of matter and form where the latter is not reducible to the former and is responsible for its organization (as soul) so that Socrates can carry on the usual, essential human activities of nutrition, perception, and thinking. This allows Aristotle to say that while accidental changes (of color, knowledge, etc.) do not affect Socrates' personhood, essential changes do so that the post-hemlock dead body is no longer Socrates except by extension. Now clearly this understanding of the self of personal identity is very different from the self that is discussed in the context of self-love. The better conception of self-love, as we just saw at the end of the previous section, is understood in terms of wishing and choosing the good for oneself and not being at odds with oneself regarding the good. But this discussion does not tell us how such a self persists. In fact, it seems that the discussion of self-love assumes rather than proves the self of personal identity. For instance, not to be at odds with oneself regarding the good presupposes but does not prove that past, present, and future actions belong to the same person. After all, one must be the same person now as in the past if one is to either agree or disagree with oneself.

I suggest, therefore, that the discussion of self-love is not so much a discussion about the nature of a self or person (i.e., the substance) as much as it is a discussion of the nature of personality (i.e., the attributes of a substance). Recall that at the end of section 3.1, we saw Aristotle thinks that there are two kinds of self-lovers, depending on whether they conceive the good in real or apparent terms. The better kind is the virtuous person who rightly conceives the good, whereas the selfish kind is one who misconceives it. So, when Aristotle speaks of distinct kinds of self-lovers, he is speaking of different attributes that qualify the substance or person (i.e., virtue or vice), rather than of the substance itself. The language of the self in self-love, then, functions like "person" does in personality. After all, a personality is an attribute of a person, self, or agent, understood here in hylomorphic terms.

Such an assumption concerning the hylomorphic conception of the self (and hence of personal identity) in Book 9 is not isolated, as many earlier discussions in the text seem to make it as well. As we will see in chapter 6, the function argument in *NE* 1.7 makes the case that happiness is an activity of the soul. Even so, the argument is chiefly concerned with the function of a human being, as expressed in a complete life in accordance with reason (*NE* 1.7 1097b21–1098a19). Even when he distinguishes external goods (such as wealth and power) from the goods of the body (such as health and beauty) from those of the soul in the very next chapter, Aristotle is quite clear that all three have a role in the good life of the agent or person. It is this agent that is held responsible for certain kinds of ignorance as opposed to others in voluntary action, and for becoming a certain kind of character (as opposed to a different kind) that eventually becomes too late to change (*NE* 3.5 1114a14–22). In other words, it is the hylomorphic compound of matter and form that is the person or self, and which is qualified by the attributes of good or bad.

Now virtue and vice, Aristotle has repeatedly told us, are activities of the soul, where the soul is the form of the body. If virtue and vice are the basis of personality and are a function of the soul, it follows that personality (i.e., the kind of self-lover) will be a function of the configuration of the soul. Since we have already seen in previous chapters that virtue is reason leading the emotions and appetites, it should come as no surprise that the virtuous configuration of the soul involves these aspects or parts of the soul. So, to confirm our response to the second question we raised at the beginning of section 3.2, the parallel to the plurality relation between friends in self-friendship is indeed a relation between the soul's parts. The problem is that Aristotle is not as explicit as he could have been in laying his version of tripartition of the soul out for us, and so we will have to work it out.

3.3 Bipartition, Tripartition, and Other Complications

The explicit problem is that Aristotle seems to suggest that the right kind of self-lover has a soul that is separated into a rational part and a non-rational part that is capable of heeding reason, and is therefore bipartite rather than tripartite. Here, the problem is that he doesn't seem to separate the non-rational part further into the emotional and appetitive. A related but different problem is that the rational part (rather than the non-rational part) seems to be divided up into practical and theoretical parts, which causes different and rather more severe problems, as we will soon see. Finally, Aristotle seems to suggest at times that the intellect is all there is to the person, which is at odds with his initial suggestion that the self is a construct of rational and non-rational parts. But let us tackle the first problem first.

3.3.1 Bipartition vs Tripartition

If the soul is the formal organizational principle of matter and not simply reducible to it, it is unsurprising that Aristotle is wary of using the language of parts (*NE* 1.13 1102a29–33). After all, material things are what can be divided into parts whereas it might be more appropriate to ask after the aspects rather than parts of soul. Aristotle's response in the context of self-love is that we can be friends to ourselves insofar as we (i.e., our souls) are "two or more" (*NE* 9.4 1166a36). While not exactly shutting the door on tripartition, his hesitation to confirm that the soul is tripartite is puzzling, but understandable for at least two reasons. First, and most immediately in context, perhaps because he explicitly has weakness of will or incontinence in mind here (*NE* 9.4 1166b6–12). For incontinence is primarily—as opposed to when it is broadly construed—about reason (*nous*) and appetite (*epithumia*) being at odds. Second, such a dichotomy is consistent with his division of the soul into rational and irrational aspects in general in the *Ethics* and in particular in the crucial function argument (*NE* 1.7 1198a3–4), where the relevant irrational aspect is broadly spoken of as capable of heeding reason as opposed to the irrational aspect (i.e., the nutritive capacity) that cannot. The discussion of the passions or feelings are only apparently missing here since these rather than the appetites are directly capable of heeding reason. But both appetite and emotion are characterized by being felt so that Aristotle might feel it is easier, rhetorically speaking, to discuss the unification of the soul in bipartite rather than in tripartite terms. Or perhaps he thinks the bipartite parallel is easier to draw with virtue friendship, which, though rare, is more likely to occur between two people.

Whatever Aristotle's reasons might be, it is quite clear that the discussion of *thumos*—the aspect responsible for emotion—is usually implicit in the context, even if it is not always explicit. The discussion of incontinence in relation to self-love mentioned above is broader than incontinence proper (which is restricted to the objects of food and sex). Hence Aristotle not only speaks of incontinence regarding things that are pleasant, but also with regard to courage, which is usually representative of *thumos* (*NE* 9.4 1166b5–11). Similar distinctions can be found in the context of the function argument in *NE* 1.7. Thus, Aristotle distinguishes the person who follows his passions (or emotions) from the incontinent (*NE* 1.3 1095a1–11). And in *NE* 1.13, Aristotle distinguishes the appetitive aspect as part of the desiring aspect, and the familiar examples of courage and temperance make clear that *thumos* is the remaining aspect (*NE* 1.13 1102b25–30). So tripartition seems to allow for a nuanced way to speak of rationality's relations with the non-rational in terms of the good or pleasure (as we saw in chapter 2 section 6). In what follows, therefore, we will take Aristotle implicitly to be speaking of the tripartite soul, understood as rational, emotional, and appetitive.[3] But whether we can stay with tripartition will depend on how we understand Aristotle's bifurcation of rationality.

3.3.2 Unifying the Practical and Theoretical Intellects

In Book 6 of the *Ethics* at least, mind or intellect (*nous*), which has the capacity to think, is spoken of in practical and theoretical terms. Aristotle's rationale for this seems puzzling. Faculties have a certain "kinship and likeness" to their objects, or else they would not be able to work together. Thus, mind and the intelligible aspects of form we discussed above must be akin in some way (the fullest implications of which we will discuss in later chapters). Here, Aristotle takes this to imply that theoretical and practical intellects must be different because their objects are different. After all, whereas the human and chicken essence remain the same no matter the thinker, in practical matters, what constitutes healthy food for humans as opposed to chickens is different (*NE* 6.1 1139a3–12; 6.7 1141a21–26). But presumably, the point also applies within human affairs. This is so because there is more variability in matters of practical concern, as we have seen, than in theoretical ones. Not only are there many means to a particular end in practical matters, but it is also often difficult to know what might actually instantiate that end in a particular situation. In other words, the good in a particular context is variable, just as what constitutes healthy food for different animals is variable.

So, when Aristotle says of the right kind of self-lover that his intellect is the most authoritative, gratified, and loved element within him, many have reasonably taken him to mean, given the practical context, the practical intellect (*NE* 9.8 1168b29–1169a3). The problem is that he does not specifically say that it is the practical intellect. Moreover, giving the practical life's primacy in this way is difficult to reconcile with the primacy that is given to the philosophical life a few pages later in Book 10 (*NE* 10.7 1177b32–1178a2).[4] There too he uses similar language prioritizing the life of intellect, which has plausibly been read to mean "theoretical intellect" in the context. But this seems inconsistent with the suggested continuities on display in chapter 2 section 2 on the relation of practical deliberation and theoretical thinking, for instance. Another way to make this point is to say that this dichotomy is phenomenologically problematic since it does not seem that we think about practical matters with one intellect and of theoretical matters with another.

Fortunately for us, there are several factors that lessen if not undermine the inconsistency. As we have already noted, Aristotle himself speaks of *nous* or intellect in general in both Books 9 and 10. Whereas the distinction between practical and theoretical intellects is made in Book 6. Moreover, Book 6 is a common book since it is also originally part of the *Eudemian Ethics*, which is usually taken to be an early ethical treatise of Aristotle's. So perhaps Aristotle changes his mind in the *Nicomachean Ethics* and that change is not reflected in the common book because of its early nature. Thus, the Nicomachean use of unqualified *nous* perhaps reflects that he does not think any longer that it is a house divided. This is clear at another, earlier iteration of the emphasis on *nous* in the same book, where he is showing how the good person's relations with himself satisfy the conditions of self-friendship (that we have already discussed). For here, he speaks of them interchangeably in the same sentence when he says that the good person wishes the good for the sake of himself or his intellect (*dianotikou*, i.e., its theoretical application) since he wishes to live and be preserved, and especially that part by which he thinks (*phronei*, i.e., its practical application) (*NE* 9.4 1166a13–23).

The implicit change of mind may be attributed to a shift of focus from the object to the faculty of cognition. The discussion in the *NE* regarding *nous* has essential continuities with the one in the *De Anima* (*DA*), where Aristotle is specifically concerned with the soul (and therefore with the subjective aspects of cognition), of which the intellect is a key aspect. For this division between practical and theoretical intellect is not forgotten in the *DA*, though there is a crucial difference. There, Aristotle tells us that the intellect *qua* theoretical contemplates nothing practical. But then he adds, " … even when it contemplates something of this kind [i.e., the practical kind], it does not straight away command avoidance or pursuit … " (*DA* III.9 432b30ff).[5] The suggestion here seems to be that while there is a difference in the activity of the intellect *qua* practical or *qua* theoretical, this is a difference in application but not in faculty.[6] Hence in III.10 he says " … [The] intellect which reasons for the sake of something and is practical … differs from the contemplative intellect in respect of end" (*DA* 3.10 433a14–16).[7] In other words, when its ends are practical, then it functions as the practical intellect, and when the ends are theoretical, as theoretical intellect.

Given the above, it may be that Aristotle thought that the practical and theoretical intellects are one and the same because he sees it is not possible to separate the practical objects of cognition from theoretical ones in practice. To use one of his examples, to know that one should eat chicken because it is a light meat, light meat being healthy for a person, combines theoretical and practical cognition. For the universal "chicken" is an object of theoretical cognition, even if determining what constitutes healthy food for a person is a function of practical cognition. This therefore seems consistent with his claim that deliberation employs the geometrical method that one would think applies to theoretical work in the main. After all, the difference arises not in the object studied but the purpose for which the study is undertaken. Aristotle likely concludes that it makes far greater sense of the phenomenon of thinking here in terms of a single faculty in different modes of application, than in terms of different faculties. It helps (and perhaps even encourages the view in the *DA*) that the thinking (or what he calls the passive) intellect is a pure potential so it can take on the cognitional form of any object without hinderance (*DA* 3.4 429b29–430a9).[8] This unification of practical and theoretical thinking that seems to be assumed in the discussion on friendship in turn means that the threat of cleaving the theoretical from the practical life is staved off. For, as we will see in chapter 9, the life of complete happiness involves both the practical and theoretical dimensions even if this ideal is only available to a select few. Still, approximations of a complete life not only involve scaling just the practical or theoretical peaks on their own, but both in some lesser way, so that avoiding a cleavage between the practical and theoretical is valuable, generally speaking.

3.3.3 Is Reason All There Is to the Person?

There is a danger of reading the crucial aspects of self-love in *NE* 9.8 discussed extensively above as suggesting that the intellect is all there is to the person or self. For Aristotle insists twice in a very short space that the intellect is, or is most of all, the self:

> But such a man would seem more than the other a lover of self; at all events he assigns to himself the things that are noblest and best, and gratifies the most authoritative element [i.e., *nous* or intellect] in himself and in all things obeys this; and just as a city or any other systematic whole is most properly identified with the most authoritative element in it, so is a man; and therefore the man who loves this and gratifies it is most of all a lover of self. Besides, a man is said to have or not to have self-control according as his reason (*nous*) has or has not the control, on the assumption that this is the man himself; and the things men have done on a rational principle are thought most properly their own acts and voluntary acts. That this is the man himself, then, or is so more than anything else, is plain, and also that the good man loves most this part of him.
>
> (*NE* 9.8 1168b28–1169a3)

Quite clearly "man" or "person" here refers to the self in "lover of self" and therefore to the self of personality rather than personal identity. But we need to be careful to take the context into full consideration before we can see what "self" refers to here. What in fact Aristotle is saying is that in gratifying our authoritative or *kuriōtatō* element, we are gratifying that aspect of us that is most dominant; but being dominant requires something to be dominant over, and this obviously is of the passional and appetitive aspects within us. Similarly, to say that reason is the person is the same as saying that the most authoritative element of the city *is* the city, which doesn't mean that is all there is to the city.[9] Moreover, we have to remember that Aristotle here is not strictly speaking of the person of personal identity as much as he is speaking of personality. If so, it would be hard to imagine one's personality being purely rather than predominantly rational. Nothing prevents us, therefore, from taking Aristotle to be saying that self-friendship is indeed a plurality relation between a unified reason, emotion, and appetite. We can now turn to how such relations within the soul can approximate the relations between autonomous and equitable friends, so that we can fully understand the place of love in Aristotle's ethics.

3.4 Equity and Harmony in Self-Love

Many careful readers of Aristotle are not convinced that friendship is based on self-love, usually because there does not seem to be friendship between the parts of the self as there is between friends.[10] One way we might respond is to show that important characteristics of friendship such as equity and autonomy apply first and as much to self-love. The autonomy requirement in friendship seems more rigid than the one for equity since equity is multi-dimensional, for it is hard to imagine friendship as a product of coercion. We cannot force two people to be friends since, as we saw, friendship is something that requires wishing each other well and choosing to act in accordance with such wishes. It is not unreasonable, therefore, to think that friends are autonomous individuals, at least to the extent that they make such choices on their own. On the other hand, since friendships can be based on different expectations between friends, clearly friendships are not equitable in that sense. Nor is it the case that friends are necessarily equals since the language of friendship, as we saw, often describes the relations between parents and their children, for instance. In the paradigmatic instance of virtue friendship, clearly there is a sense in which the friends are equals in virtue (*NE* 8.6 1157b36; 8.7 1158b27–28), if not in everything else (for example, wealth or social standing). Let us therefore begin with a more detailed consideration of how equity might apply in the case of self-love before we move to the challenge of thinking about autonomy in this context.

Unequal yet viable friendships allow us to see how similar inequalities might exist in self-friendship, since the tripartite aspects of personality are so different from each other. If the inequalities (say of power or knowledge) become too extreme, Aristotle suggests that friendships can become unviable because of a loss of common ground (*NE* 9.3 1165b23–28).[11] But, for the most part, the inequalities are neutralized in the relationship since " … the superior person gets honour and the inferior, more gain" (*NE* 9.14 1163b3). Of course, the problem is that since the agent usually reciprocates in terms of what he expects from the friend, it is the case that these friendships don't last, as we have already seen. For in unequal friendships, the friend doesn't necessarily want the same thing in return. But Aristotle's point seems to be that it is *possible* to sustainably expect different things from each other, as is clearly the case with parent-child relations, which we saw are a form of friendship. Thus, while parents care for the well-being of the child, the child repays them with honor, even though no honor can fully repay the debt of existence that is owed here (*NE* 9.1 1164b3–5). Self-friendship, then, in one important sense, resembles the unequal relationship between parent and child. This is so because Aristotle repeatedly emphasizes the intellect's superiority over the non-rational aspects as we saw at the end of the last section, and not just in the discussions of friendship (for instance *NE* 1.13 1102b14–18; *NE* 10.7 1177a20; 2077b30; 1178a5–8, etc.). Clearly, the different aspects of the soul are satisfied by different objects so that the appetite for food and sex in a virtuous person, for instance, is satisfied in a sustainable manner in exchange for the suzerainty and the accompanying honor afforded to the intellect.

Honor for the better is in proportion to the lesser's love, if Aristotle means honor (or respect) as opposed to honors (which are public displays that may or may not be representative of honor).[12] For we honor those who we love. Hence Aristotle also makes the point about equalizing in terms of love when he says:

> In all friendships implying inequality the love also should be proportional, i.e., the better should be more loved than he loves, and so should be more useful, and similarly in each of the other cases: for when the love is in proportion to the merit of the parties, then in a sense arises equality, which is certainly held to be a characteristic of friendship.
>
> (*NE* 8.7 1158b24–28)

Parents are not just honored by their children but loved as well, just as the better friend is honored and loved by the lesser. What love brings to the relationship is reciprocity, since clearly parents love (i.e., *philein*) their children too as much as the better loves the lesser in a friendship. Ideally, this love is in proportion to merit, though this does not always happen since parents often love their creations more than they ought, and children love their parents less than they should. So, what likely makes the love proportional is when what is deemed worthy of merit (i.e., the good) is accurately perceived. Such perception of the good is clearly possible to the virtuous parent (as discussed in chapter 2 section 3), and to an approximate extent, then, to the child on its way to virtue.

But if love has the ability to bring parity to a relationship between friends, we can ask how this might be so in the case of self-love (which is, after all, the verb form of self-friendship). The answer likely is that what is true for relations between friends must be so for what is the case within the self and should therefore be seen in terms of the relationship between love and goodness. In the case of self-friendship, as we have already seen in chapter 3 section 1, the right kind of self-lover consistently wishes and chooses the real as opposed to the apparent good without being at odds with herself. In our discussion of love and virtue in chapter 2 section 6, we saw that loving something means to desire it for its own sake (for example, health), as opposed to wanting it for the sake of something else (as in the case of a medical procedure which is for the sake of health). Moreover, the virtuous person is one in whom reason, emotion, and appetite are aligned because reason *qua* wish perceives the good. Emotion and appetite, on the other hand, are cultivated to love the good (in terms of the fine/noble or pleasure) and are manifest in the choice that instantiates wish. It is no wonder then that the right kind of self-lover is in sync with herself; for even though emotions and appetites cannot conceive the good, they can apprehend it *qua* good or *qua* pleasure. Yet it is also through the mediation of the good, for instance, that the intellect can enjoy the appropriate satisfaction of appetite (i.e., as a good); or else, we would not have the reciprocity in self-love that we do in friendship. Thus, the virtues involve relations between reason, emotions, and appetites that are based in love and thereby constitute what Aristotle means by self-love.

Yet given the primacy and superiority of the intellect and reason in Aristotle, it is important to remind ourselves that the relation between the rational and non-rational is not simply top down if in fact it is to be more than minimally reciprocal. Recall that the crucial, desiderative component of wish, which is rational desire, is inculcated through action. Wish's perception of the real (as opposed to the apparent) good in the virtuous person is a function of character, which is inculcated through cultivation (*NE* 3.4 1113a25–35). Thus, it is not simply the non-rational aspects of character (and specifically their desiring) that a good upbringing is concerned with, but with the rational as well. Such rational desire, then, is for acting well in general, which takes time to acquire, like the desire to continue to be healthy. This desire is instantiated in a particular context by choice, which brings together deliberation and non-rational desire. Hence the inculcation of rational and non-rational desire for the good comes from the bottom up, through action. Moreover, it is the unity of desire in wish and choice that results in harmonious action that is characteristic of virtuous action for Aristotle and therefore of the right kind of self-love.

Thus, it would seem that the issues of harmony and equity are closely related. We cannot have a harmony if its potential constituents are not in some kind of equitable relationship. Or else we would have either a discord or even a disconnect on the one hand, or a hegemony rather than harmony on the other. While it is true that the rational and non-rational aspects of personality are unequal in important ways, as Aristotle is often keen to emphasize, they are equals in virtue. It is this equality in virtue understood in terms of a shared love of the good that allows them to work together in harmony. After all, if the equity in the best kinds of friendship is based on virtue and not on considerations such as power and position, and such friendships are modeled on self-love, it makes sense that equity in virtue is the basis of self-love as well.

The harmony that self-love makes possible also has important implications for unity and autonomy. If, as we saw in chapter 2 section 1, the virtues are defined in terms of their stability, then the common and pleasurable pursuit of the good by both the rational and non-rational aspects of the personality cement this stability into a harmonious unity. If these in fact are pursued as different goods, then at best what we could have is a neutral status quo when the rational and non-rational balance each other out; but Aristotle in fact thinks that such disagreement about the good usually leads to discord within the person (*NE* 9.5 1166b1–29). Such unity then begins to approximate that of the Divine in ways that will allow us to access the contemplative activity of the Divine (understood as a necessary first principle that is fine/*kalon* (*Metaphysics* 12.7 1072b10–11[13])), and which is key to human happiness, as we will see in chapter 9 (*NE* 7.14 1154b21–30). Yet if we are to have a truly harmonious unity here, as I think Aristotle wants, we need to see how such unity is autonomous in some essential way, and not coerced; for a coerced harmony sounds like an oddity, if not a downright contradiction.

3.5 Autonomy (as Self-Governance)

Autonomy/*autarkia* in contemporary discussions means self-determination or self-governance, a meaning that originates with the Greeks and especially

Aristotle. Practical wisdom (*phronēsis*), which is the acme of practical virtue for Aristotle, is defined in terms of knowing what is good for the agent in general and being able to attain it. In fact, Aristotle thinks it is this ability to self-govern that is the basis of such an agent's ability to govern the state (*NE* 6.5 1140b4–11); hence, he goes so far as to say that they are the same disposition (*hexis*) and only differ in application (*NE* 6.8 1141b23). This reference to self-governance is unsurprising, given that such self-governance presupposes an internal harmony that we just saw the virtuous kind of self-lover possesses. Interestingly enough, Aristotle explicitly uses the language of *autarkia* in *NE* 1.7, to speak of how humans as rational, social beings can be independent or self-sufficient because they are virtuous. That discussion, as I will show in chapter 9, implicitly understands such independence in terms of self-governance discussed here. Returning to the matter at hand, then, we will have to see how autonomy of the individual transmutes in the context of the aspects of personality.

Clearly, autonomy as self-governance is something that can apply at best to the rational rather than the non-rational aspects of the soul. But even if the non-rational aspects are not quite self-governing, they do have a natural orientation of their own, as discussed in chapter 2 section 5. While different kinds of cultivation change this orientation, in general Aristotle thinks humans will follow their appetites if left to themselves. This is perhaps because our animal nature is such a large part of us in comparison to the rational (*NE* 10.7 1178a1); and it explains why in general we think that those who indulge their appetites less, are better than those who indulge them more (*NE* 2.9 1109b6–12). Similarly, different people are more or less courageous by nature (courage, as we saw, being representative of the archetypical emotion of *spiritedness/thumos* for Aristotle), so lacking the natural sight that reason provides can lead to stumbling and perhaps even falling (*NE* 6.13 1144b3–14). This in turn suggests that reason, if left to its own devices, has its own teleology, one that is often subverted in turn by strong appetites and passions (as is manifest in regret). Of course, cultivation, which is often guided by parents or tutors, directs the natural teleology of the non-rational parts as much as education does of reason, and by implication, of the person as a whole. The issue, then, in the context of our concern here with autonomy as self-governance, will be to see if somehow the process of cultivation is not entirely coercive.

Now understanding how a virtuous person becomes self-governing requires a discussion of Aristotle's important if controversial distinction between virtue and skill/*techne*. We have seen that a virtuous person is the product of a long process of education and training, overseen by a moral tutor. So, it might be appropriate to say that the overall expertise in the tutor plausibly produces virtue in the tutee and eventually in the virtuous person herself. But this tutor/tutee distinction separates the skill from its product too neatly; for completing the process essentially involves the tutee's own hand, as we will see below. An understanding of the virtue/skill distinction will help us see the tutee's role in completing the process that makes it possible for her to become a self-governing actor.

3.6 Virtue and Skill

Aristotle divides knowledge into theoretical, practical, and productive. Theoretical knowledge, Aristotle tells us, is pursued for its own sake and is the aim of both the speculative and empirical sciences such as metaphysics, physics, biology, and mathematics. Practical knowledge is concerned with the good attainable by action, which therefore differs from species to species because their respective goods do as well (*NE* 6.7 1141a21–23). Practical knowledge in the human arena involves politics and ethics and is concerned with our relations with others and therefore with action, rather than with knowledge for its own sake. Productive knowledge is concerned with making artifacts as in medicine, shipbuilding, and art (*Topics* 6.6 145a15–16).[14] Thus, the virtue/skill distinction seems to separate the virtuous activity from the making of virtue into two very different arenas of practical and productive knowledge in Aristotle.

The key difference between action and production is that the latter is essentially concerned with the rational production of an artifact, whereas the former is about the rational capacity to act (*NE* 6.4 1140a5–21). Products are not simply non-living things like chairs, but things like health and therefore healthy people as well, who are an outcome of the skill of medicine for Aristotle. By extension, therefore, it is not unreasonable to think that virtue and the virtuous person is a product of a craft, such as character education. Aristotle insists that the focus of the assessment, when it comes to skill, is very much on the quality of the product. But a skill is a process/*kinesis* that takes time and is complete only when we have a complete product (for example, virtue) and is incomplete at every stage before that (*NE* 10.4 1174a19–23). Whereas in the case of the activities of someone who is already virtuous, the focus for Aristotle is on the doing, which as we saw in chapter 2, presupposes knowledge, virtuous character, and choice that is undertaken for its own sake. Interestingly enough, in his contrast with making, Aristotle focuses on how virtuous action is a doing that is an end in itself, and therefore an activity/*energeia*, which by implication does not take time since like seeing it is complete from moment to moment (*NE* 10.4 1174a14–21; 6.5 1140b4–7).[15] Now we saw that practical activity is defined as being concerned with goods attainable in action, which therefore must include things like victory in a skirmish that in fact do take time. Indeed, we have spoken of such outcomes as the aim/*skopos* of virtuous action that is the result of deliberative choice, even if outcomes are not artifacts though clearly both are the result of processes.[16] The difference is that without the appropriate *telos*—of choosing action for its own sake which plausibly does not take time—we no longer have virtuous activity even if we have the right outcome (such as victory) since the right *telos* is an essential condition for virtuous activity. Whereas with skill, the outcome (that is, the artifact) *is* all that counts. While there is much value in defending Aristotle's explicit distinction between virtue and skill, we will look at an instance where they seem to come together in the construction and maintenance of virtuous character; for this convergence in turn has interesting implications for the role of fortune in happiness.[17]

We have spoken broadly of the cultivation of character in the previous chapter, and it will be useful to remind ourselves of the broad features of that discussion from the perspective of the skill necessary to develop the right kind of personality. The obvious one to begin with is that the making of a good person takes time both in terms of cultivating character and in the education of reason. This is so whether we are speaking of learning to enjoy the right kinds of food in cultivating the appetites' development towards temperance; or of learning to stand one's ground in battle to cultivate the seemingly contradictory emotions of fear (to help assess the dangers appropriately) and confidence (that is the ground of positive action without being reckless) in their evolution towards a courageous disposition.[18] In the latter case, the cultivation of the emotions occurs in the context of learning battle skills such as sword-play, which involves learning, among other things, how to lunge, thrust, parry, and riposte.[19] Moreover, such development requires variation in opportunity so that the tutee can learn to distinguish the relevant features of the situation before learning to respond to them. Such responses, one learns over time, need to be modulated so that the eventual virtuous choice that instantiates wish hits what Aristotle calls the Mean (as we will discuss in chapter 6).

The second important feature of such development is that it presupposes a tutor, and not just for the rational dimensions, but for the cultivation of moral dispositions as well. Learning to eat the right food or to make the right moves in battle and learning how to develop the right kinds of wish requires someone with knowledge and insight. Aristotle thinks that the tutor ideally must be a citizen and hence a lawmaker, but, as we will see in chapter 6, his training regime has to be consistent with the law (*NE* 10.9 1179b30–1180a5). Otherwise, it is hard to see how the tutee himself ideally becomes a virtuous citizen. Aristotle insists, therefore, that the laws that govern the education of youth are ideally common to all citizens in the state and not simply the law of a particular household, as is usually the case. Of course, the application of law to the education of individuals has to be customized, and this is done best by those who know the law by dint of being its authors (*NE* 10.9 1180a26–1180b20).

Even so, the process of self-construction that the tutor initiates and undertakes is eventually only completed in the hands of the tutee herself. A virtuous person, we know, must wish and choose to act temperately and do so for the sake of the action itself. Whereas the tutee's actions are an approximation to temperance because the tutor asks her to do so. In between lies a transition to autonomy. We may ask how this happens, especially since one way to deny this is to suggest that the tutee merely thinks she chooses the actions for their own sake eventually, when in fact she has been coercively trained to do so. But Aristotle suggests what makes it a transition is that it is still up to the tutee to wish and choose otherwise than she does, though after her character is set it becomes a moot issue (*NE* 3.5 1114b15–25). This I think we can appreciate from our experiences with or as children. No matter how well brought up, there is always a transition period in which a young person may make mistakes on her way to self-determination, even if these missteps sometimes end disastrously. Since such mistakes arise frequently enough regardless of the socio-political context and can just as often be crucial to the ideally self-correcting processes that lead to self-governance, they suggest that virtue is not simply the result of coercion. For it is not enough to be taught about the good; one must come to wish and choose it for itself and by oneself (that is, out of love in all its forms), which often occurs in the good's absence when one falls away from the path to virtue.[20] Nor must Aristotle's suggestion be taken to mean that one cannot act otherwise once virtue is established. It is just that such divergences are no longer a live option in the way they might be for the tutee in transition, and perhaps even more so for one who is weak-willed.

But reason's pursuit of the good for its own sake is not all there is to virtue and hence to self-love; for virtue requires this be so for the non-rational aspects as well. Making a case for the autonomy of the non-rational aspects of personality is more challenging since self-governance is usually associated with reason. This is so especially since the non-rational parts are rationally cultivated rather than educated, for the line between cultivation and coercion is difficult to discern.

Such discernment might be aided by recalling that the non-rational aspects come to love the good conceived by reason despite having natural orientations of their own. This love clearly relies on the familiarity provided by cultivation but is more than that in important ways. First, since it is directed at the good perceived as fine or as pleasurable, it is not merely an automatic response, but a deeply felt committed one that an agent's drives come to on their own during the transition. For one cannot be brought to love through coercion even if one can be coerced because one loves.

So, it seems that the skilled process of character-building of the tutee that begins with the tutor is ultimately completed and maintained in the hands of the tutee herself. The self-skilling is completed by actions that closely approximate fully virtuous actions but are still processes since they are involved in the self-construction of the virtuous person. Fully virtuous activity, then, is only possible once we have the virtuous person. It is as if Aristotle had just this point about self-construction in mind when he explains why the benefactor loves the benefited friend more, rather than vice versa; for he says:

> The cause of this is that existence is to all men a thing to be chosen and loved, and that we exist by virtue of activity (i.e. by living and acting), and that the handiwork *is*, in a sense, the producer in actuality; he loves his handiwork, therefore, because he loves existence. And this is rooted in the nature of things; for what he is in potentiality, his handiwork manifests in actuality.
>
> (*NE* 9.7 1168a5–9)

Aristotle is clearly speaking here about the agent's involvement in the making and hence loving of her friend, and how much of the agent *qua* handiwork is in the friend as a result, which eventually allows him to justify his view that the friend is another self (*NE* 9.4 1166a3–32; 9.9 1169b6; 9.10 1170b6). But this is literally truer of the agent's loving herself as she is critically involved in her own self-construction, wherein the handiwork really is the producer in actuality.[21] Moreover, the self-love is an ongoing activity since self-construction, or, at the very least, self-maintenance, is an ongoing enterprise.[22] For the virtuous disposition is maintained by virtuous activity (understood in terms of the undertaking of its *telos* as much as of its *skopos*), much like health is maintained by exercise. But most importantly, it is quite clear that the love of virtuous action is not distinct from one's love of oneself or self-love since action is the producer/character/personality actualized, and these are simply different ways of speaking of the same thing.[23]

I want to discuss two related implications of Aristotle's views here before I end this chapter. The first has to do with how the harmony that is emphasized in the discussion of equity is enhanced here by the unity that our assessment of autonomy brings to light. Reason leads on this view, both in the process of cultivation and the exercise of virtue, and its leadership is non-coercive and in harmony with the non-rational. Thus, we have a stable, joyful personality that expresses this internal consistency in the ability to pursue sustained practical activity, and is essentially presupposed, I will suggest, in the pursuit of theoretical ones. The second has also to do with the issue of stability, which arises when we think about the agent's life as an artifact rather than just in terms of the activities of virtue. Aristotle speaks, as we will see later, of the activities of virtue as an essential constituent in the life of happiness. But such doing presupposes an ongoing making not just because the maintenance of virtuous dispositions are ongoing processes but because the agent's virtuous activities involve processes such as building another's character or sword-fighting that have outcomes. This in turn will be important to understand Aristotle's views in chapter 9 on the role of fortune in happiness. For a life might be virtuous yet have its outcomes grievously affected by ill-fortune in ways that suggest that Aristotle thinks of it as a self-constructed artifact. As we will see, this assessment in turn will have important implications in chapter 9 for the pursuit of philosophy and its highest actualization in contemplation/*theoria* (and thereby for happiness).

But now it is time to turn our attention to our first discussions of the *Bhagavad Gītā* on intentionality and the self so that we can set the stage for a dialogical discussion on these issues between the *Gītā* and the *Ethics*.

Notes

1 See Aristotle, *Nicomachean Ethics*, trans. Terence Irwin, 3rd ed. (Indianapolis, IN: Hackett Publishing Co., 2019), 377.

2 Hence, I think it is not ideal to read Aristotle as an egoist or an altruist. For examples of the egoism reading, see Bradford Jean-Hyuk Kim, "Aristotle on Friendship and the Lovable," *Journal of the History of Philosophy* 59, no. 2 (2021): 221–45, and Thomas Hurka, "Aristotle on Virtue: Wrong, Wrong, and Wrong," in *Aristotelian Ethics in Contemporary Perspective*, ed. Julia Peters, Routledge Studies in Ethics and Moral Theory 21 (New York: Routledge, 2013), 9–26, who thinks it is about the agent's own happiness. For examples of the altruistic reading, see Charles H. Kahn, "Aristotle and Altruism," *Mind* 90, no. 357 (1981): 20–40; John M. Cooper, "Friendship and the Good in Aristotle," *The*

Philosophical Review 86, no. 3 (July 1, 1977): 290. Whereas I think Annas is right in saying that Aristotle's position here is not reducible to altruism or egoism but takes a path between them. See Julia Annas, "Virtue Ethics and the Charge of Egoism," in *Morality and Self-Interest*, ed. Paul Bloomfield (Oxford: Oxford University Press, 2007), 214.

3 Whereas some think such a view is incipient but not implicit; see John M. Cooper, "An Aristotelian Theory of the Emotions," in *Reason and Emotion: Essays on Ancient Moral Psychology and Ethical Theory*, ed. John M. Cooper (Princeton, NJ: Princeton University Press, 1999), 421–22. Or else we can less plausibly reduce the discussions of appetite that are consistent with tripartition to the "Platonic portion of the *Ethics*," as does William W. Fortenbaugh, *Aristotle on Emotion: A Contribution to Philosophical Psychology, Rhetoric, Poetics, Politics, and Ethics* (London: Duckworth, 1975), 86.

4 Important discussions that think that Aristotle is referring to the practical intellect in Book IX and the theoretical one in Book X include: John M. Cooper, *Reason and Human Good in Aristotle* (Cambridge, MA: Harvard University Press, 1975), 168–77; and Richard Kraut, *Aristotle on the Human Good* (Princeton, NJ: Princeton University Press, 2021), 128–30, among others.

5 Translation from Aristotle, *De Anima Book II, III*, trans. D. W. Hamlyn (Oxford: Oxford University Press, 1983).

6 See Kathleen V. Wilkes, "The Good Man and the Good for Man in Aristotle's *Nicomachean Ethics*," in *Essays on Aristotle's Ethics*, ed. Amélie Rorty, Major Thinkers Series 2 (Berkeley: University of California Press, 1980), 352–4; Jennifer Whiting, "Human Nature and Intellectualism in Aristotle," *Archiv fiir Geschichte der Philosophie* 68, no. 1 (January 1, 1986): 83–5.

7 Ibid.

8 I will say more about the nature of the passive intellect in chapter 9, where it becomes pertinent to the nature of contemplation.

9 See Howard J. Curzer, "The Supremely Happy Life in Aristotle's Nicomachean Ethics," *Apeiron* 24, no. 1 (March 1, 1991): 52–3. For more on this issue, see chapter 9 section 7.

10 See, for instance, Julia Annas, "Plato and Aristotle on Friendship and Altruism," *Mind* 86, no. 344 (1977): 539–40, and more recently, Jerry Green, "Self-Love in the Aristotelian Ethics," *Newsletters for the Society for Ancient Greek Philosophy* 11, no. 2 (2010): 12–18.

11 Something that can happen within a person who is at odds with himself and can be, as Irwin puts it, a stranger to himself. See T. W. Irwin, *The Development of Ethics: A Historical and Critical Study*, vol. 1, *From Socrates to the Reformation* (Oxford: Oxford University Press, 2011), 226–8.

12 See Irwin, *The Development of Ethics*, 77.

13 Jonathan Barnes, ed., "Metaphysics," in *The Complete Works of Aristotle: The Revised Oxford Translation*, by Aristotle, trans. W. D. Ross, vol. 2, Bollingen Series 71 (Princeton, NJ: Princeton University Press, 1984), 1552–728.

14 Jonathan Barnes, ed., "Topics," in *The Complete Works of Aristotle: The Revised Oxford Translation*, by Aristotle, trans. W. A. Pickard-Cambridge, vol. 1, 2 vols., Bollingen Series 71 (Princeton, NJ: Princeton University Press, 1984), 166–277.

15 See Appendix 1 for more on the *energeia/kinesis* distinction.

16 Thus the fact that virtuous activity has outcomes may not by itself be reason enough to collapse the virtue/skill distinction, as suggested by Tom Angier, *Techne in Aristotle's Ethics: Crafting the Moral Life* (London: Bloomsbury Publishing, 2010), 42–3.

17 See Jozef Müller, "Practical and Productive Thinking in Aristotle," *Phronesis* 63, no. 2 (April 2, 2018): 148–75. Müller thinks that it is possible to separate productive but not practical activity from ethical agency (by delegation, for instance). I will show below how this is not possible when it comes to the final stages of becoming a virtuous character, and indeed, for its ongoing maintenance.

18 Important discussions of how the courageous disposition unifies the seemingly conflicting emotions of fear and confidence include: Stephen R. Leighton, "Aristotle's Courageous Passions," *Phronesis* 33, no. 1–3 (January 1, 1988): 76–99, and Susan Stark, "Virtue and Emotion," *Noûs* 35, no. 3 (2001): 440–55. The latter is especially useful for explaining how the conflicting emotions of fear and confidence help in assessing situations without generating conflicted actions.

19 Such a process, we have seen, is not mechanical but involves the interwoven development of both the non-rational and rational aspects of the personality including rational wish. See Myles Burnyeat, "Aristotle on Learning to Be Good," in *Aristotle's Ethics: Critical Essays*, ed. Nancy Sherman, Critical Essays on the Classics (Lanham, MD: Rowman & Littlefield, 1999), 205–30; and Nancy Sherman, "The Habituation of Character," in *Aristotle's Ethics: Critical Essays*, ed. Nancy Sherman, Critical Essays on the Classics (Lanham, MD: Rowman & Littlefield, 1999), 231–60, whose case is more nuanced but more focused on the development of choice rather than, as is mine, on choice and wish. But Sherman importantly emphasizes the otherwise impossibility of the transition from cultivation to moral maturity. I will attempt to briefly fill in the details of how this transition occurs below.

20 Thus coming to love in all of its dimensions is what I take Aristotle to mean when he says that a person is " … somehow responsible for the state he is in … " in the crucial discussion of how moral responsibility is possible on views that make cultivation and education central to its development (*NE* 3.5 1114b2). Such a view has the advantage of affirming that undertaking virtuous action for its own sake (which is a function of rational choice) is incrementally developed in cultivation but

without reducing it to the development of the moral disposition (as does Jimenez) which is after all non-rational. See Marta Jimenez, "Aristotle on Becoming Virtuous by Doing Virtuous Actions," *Phronesis* 61, no. 1 (December 10, 2016): 3–32.

21 See Appendix 1 for more on Aristotle on actuality.

22 See Angier, *Techne in Aristotle's Ethics*, 43–44, who I follow here. See also Cremaldi who usefully details how a subset of an agent's virtuous actions are self-constructive in the case of the mutually nurturing, shaping and beneficial relations of virtue friendship. For details, see Anna Cremaldi, "Aristotle on Benefaction and Self-Love," *Epoche: A Journal for the History of Philosophy* 26, no. 2 (2022): 287–307.

23 I do not think that Aristotle means as Nietzsche might that there is no other self than in action, since Aristotle's views here presuppose a hylomorphic substance, as discussed earlier.

4

The Nature of Moral Intentionality in the *Bhagavad Gītā*

4.0 Introduction

As we turn our attention to the *Gītā* on intentionality and personality, it might be useful to recapitulate what we have seen in the *Ethics* so far. We began with a focus on the form rather than the content of morality, which tells us why an agent does what s/he does. This translated into an investigation of moral intentionality which turned out to be more than just about reason, since the non-rational drives of emotion and appetite are important for ethical orientation as well. The unification of personality for Aristotle is a function of harmonization of these three drives by way of the virtues that culminates in the right kind of self-love. But personality is not the same as personhood, since Aristotle seems to suggest that an integrated personality presupposes and characterizes the person or substance as virtuous.

Framing the discussion in the *Gītā* by starting with the *Ethics* needs to be undertaken with caution. Such framing could result in the unintended straight-jacketing of the *Gītā* and the issues that it considers. On the other hand, framing the issues in terms of the *Ethics*' may help us see issues more clearly in the *Gītā*. Specifically, the discussion of personality or character formation and integration in the *Ethics* will aid us to begin reframing the standard readings of the *Gītā*'s views on intention and selfhood. But this preceding (and perhaps privileging) treatment of the *Ethics* will not always be so, as we will see later; for understanding Aristotle's discussion of the relation between the practical and theoretical lives is better understood when it is in turn framed by a discussion of the *Gītā*'s views on the different paths (or *yogas*) to the final good of human freedom.

We will begin, then, with an attempt to understand the *Gītā*'s views on intention by investigating its key notion of detachment. The initial scrutiny will hopefully show that detachment requires the harmonization of both rational and non-rational dimensions that parallel and, in some ways, go beyond the discussion in the *Ethics*. Where the comparison is useful is in thinking about how the faculties involved in the intellectual aspects of action determine one's duty/*dharma* and its relation to the social order. The discussion of perception, passion, and desire in the *Gītā* is also enhanced by the comparative context, even as the text's moral psychology goes further than the *Ethics* because of the central role of the faculty of will.

This initial understanding of detachment will allow us to explore more deeply (in chapter 5) the *Gītā*'s discussion of character development and transformation which in turn will heighten our understanding of what detachment means in the fullest sense. The discussion will involve the *Gītā*'s complex (and controversial) notion of selfhood, and its theory of strands (*guṇa*s, or what we might call "elementary ontological entities") which is key to understanding the text's insights in character development and transformation.

4.1 Setting up the Dilemma

In the Introduction, we saw that Arjuna finds himself faced with the full force of partaking in a civil war that will tear his family and society apart. He will be forced to fight and to kill his cousins, uncles, former teachers, and erstwhile friends and countrymen. He realizes that there will be no easy way to live with these consequences, even if he gains wealth and power in the bargain. His initial response to standing at the edge of this precipice is to withdraw from it; he thinks it is better for him not to fight and face death unresistingly, than it is to partake in the battle that will stain his hands with tainted blood. Yet Arjuna's decision is not final, since in asking for Krishna's advice, he is clearly leaving open the possibility of partaking in the upcoming battle.

To fight or not to fight, then, is Arjuna's question, the more general version of which is: "What ought I to do?" Clearly, these are the kinds of moral (and hence rational) questions that we all ask in particular situations, as well as more generally when we are thinking of broader considerations of career, life goals, etc. But the question that Arjuna asks is more acute since he is faced with a moral dilemma, i.e., he is faced with two choices, both of which have undesirable moral consequences. He articulates the choice to fight and kill his extended family and friends or not to fight and be killed, in terms of duty when he says in *BG* 2.7: "My mind is confused as to my duty/*dharma*. I ask you which is clearly preferable?"[1] Arjuna seems therefore to be suggesting that confusion arises because fighting for him is a duty but so is not fighting, so that discharging one means violating the other.

There is some controversy about which duties are at odds here. There is agreement that to fight is to live up to Arjuna's personal duty/*svadharma* as a warrior/*kshatriya*, something that he has been born and trained to do (more on this below). Some think that fighting violates his duties to his extended family/*kuladharma* including his cousins and uncles; but the problem is that not fighting does that as well, towards his immediate family (i.e., his brothers, wife, and mother). So fighting and not-fighting violate the same duty, which is a different kind of problem from the one that Arjuna thinks he faces.[2] A more plausible option might be the violation of the universal duty/*sāmānya dharma* of non-violence if Arjuna fights.[3] Such a duty might not usually apply to a warrior like Arjuna whose life is shaped by the possibility of war, since this would mean that he would always find himself in a dilemma when going to war. But Arjuna's despondency is clearly based on the extraordinary nature of the battle that faces him, and therefore by the inappropriateness of the ensuing violence.

If this view is correct, then the dilemma is this: by fighting, Arjuna lives up to his duty as a warrior/*svadharma* but not as a human being/*sāmānya dharma*. But by not fighting, Arjuna may be doing the more humane thing and living up to his duty as a human being but violating his duty as a warrior. It would seem, therefore, that he is damned if he does, and damned if he doesn't, which is why moral dilemmas are so difficult to navigate. We will see that Krishna's response comes in stages and it is only in chapter 7 that we can discuss how the dilemma is navigated. Here, a great deal must be done first to set up Krishna's eventual response.

4.2 Intellect, Mind and I-Sense: A Different Kind of Tripartition

Now clearly the *Gītā* sees Arjuna's dilemma as an intellectual one. His is a problem of choice, something that is usually conceived by an intellect/*buddhi* and acted upon, as we will see, by the will. Moreover, the choice presupposes distinguishing different duties and understanding their social context, thinking about how these duties might best be undertaken, and unifying these activities in terms of the overall purpose these serve in the individual's life (*BG* 18.30).[4] Such purpose (or the highest good) in the *Gītā* is freedom/*mokśa* that is the result of knowledge/*jñāna*, which makes the intellect a key human faculty (*BG* 4.33–39). This reading may sound strongly intellectualist, when in fact it is not.

For what the *Gītā* is not saying here is that only through the life of philosophy may one obtain the kind of ultimate knowledge that leads to freedom. What it is saying is that, as we have seen in chapter 1, knowledge results from a variety of paths/*yogas* all of which can therefore lead to freedom. But our focus here—given the nature of this exercise and Arjuna's dilemma—is on the ethical path or the path of action/*karma yoga* and therefore on the intellect's role in practical action, and how this in turn might lead to knowledge and hence freedom. Moreover, this is not simply a theoretical exercise just as in the case of Aristotle's *Ethics*, but one in which the theoretical dimension of practical ethics has immediate and enormous practical import. In fact, the dialogue between Arjuna and Krishna may be seen as one kind of exercise in collective deliberation that Aristotle says we undertake on " ... important questions, distrusting ourselves as not being equal to deciding [by ourselves]" (*NE* 3.3 1112b10).

Since we are focusing on practical action, we need to discuss agency in general and what "*manas*" and "*ahamkāra*" mean in the *Gītā* and their relation to the intellect in particular. I have translated "*buddhi*" as "intellect," when the more appropriate contemporary English translation might be "mind." But usually "mind" translates "*manas*" in the *Gītā* and in other Indian philosophical texts, which is clearly distinguished from the intellect/*buddhi*. Yet the *Gītā* only hints at the mind's nature: for instance, it suggests that the mind is like a sixth sense organ (in addition to sight, hearing, taste, smell, and touch) (*BG* 15.7); and that it can control these senses which are the gateways of the body (*BG* 8.12). We will start unpacking these suggestions by starting with the mind therefore rather than the intellect.

In suggesting that the mind/*manas* is a sixth sense, the text is not saying that the mind has extra-sensory perception, but then it is unclear what the mind, insofar as it perceives—or what I call mind-as-sense/*manas*—does do. One obvious answer is that the mind-as-sense perceives sense objects as sense objects per se. Taking our cue from Aristotle in the *De Anima*, it is not unreasonable to think that the individual senses perceive color, taste, texture, sound, and smell, but none of them sees the whole object. It is true, sight sees the apple, but our apprehension of it as sweet and tangy in taste and smell, etc.—and therefore as what makes the visually perceived apple appear desirable—comes from the other senses. It is the mind-as-sense, then, which perceives the object as a whole, or as an apple per se (*BG* 6.35, 17.11). We saw that in Aristotle there is a very close relation between sensing and desiring, which we also see here. For if I am right that the mind-as-sense perceives the object per se, then it is unsurprising that the text thinks it is also the source of desire (*BG* 2.55). After all, we usually think that desire, even when it is driven by a sight object, for instance, is desire for the object per se. Where the *Gītā* seems to go beyond Aristotle is in the suggestion that it is the mind/*manas* that controls the senses so that sensation, desire, and willing occur within the same faculty. This is not to deny that rationality has a role in determining what the choices are, but that it is the mind-as-will/*manas* that does the choosing. Thus, it is the mind that chooses between fighting and not fighting, even if it is the intellect that conceives the choices. The mind can rein in the senses, just as it is capable of merely following them (*BG* 2.67). Whereas Aristotle does not seem to have an obvious conception of the will, since action we saw is based on desire itself, rational or otherwise, educated or not.[5]

The intellect/*buddhi* is concerned with knowing and understanding and therefore with the truth, and for this reason is considered the highest of human faculties (*BG* 3.42, 6.21). But the intellect is important on the practical front as well, since it tells us right from wrong (*BG* 13.30–31), sometimes on the back of the kind of deliberative exercise we see in the *Gītā* as a whole. Yet this is indicative of the intellect's deep integration with the mind, since it is the mind-as-will that chooses one kind of action over the other, even if it does not conceive them. This seems plausible since the mind-as-will makes decisions directly about both sense objects—when it decides to pursue them or not—as well as indirectly when it directs the mind to consider intellectual ones such as what constitutes duty/*dharma* (cf. *BG* 6.14; 6.25). Often, the mind-as-will mediates between sensual and intellectual considerations, as when it decides between playing and studying. In such cases, the essential interconnectedness of mind, intellect, and senses becomes obvious, and lays the groundwork for how the will is determined in the *Gītā*.

To complete our initial understanding of practical agency, we look next at the *ahamkāra* or literally the I-sense (often translated as "ego"). This faculty, as the literal translation suggests, is the basis of attribution of perception to me, so that I perceive the apple, rather than there simply being a perception of the apple (*BG* 3.27). We will see later for Aristotle that thinking particular thoughts is the basis of reflexively recognizing that there is a thinker doing the thinking. But the *Gītā* thinks that the I-sense is the basis of such attribution. Thinking, perceiving, and willing are therefore not just deeply integrated but are so because they are grounded in the I-sense; for even in the most abstract of thinking the thinker is present, even in the most unthinking of sensations there is a perceiver, and in every act of will, an I. Interestingly enough, while the I-sense is therefore not only the cornerstone of agency and practical knowledge, it is also a key stumbling-block to freedom based on the highest knowledge, as we will see. But it is precisely because the sense of I emerges from a distinct faculty that it will be possible to work through the problems its existence creates for the highest goal of human freedom/*mokṣa*.

The intellect, mind, and I-sense together are what the *Gītā* calls "the doer" (*kartā*), or what we might say constitutes the psychological aspects of agency (*BG* 7.4). The doer/*kartā* is constituted by the subtlest of physical elements even as it animates the gross physical body, both of which together gives us the person (*BG* 18.14). Thus, while a different trichotomy emerges here (intellect/mind/I-sense) from Aristotle's (reason/spirit/appetite), for our purposes there are also very interesting parallels. We saw that Aristotle—despite the trichotomy—is really interested in the dichotomy between reason and unreason which is ultimately mediated by desire in the form of love. The *Gītā* too seems to be interested in this dichotomy between reason and desire. Reason because the intellect is the basis of knowledge and hence freedom, and desire because of the emotions that arise because of the interest that the senses generate in sense objects. As we will see, it is because the *Gītā* is concerned with checking these emotions and encouraging a turn towards knowledge that it emphasizes sense-control. But like Aristotle, the *Gītā* also speaks of desire as the common denominator of the dichotomy, even if decisions are ultimately made by the will.

4.3 The Four Classes, Stages, and Aims of Life in the *Gītā*

But before we think about the dichotomy between reason and desire in the *Gītā*, it is important to contextualize its views in relation to the orthodox tradition. Much of this context concerns the nature of moral obligation in relation in turn to one's place in society and stage in life/*varṇāśramadharma* and their relation to the aims of life/*puruśārthas*.[6] What we see is that there is much in the *Gītā*'s own discussion of *dharma* that is continuous with that of the tradition. Broadly speaking, the four classes/*varnas* of society are explicitly mentioned and their roles and priority upheld (*BG* 4.13), as are the duties or virtues/*dharma* of each of the classes (*BG* 18.42–44). The text insists that all physical entities are forced to act by the very impulses in nature itself (*BG* 3.5). This is true of the individuals as well, for all of us have to follow our particular natures (*BG* 3.33). The stage and station scheme/*varṇāśramadharma* as a part of the larger *dharma* of the cosmos, anticipates the broad tendencies of our individual natures and slots them in appropriately in ways that take for granted the reality of transmigration. Hence the text specifically says that past actions/*karma* determine one's nature by determining birth, and birth in turn determines one's station in life

(*BG* 6.40–45, 8.3). So here too we find that an individual's obligations in life are tightly prescribed by their stage and station *varṇāśramadharma*. In fact, the *Gītā* repeatedly tells us that we ought to do our duty regardless of what it is and how poorly we end up doing it, even if we could conceivably undertake someone else's duties better (*BG* 3.35, 18.47). More particularly, as we saw above, and as Arjuna explicitly says (*BG* 2.7), his dilemma is conceived in terms of the *dharma* scheme. Finally, *dharma* as a means to *mokṣa* is one of the central themes of the *Gītā* and is repeatedly insisted upon in the text (*BG* 2.47–53, 5.22–23, 3.31, 9.31, 17.25, etc.). So, at an important level, the *Gītā* wants to maintain much that is important to the tradition, even if it seems to come at the cost of accepting its critical drawbacks. But it is not unmindful of the tradition's shortcomings, as we will soon begin to see.

The complex of considerations that confront Arjuna, therefore, are not just about the dilemma. He must consider his *dharma* in relation to his overall ends in life/*puruśārtha* including considerations of power and well-being/*arthā*, and of ultimate freedom/*mokṣa*—as well as how his actions might fit into the upholding of the social order. Unsurprisingly, these are the very considerations that ground his hesitation in initiating the war, as we saw at the beginning of this chapter. Krishna's response, one would think, would consequently be to give Arjuna some kind of theoretical principle to adjudicate between his duties and their relation to his other ends in life as well as to the larger scheme of things.

Curiously enough, Krishna's initial response comes in terms of theoretical wisdom (*Saṁkhya*), which seems not to be as useful as the one that follows from a more practical perspective (*Yoga*).[7] The theoretical considerations can be captured by two arguments. First, Krishna says Arjuna should fight because it is the lower self or person that dies whereas the Higher more important Self does not. Since the relation between the lower self and Higher Self is that of replaceable clothes to a body, Arjuna should not worry about killing his relations, since their higher Self or Selves are not affected (*BG* 2.11–30). Second, Arjuna as a warrior should undertake his duty and fight a war that is unavoidable, or else what will people say (*BG* 2.31–38)? There are obvious problems with both arguments. The first is problematic because it seems to allow for the possibility of killing *anyone* on a whim, for instance. The second is problematic because it seems to suggest that public opinion is the appropriate criterion for right action, when we know that it often is not.

But these initial, theoretical arguments serve multiple goals, which I can only indicate here, before we turn to what Krishna calls his response from the perspective of *Yoga*. The first argument—that the higher, essential Self is not affected by death—is meant to initiate the discussion of the metaphysical framework centered around the Higher/lower self, which will be a central theme of the text (and which we will examine more closely in chapter 5). The first argument also serves the provocative purpose of seeing if Arjuna will simply accept Krishna's answers or will ask for clarification. Only if he asks for clarification (which he does) would fuller, more considered answers be forthcoming. This first argument has therefore to do with testing Arjuna's preparation, to see if in fact he can understand the initial answers—something that Krishna thinks becomes obvious by the kinds of questions and objections Arjuna might further ask.[8] The second argument—that involves the "what will people say?" refrain—is meant to articulate Krishna's position explicitly in terms of the dilemma: that Arjuna should discharge his own duty/*svadharma* as a warrior and fight. At the same time, Krishna's response here indicates why it is not acceptable to kill on a whim, since such killing must be based on one's duty/*dharma* as we will see. So, Krishna's theoretical considerations here are preliminary at best and do not provide us with a justification for why he thinks Arjuna should uphold his personal duty/*svadharma* over his more universal human obligations/*sāmānya dharma*. Let us turn to his insights from the practical/*yoga* point of view.

4.4 Understanding Detachment: A First Attempt

The key principle of the practical point of view is found in *BG* 2.47–48:

> Your right is to action alone;
> Never to its fruits at any time.
> Never should the fruits of action (*karmaphala*) be your motive (*hetur*);
> Never let there be attachment (*saṅgo*) to inaction in you.
>
> Fixed in Yoga, performing actions,
> Having abandoned attachment (*saṅgam tvaktvā*), Arjuna,
> And having become indifferent to success or failure.
> It is said that evenness of mind is yoga.[9]

So Arjuna is asked to focus on the action and not its consequence (i.e., its fruit), based on what we can call "the principle of detachment," or just "detachment."[10] But we need to determine what kind of action and consequence the principle applies to and why. For instance, it would be odd if he means Arjuna should not pay attention to any consequence, for that may make it difficult to undertake purposive action. The immediately preceding verses provide context and clarity (*BG* 2.42–46). There, the priest/*brahmin* with true knowledge is contrasted with one who merely uses his scriptural knowledge to obtain enjoyment and power for himself. Presumably, power accrues by the partisan enforcement of Vedic injunction, and enjoyment from the payment received for performing ritual sacrifice for others. (So, we see here that the *Gītā* is not blind to the shortcomings of the tradition. Yet it will take some doing to see how exactly the principle of detachment on offer here helps reform the tradition.)

The context, therefore, clarifies that the actions in *BG* 2.47 are those sanctioned by the *Vedas*, or, in other words, actions in accordance with *dharma*. It makes clear that the consequences being referred to are "enjoyment and power," and thereby what we might call "personal fruit." This does not preclude Arjuna from considering other, more relevant, and indeed necessary kinds of fruit of his action such as victory, so long as these are not conceived as personal fruit—i.e., fruit that accrues to him in ways that aggrandize him. After all, the pursuit of victory is a kind of fruit that he is required to pursue because of his *dharma* as a warrior. Thus, the difference may be subtle yet important and reminiscent of Aristotle's view on right intention in virtue: Arjuna should pursue victory because it is his *dharma*, not because it accrues personal fruit such as wealth and power.[11] Like Aristotle, the focus here therefore seems to be on the nature of a certain kind of intentionality: how must *dharma* or virtue be undertaken? Aristotle might say "for the sake of the fine/*kalon*" and Krishna would say "for the sake of duty/*dharma*." This then explains why Krishna sounds like Kant who also asks us to undertake duty for duty's sake and not because it is to the agent's advantage. But unlike Kant, Krishna is interested in a kind of consequentialism, as we will see in chapter 6, precisely because *dharma* is essentially consequentialist in nature since its concern is world-welfare. In Aristotelian terms, the *telos* of the action is to act for the sake of *dharma*, even if its *skopos* is to be understood in terms of the world's welfare and not that which is conducive to flourishing.

Clearly, there are many considerations at work here that are purely rational, even if they do not seem to resolve the dilemma. Which kind of consequence one should or shouldn't consider is a rational exercise, as is deciding to act with the right kind of intent based on such considerations. In fact, as was suggested before, emphasizing different consequences can change the way in which a duty, such as helping a friend in distress, is willed, and instantiated. Thus, if the focus is on consequences that accrue to the agent, then the ensuing action that is willed could be quite different from the one in which the focus is on what is best for the friend. Even so, it is unclear how the principle of detachment on offer here gives us a rational way out of the dilemma. After all, Arjuna focusing on doing his duty because it is his duty is no help in determining which duty he should undertake, even if Krishna thinks it should be his duty as a warrior. In other words, the principle of detachment does not seem to give Arjuna enough justification to see why he should pick one duty over another. But it may be granted that once Arjuna has justification for knowing that his duty is to fight, then the principle has significant impact on how the duty is instantiated.

Several related considerations might be relevant in response. The first is that focusing on detachment is consistent with our initial focus on a certain kind of moral intentionality as with Aristotle. It also needs to be emphasized that this is only the first stage in Krishna's reply since he seems to be considering the broadest and thereby most general application of the principle. The thought seems to be that for the most part an orthodox individual's duties and obligations are quite clear, based on considerations of one's stage-and-station-in-life. Hence, a student's main obligations are centered around study as much as an ascetic's are on meditation/*dhyāna*. For the most part, then, what the principle of detachment does is significantly improve how duty is to be willed. And as mentioned above, in chapter 7 we will see that this refocusing of intention away from the agent realigns it with the purpose of *dharma*, which is as we saw overall social well-being. In fact, as we will see in that chapter, it is the explicitly articulated principle of social welfare in *BG* 3.20–25 that is the basis of adjudicating moral dilemmas. But we have some work to do on the more basic aspects of the principle of detachment before we can get there. In sum, right action in the *Gītā* involves the intellect in at least three important ways: in determining and accepting one's goals in life, in the intentionality with which actions that fulfill these goals are undertaken, and in the way in which deliberation is involved in determining the action that constitutes one's duty in a particular situation.

Yet the intellectual dimension of action is not enough to successfully undertake action in accordance with duty/*dharma*. Individual agents may know what *dharma* requires of them in any given situation in relation to their other goals in life and may even intend to undertake such action because it is their duty to do so. But this by itself does not guarantee success, since agents do not always live up to what they know they should do. In Aristotle, we saw this inability has to do with emotion and appetite, and here the explanation is not very different, even if there is more to it as we will see in chapter 5. We can start by seeing that the focus is on the objects of attachment to which detachment applies—wealth and power as we saw above—are sense objects and therefore the subject of the mind/*manas*. Wealth is usually understood in terms of objects it can buy, or, at the very least, its physical tokens such as currency and metal. Power has to do with the ability to command control or influence other people who are embedded in social frameworks. People are also objects of lust, an additional kind of attachment that the *Gītā* consistently mentions (for example, *BG* 7.11, 8.1).

So, then it would seem that the mind/*manas* plays a crucial role in detachment in three important ways. First, the mind-as-sense works with the sense object per se to give us the object of detachment, as we saw above. This is so even if substantial intellectual elements are involved in conceiving these objects. Second, the mind-as-sense not only perceives objects per se, but it is also that which desires them (*BG* 2.55, 2.60), even if we sometimes speak as if the individual senses do (*BG* 3.34, 16.2). (I will say more on why the *Gītā* thinks there is such a close connection between perception and desire in the next section.) Third, since *manas* is also mind-as-will, it is the faculty that chooses between the intellect's determination to pursue duty with detachment, and of its own determination as sense (i.e., as mind-as-sense) to act with attachment. The *Gītā* thus implies that acquiescing to attachment is easier because of the grounding of willing and perception in mind/*manas*, and indeed this seems to be borne out by experience. If so, it is not surprising that sense-control is critical for the consistent possibility of detached, duty-bound action that is in accordance with reason.

4.5 Sense-Control

We have seen that for Aristotle, reason by itself cannot move us to act since desire in general must cooperate. The view in the *Gītā* seems to agree since it consistently tells us that desire for sense objects can undermine the intellect's goals (*BG* 2.58, 2.61-63, 2.67, 3.41, 4.39). You would therefore expect there to be a discussion here of a kind of cultivation where sense-control is discussed, and indeed there is one even if it is quite brief. The brevity has to do with the fact that so much of this cultivation is already assumed in the stage-and-station/*varnāśrama* framework. For instance, studentship/*brahmachārya* is a case in point in the teaching and learning of such sense-control. Not only is sexual abstinence a strict requirement of such a stage, as discussed earlier, but the student's diet avoids spice, meat, and foods that are thought to stimulate sexual desire (*MS* 2.177).[12] Thus, the discussion in the *Gītā* on sense-control seems to be more conceptual than detail-oriented, and we will attempt to unpack some aspects of it here.

The lack of sense-control arises in the fundamental act of perception, which is so basic and natural to us. The problem is that we do not simply use perception to navigate the world but come to dwell on its objects (*BG* 2.62). This dwelling has perhaps to do with the fact that our contact with these objects is so very sweet, yet beguiling since the text tells us that it is eventually poisonous (*BG* 18.38). The "dwelling" therefore suggests the basis of attachment: we want to keep owning and to hold on to these various objects in hope of extending their pleasures' tenure, which means several different factors come into play that we will see later are basic to the mechanism of *karma*. The first is the want or the desire. Clearly, there is a desire for food and sex for instance whose satisfaction is natural, which is different from, even if it is continuous with, the desire to dwell, to hold, and to possess. The second is the implicit reference to the possessor, the sense that something is mine, which originates in the I-sense/*ahamkāra*, that strengthens its position in relation to the other aspects of agency with such possessive activity (*BG* 5.8–9). The third is the relation of desire to emotion, since desire's satisfaction or the lack thereof leads to delight, pleasure, satisfaction, anger, pain, fear, jealousy, and so on. Once again, the implication in the *Gītā* seems to be that the emotions, which are clearly connected with desire and perception, likely also originate in the mind-as-sense (*BG* 3.34). (And, interestingly enough, the text says that excessive emotion affects memory, which suggests that memory is housed in, or is closely connected to, the mind as well (*BG* 2.63).) Since emotions have a strong influence on the will's ability to act in accordance with the intellect, the imperative for sense-control makes even more sense.

As the locution implies, control of the senses means not to be driven by sense objects but does not necessarily deny a place for such objects in human life (*BG* 3.8). In the orthodox Indian context, the place of sense objects in human life is based on our natural need for food, sex, security, etc., even if it is finely tuned by the stage-and-station setup. Not only will the different class's activities determine much of the detail regarding material goods, but so will the stage in life, as we have seen. Beyond this, and to prevent the problem of dwelling, the text advocates a withdrawal from sense objects like when a tortoise retracts its limbs into its shell (*BG* 2.58). The idea seems to be that such withdrawal is compatible with the prescribed *dharm*ic place for such objects in one's daily life (*BG* 7.11, 2.64). For Krishna is not just speaking of the ascetic renunciant/*sanyasi* here since his advice is an immediate prescription to Arjuna's predicament. Still, this is easier said than done, and not just because the mind-as-sense would seem to need an object of some sort, and it is unclear what an internal substitute for sense objects—that the language of withdrawal hints at—might be. But the problem is not easily mitigated since the senses are naturally made to function in relation to external objects, even if the text thinks this does not mean dwelling on them is essential to their functioning.

By way of response, the text seems to provide internal objects for the mind-as-sense as a substitute for sense objects and allows that sense-control is very difficult (*BG* 5.35). In the Introduction, we saw that the *Gītā* presents us with a variety of paths/*yogas* to freedom, including the path of action/*karma yoga*, of knowledge/*jñāna yoga*, and of devotion/*bhakti yoga*. As a result, the text offers up different internal (and therefore non-sensuous) objects which the mind can direct its attention to instead. God is advanced as the object of devotion (*BG* 11.55), the Self as the object of knowledge (*BG* 6.25), and what is relevant for us here, *dharma* or world-welfare (*BG* 3.25) as the object of action. If the latter seems too abstract and therefore intellectual, the text suggests that the agent/*karmayogin* can keep an imagined or actual moral exemplar at the forefront of their mind as the standard to follow (*BG* 3.21).[13] Given that the mind-as-sense is naturally inclined to pursue sensuous rather than non-sensuous objects, and that the latter are partly conceptual and partly imagined, it is not difficult to see why self-control is challenging. Krishna even points to how relapses are possible for those on their way to self-control since the taste for sense objects is very difficult to remove (*BG* 2.59). However, he insists that sense-control is possible through constant practice and striving (*BG* 6.35–36), something that we have seen the stage-and-station schema encourages in all of its particular details.

Thus, sense-control is essential for detachment in two important but related ways. Sense-control makes it possible for the intellect's goals to be realized in accordance with *dharma*'s dictates, because it allows the agent to set aside considerations of personal fruit. The agent can set aside considerations of such fruit precisely because these are understood in terms of sense objects. Hence, as we saw, Arjuna speaks of just such fruit in relation to his dilemma in terms of kingdom, wealth, and loss of friends and family. Such attachment to personal fruit we know is a function of desire, which is the cause of both positive and negative passions that can cloud and even undermine judgement and not just in the case of moral dilemmas. Thus, sense-control allows us to set aside considerations of personal fruit precisely because it is concerned with the abatement and control of desire.

4.6 Detachment: A Second Approximation

A fuller sense of detachment therefore presupposes a harmony between intellect and mind-as-sense/*manas*—which seems to parallel Aristotle's views on virtue. But this is beguiling just as it is in Aristotle, since wishing, we saw, is a form of rational desire; the contrast here is also not straight-forwardly between reason and desire since the mind-as-will is ultimately determined by rational or non-rational desire.

But to see this contrast clearly, we first need to distinguish those who are trying to act with detachment from those who are already detached. In Aristotle we saw that those who are in training towards virtue are different from those who act from (or in accordance with) virtue mainly because of a difference in education and cultivation. Harmony for Aristotle is when reason and desire speak with one voice and that applies in the main to those who are virtuous as opposed to those who are working towards virtue. Here in the *Gītā* we see that detachment in the fullest sense is the case when the mind has control over the senses and can act in accordance with the intellect's injunctions. (We will see that this denouement of detachment is provisional at best and will need to be reconsidered in light of later conclusions.) An easy way to capture the difference is to think of Krishna as the exemplification of a detached sage (even if the tradition thinks he is much more than that);[14] and a reform-minded Arjuna who takes Krishna's injunctions to act with detachment to heart, as a work in progress. Thinking about the text with this distinction in mind will begin to clarify much about detachment that will come to complete fruition in chapter 5.

Where the *Gītā* differs from Aristotle is when it comes to the place of the mind-as-will/*manas* in action. The text consistently suggests that in the case of most of us who are like Arjuna, knowledge is obscured by desire, so that controlling desire naturally leads to wisdom (*BG* 2.60, 3.39, 5.15). This is somewhat misleading since the intellect must be educated and the will/*manas* has to choose to follow the intellect. But it is difficult to see how the will can mediate between desire on the one hand and reason on the other, given that reason and desire are very different. Krishna thinks mediation by the will is possible precisely because the will deals in desire, and that the desire for knowledge and freedom (and by implication the desire to act in accordance with duty) is just as much a desire as the desire for wealth (*BG* 7.16, 8.11), something we saw in Aristotle in terms of rational desire or wish.

What sense-control by the mind-as-sense therefore allows for is the possibility that the mind-as-will can choose to be determined by the intellect's desire to act in accordance with duty. This seems plausible because the mind-as-will is not a rational faculty even if it works closely with reason, so that acquiescing to rational desire is also to acquiesce to its various modalities of intention. Thus, depending on the agent's stage of moral progress, she could intend not to act from more obvious considerations of personal fruit that are contrary to duty; or more subtle ones that are consistent with it. It also means that when the mind-as-will lacks sense-control it doesn't necessarily do so because it rationally considers the personal fruit that will accrue, as much as it succumbs to non-rational desire. In better case scenarios, she begins to act precisely because the action appropriately instantiates duty/*dharma* even if this is only to approximate how the sage acts.

Yet our understanding of this approximation of detachment does not get at the full transformation of the sage. To see why, we can start by examining the place of the I-sense/*ahamkāra* in action, even if the transformation affects the intellect, willing, passion, and desire just as much. We saw very briefly that the pursuit of sense objects strengthens the sense of I and therefore the role of the I-sense in the doer/*kartā*. After all, the dwelling on sense objects and the resulting desire to possess them and to extend that possession is plausible precisely because an enduring sense of possessing them is possible. Also, it stands to reason that sense-control and detachment influence the I-sense. Detached sages are not driven by personal fruit precisely because their senses are controlled. This means that their actions do not emphasize the I-sense in the way that is the case with those who lack such sense control. Given that there are various path dependent, internal, non-sensuous objects in place for those pursuing detachment, we will have to determine the implications of these substitutions for the I-sense. The matter is complicated by the fact that the text and the tradition in general speak of not one but two types of selves that are different from but related to the I-sense. We therefore turn our attention to these discussions so that we are in a position to better understand the nature of detachment in the *Gītā*.

Notes

1 Winthrop Sargeant, trans., *The Bhagavad Gītā: Twenty-Fifth–Anniversary Edition* (Albany: State University of New York Press, 2010).

2 Richard Berg, "An Ethical Analysis of the *Bhagavad Gītā*," in *The Contemporary Essays on the Bhagavad Gītā* (New Delhi: Siddharth Publications, 1995), 21–22; Simon Brodbeck, "Calling Krsna's Bluff: Non-Attached Action in the Bhagavadgītā," *Journal of Indian Philosophy* 32, no. 1 (February 1, 2004): 87; and Kenneth Dorter, "A Dialectical Reading of the Bhagavadgita," *Asian Philosophy* 22, no. 4 (2012): 311–12, suggest that the dilemma arises because of a conflict between duties to family and to class. Other suggestions include M. Agarawal, "Arjuna's Moral Predicament," in *Moral Dilemmas in the Mahābhārata*, by Bimal Krishna Mattilal (New Delhi; Varanasi: Motilal Banarsidass, 1992), 134–35, who thinks that the

dilemma arises from a conflict between utilitarian considerations and duty, though this does not sit well with Arjuna's specific claim in the quote that the confusion arises with regard to a choice between duties. In any case, it should be quite clear that Arjuna sees his situation in terms of a couple of competing options neither of which is palatable, and responds to Paul Weiss, "The Gita: East and West," *Philosophy East and West* 4 (1954): 257–58, who thinks that the conflict is not grasped in the text.

3 So, for instance, as articulated in *MS* 10.63 along with truth-telling, not stealing, keeping oneself pure, and keeping the senses under control.

4 The *Gītā*, on my view at least, seems to take a compatibilist stance on human freedom. That is, while it claims that events on a global scale are determined (*BG* 11.26–29, for instance), human beings act and intend freely based on the determinations of their own empirical nature.

5 See Bal Gangadhar Tilak and S. B. Sukthankar, *Śrīmad Bhagavadgīta Rahasya, or, Karma-Yoga-Śāstra* (New Delhi: Asian Educational Services, 2007), 179–86. Tilak distinguishes the two roles of *manas*/mind based on *BG* 3.42 but does not translate them as I do here as "mind-as-sense" and "mind-as-will."

6 See Appendix 2 for more details.

7 See Appendix 2 for more details on the use of "Saṁkhya."

8 See a similar trajectory in the instruction of Indira by Prajāpati in *Chāndogya Upanṣad* 8.7–8.15.

9 Sargeant, *The Bhagavad Gītā*, 131–33.

10 I take detachment as the English shorthand for several Sanskrit terms: *karmaphalahetur* above and *tyaktvā karmaphalāsangaṁ* having abandoned fruit of the action (*BG* 4.20); *gatasañgasya* free from attachment (*BG* 4.23); *sañgam tyaktvā* having abandoned attachment (*BG* 5.10, 5.11); *karmaphalaṁ tyaktvā* having abandoned fruit of one's actions (*BG* 5.12); *asaktaś* (*BG* 3.7, 3.9, 3.25, 5.21), literally "not attached"; *na sajjate* (*BG* 3.28), literally "not joined or attached"; *tyaktasarvaparigrahaḥ* (*BG* 4.21), literally "abandoning all acquisitiveness"; *sarvakarmāṇisaṁnyasa* (*BG* 5.13), literally "renouncing all action"; *sarvakarmaphalatyāgaṁ* (*BG* 12.11, 13.2), literally "sacrificing the fruit of one's actions"; *saṅgarahitam* (*BG* 18.23) or *asaṅgam*, literally "free from attachment"; *aphalākāṅkṣibhir*, literally "the fruit not desiring ones"; and variants thereof. As pointed out, the often discussed *niṣkāmakarma* is not actually found in the text. Cf, for instance, Sandeep Sreekumar, "An Analysis of Consequentialism and Deontology in the Normative Ethics of the Bhagavadgita," *Journal of Indian Philosophy* 40, no. 3 (2012): 296.

11 Such a view is broadly supported in the scholarship, though there are exceptions—such as Christopher G. Framarin, "The Desire You Are Required to Get Rid of: A Functionalist Analysis of Desire in the Bhagavadgita," *Philosophy East and West* 56, no. 4 (2006): 604–17—who I discuss more fully below. Yet there is more

to detachment than not being concerned with personal consequences, as my discussion in section 3 of this chapter will show.

12 Manu, *The Laws of Manu*. Penguin Classics (London; New York: Penguin, 1991).

13 Hence there is a parallel here with Dhand who thinks that the great Indian epics of the *Mahābhārata* and *Ramayana* represent idealized behaviors in the characters for the many to follow in ways that are consistent with though less abstract than the more technical discussions of the *Dharmaśastras*. See Arti Dhand, "The Dharma of Ethics, the Ethics of Dharma: Quizzing the Ideals of Hinduism," *Journal of Religious Ethics* 30, no. 3 (Fall 2002): 360.

14 I have a great deal of sympathy for readings like Gandhi's that suggest that Krishna is simply the goal of human perfection since these are more consistent with my understanding of *bhakti yoga*, as will become obvious by chapter 8. See David Atkinson, "The Gītā and Gandhi's Moral Vision," in *The Contemporary Essays on the Bhagavad Gītā*, ed. Braj M. Sinha, 1st ed., Siddharth Indian Studies Series (New Delhi: Siddharth Publications, 1995), 9.

5

Personhood in the *Bhagavad Gītā*

5.0 Introduction

Our task here has been set by considerations from the previous chapter. There, we saw that a preliminary understanding of detachment parallels Aristotle's discussions of harmony between the rational and the non-rational, even if the discussion of selfhood is more extensive in the *Gītā* than in the *Ethics*. Thus, a fuller understanding of detachment will require us to explore the *Gītā*'s extensive discussions of selfhood and their relation to the I-sense/*ahamkāra* before we are in a position to engage in a dialogical exercise between them.

The challenge here is to determine the relation between what the *Gītā* calls the Higher Self/*Ātman*/*Dehin* and the lower self/*deha*, which in turn is complicated by the controversy concerning the relation between the Higher Self/*Ātman* and the Universal Self/*Brahman*. Our discussion here of the Higher and Universal Selves will be limited and provisionally non-committal, as we focus on the light that connection might throw on the lower self/*deha* and its relation to the I-sense/*ahamkāra* and the doer/*kartā*.

These discussions will require us to consider many of the issues that we have already seen in Aristotle: the nature of personal identity, of moral agency, and of character (or personality). The *Gītā*'s discussion of character development and transformation will deepen our understanding of what detachment means in the fullest sense and will involve its theory of strands/*guṇa*s, or what we might call "elementary ontological entities."

What we will see is that the sage represents the impersonal, desireless culmination of detachment that is a stark contrast in many ways with Aristotle's virtuous and happy human being. This in turn will set the stage for an interesting conversation between them.

5.1 Higher Self (*Ātman*), Universal Self (*Brahman*)

The Higher Self in the *Gītā* is *Ātman*, though the text also uses the language of *Dehin* and *Puruṣa* to refer to it. "*Dehin*" literally means that which is embodied, whereas that in which it is embodied, what I call the lower self, translates "*deha*." "*Dehin*" is therefore often used when the text wants to emphasize that the Higher Self has a place in the world through the body (e.g., *BG* 2.13, 8.4, 9.15, 13.32, etc.). "*Puruṣa*" denotes "spirit" in the text and is usually used to emphasize the Higher Self's difference from the body and the material world (*BG* 13.20–22).[1]

The Higher Self/*Ātman* is characterized in a variety of ways in the text. It is higher because it sits above the hierarchy of senses, mind, and intellect (*BG* 3.42–43), and because it is the very being or essence of humans (*BG* 8.3). The *Ātman*'s primacy in the hierarchy has to do with spiritually powering the activities of the senses, mind, and intellect (or doer/*kartā*) because it shines like the sun (*BG* 5.16). This is usually taken to mean that the Higher Self is the origin of embodied conscious activity, even if its shining like the sun is not an action in the usual sense as that which is undertaken by the doer/*kartā* (*BG* 13.14,13.29, 13.33, 5.13). Being a source in this sense perhaps partially explains why the text thinks the *Ātman* is the essence of human nature. Additional considerations are forthcoming when the *Gītā* tells us knowledge of the Higher Self/*Ātman* (which we know can be sought through various paths/*yogas*) obtains for us the highest human end of freedom/*mokṣa* (*BG* 6.10–11, 3.17, 4.33–39). But why this might be so only becomes clear when we understand the possible relations between the Higher Self/*Ātman* and the Universal Self/*Brahman*.

The *Gītā*'s views on the nature of reality are broadly monistic so that all existing entities are the manifestation of a single world principle or Self, which following tradition, it calls "*Brahman*" (*BG* 3.15, 4.24–25, 4.31–32, etc.). Traditionally, this has mainly played out in two ways when it comes to relating the Higher (Individual) Self/*Ātman* and the Universal (World) Self/*Brahman*: either that they are identical or that there is a parts-to-whole relation between them. On either view, we can see why the *Ātman* is the very being or essence of the human being since it is either the same or an aspect of the essence of the universe. But on other matters, the difference in the views is significant. Śaṇkara, whose monism takes the *Ātman*/*Brahman* relation to be one of hard identity, is an idealist of sorts, which means that the distinction between matter (or Nature/*Prakrati* broadly construed) and spirit for him is ultimately provisional. This is not the case for Rāmānuja, who maintains the materiality of Nature and the distinctness of individual *Ātmans* from *Brahman* while still holding a qualified monism.

The problem when it comes to deciding between them is that there is evidence for Śaṇkara's views (*BG* 4.35, 11.2, 7.29) and for Rāmānuja's views (*BG* 6.15–29, 6.47, 9.34) in the text.

Fortunately, we do not have to decide between them in this chapter since both views agree on some key issues that are relevant for us here, even if the disagreements on other matters are substantial and irreconcilable. First, they agree that in relation to the lower self, the Higher Self does not act as much as it enables that in which it is embodied to act by its presence (*BG* 4.13, 13.31).[2] Second, that this lower self is what acts even if there is disagreement about its ultimate ontological status. Since our interest is on moral action and agency here, we can focus for the moment on the lower self rather than on the Higher.

5.2 The Lower Self

"Body" usually translates "*deha*," to contrast with the spiritual *dehin*, and this is not entirely inaccurate; but the *deha* is also more than just the body, which is why I have translated it as "lower self." This is especially clear when the *Gītā* uses the language of "*adhisthanam*" (literally "ground" or "place") in the context of four other factors of action: the senses, the doer/*kartā*, Providence, and predispositions (*BG* 18.14). Together, it is these five factors of action that constitute the empirical agent or lower self/*deha*.

The lower self/*deha* is therefore a complex construct grounded for the most part in the body. The body is home to the senses, since the sense organs partially constitute it, but also because sensation is a bodily phenomenon. But, as we have seen in chapter 3, the perception of the sense object per se is a function of the mind-as-sense/*manas*. This connection is not overlooked here since the *manas* is integrated in the lower self/*deha* as part of the doer/*kartā*, along with the intellect/*buddhi* and the I-sense/*ahamkāra*. Nor are there any deep discontinuities here between the material body and senses on the one hand and the psychological dimensions that the doer represents on the other, as we have already seen in chapter 3. For, as we are told, all that acts and therefore all five factors of action are constituted by material elements, subtle and gross (on which more shortly) (*BG* 8.5, 12.6).

What remains unclear is the nature of the two remaining factors—Providence and predispositions—and how they are related to the body. Providence/*daivaṁ* here clearly has religious dimensions since its root, "*deva*," means "divinity."[3] The thought here seems to be that individual human action involves a factor that is not in that individual's control because it involves other human and natural activity that forms the larger backdrop to it. For instance, Ram's deciding to go to the market can be influenced by a friend's dropping in for a visit, the weather, or the illness of a spouse, and so on. While we might agree that there are outside influences beyond an agent's control that influence his action, we may not agree that there is a Divine plan according to which these influences play out. The *Gītā*'s theistic stance, given the centrality of Krishna's divinity to its narrative, is unequivocal. The interesting thing is that the *Gītā*'s position here is likely in response to early, atheistic Buddhism, which therefore does not believe in Divine Providence. But where the *Gītā* does agree with Buddhism is in thinking that this external influence is causal.[4] Ram's decision about market-going causally affects and relates to other decisions he makes going forward (for instance, to entertain his friend at home, or to buy things at the market, etc.). Moreover, Ram's decision itself is causally related to and affected by his friend's decision to visit, or by natural events such as the weather. Providence (or its atheistic version) is therefore grounded in the body insofar as it is expressed through the body (and indeed all bodies). Providence, then, will have interesting implications for the place of human freedom in general and Arjuna's choice in particular, as we will see towards the end of this chapter. But, for the moment, we need to think about the implications of such a causal understanding of Providence for the last remaining factor: predispositions/*ceṣṭa*s.

"*Ceṣṭa*s" literally means "actions" or "motions," which is puzzling since as one of the five factors of action it is meant to explain action. But if we see that the text is pointing to how past actions (or motions) are a causal factor in present ones, it might justify my use of "predispositions" instead.[5] For the suggestion seems to be that our past actions predispose us to act in certain ways that causally influence present and future actions. The Aristotelian language of "disposition" may seem misleading, and perhaps "momentum" might be more appropriate, especially as we begin to unravel the mechanism of *karma* here. But we will soon see that there is a place for both these senses, and at the very least, it is obvious here how *ceṣṭa*s are grounded in the body. After all, we are speaking here of the past actions of the body, and ultimately, of the subtle body (as I show below).

We are now in a position to review the various kinds of self that the *Gītā* discusses, and it might be useful to do so before moving forward. We saw that the most basic I-sense/*ahamkāra* is a part of the doer/*kartā* which is the psychological aspect of agency that also involves the *manas*/mind-as-will, the *manas*/mind-as-sense and the intellect/*buddhi*. The I-sense is responsible for generating the sense of ownership of thoughts, decisions, and perceptions that originate in the rest of the doer/*kartā* so that they can be said to belong to that doer. The doer represents the psychological dimension of the lower self or empirical agent who has a certain history in the world and a place in the larger Divine scheme of things. The lower self/*deha* is empowered by the Higher Self/*dehin* or *Ātman* which in turn is associated with or identical to the Universal Self/*Brahman*.

Thus, a rather complicated picture of human nature emerges here, and it may seem that it is unclear where we might go next, since it is uncertain which of these is impacted by detachment. Perhaps recalling the framing considerations from our discussion of Aristotle may be useful here: how might we think of personal identity in the *Gītā* and what is the nature of character or personality in this context? Responding to these questions, I hope to show, will keep us on track to understand what detachment in the fullest sense means, and which self is impacted in the process.

5.3 Personhood and Personality

The question of personal identity asks how it is possible for the person to remain the same (i.e., to be identical with oneself) over time (i.e., through the past, present, and future). One reason we often ask this question in the human context is to explain how a future self can be held morally responsible for the actions of a past version. In Aristotle's case, it is the hylomorphic substance (which is a combination of form/essence/soul and matter) that is the basis of personal identity. Personality or character for him, on the other hand, has to do with the relations between the rational, emotional, and appetitive aspects of the soul. The question of personal identity in the *Gītā*'s context is complicated by the fact that it thinks it is possible for the same person to exist in previous and future lifetimes. Hence, as we have already seen in chapter 3, the text specifically says that past actions (*karma*) determine one's nature by determining birth, and birth in turn determines one's station in life (*BG* 6.40–45, 8.3). So let us look at the various possibilities discussed above as candidates for personal identity.

It could be argued that the Higher Self/*Dehin*/*Ātman* is what persists through the different lives since the text repeatedly tells us that it is unchanging and immortal (*BG* 5.13, 13.29). But while *Ātman* like Aristotle's form is the essence of human nature (*BG* 3.42–43), it is not the basis of personal identity. For, regardless of *Ātman*'s relation to *Brahman*, it does not distinguish individuals from each other, which is what we really need for personal identity (*BG* 6.29,

11.2).[6] If *Ātman* is identical to *Brahman*, as in Śaṇkara's view, then all individuals share the same *Ātman* and cannot be distinguished from each other on the basis of their *Ātman*. If there are many *Ātmans* that are an aspect of *Brahman*, as on Rāmānuja's view, their common nature as eternally changeless non-actors make them less than ideal candidates as the basis of personal identity (*RGB* 4.35, 8.21).[7]

Nor can the material, lower self/*deha* be the basis of personal identity since it involves the body. The problem is not that the body is material as much as it is quite clearly not the same body across different lives, which we saw the tradition accepts as true in the stage-and-station in life discussion in chapter 3. The only remaining plausible candidate for personal identity is that which transmigrates, or the lower self without the body. This may make sense since the doer/*kartā* as intellect, mind, and I-sense—which are constituted by subtle matter—may satisfy the core needs for moral responsibility, even if one key feature seems to be missing. For we usually say that a person's ability to remember their past self is an important feature (even if not the basis) of their being continuous with that person. Here, we have seen that while memory is an aspect of the mind, memory does not seem key to personal identity. For clearly most people don't recall their past lives even if the text (following tradition) very clearly believes that such *anamnesis* (as it is called by Plato) is possible (*BG* 4.5). How then can everybody be held responsible for their past lives?

The *Gītā*'s implicit answer, I think, is that the details of past lives are not necessary to acknowledge their broad impact on the present; and this is manifest through the predispositions/*ceṣṭa*s that we are born with and our place in the larger scheme of things (or Providence/*daivam*). Not only do the actions of my agency in a previous life have an impact on my mind and intellect so that they shape and change me in that life, but they do so in this one as well. Interestingly enough, the impact of past actions in relation to Providence on the doer/*kartā* is quite fine grained and detailed enough to distinguish individual lives and be the basis of personal identity.[8] But of greater relevance to us is the impact of past actions on human nature so that we can distinguish different types of people by class and personality; for this then begins to explain the philosophical basis of the class/*varna* system championed by the tradition, which for the *Gītā* is crucially grounded in the notion of detachment. Our next step, therefore, is to understand how predispositions that are the basis of the transmigrating doer/*kartā*—which are made of subtle matter—are formed, how they are the basis of character and hence class-membership. To do so, we will have to look at the basic constituents of matter before we can understand how these are shaped by action.

5.4 *Guṇas* and Personality Traits

In chapter 3 we saw that the *Gītā* takes the traditional class setup to be sacrosanct, even if it is critical of it in the initial discussion of detachment in Book 2. Now we begin examining the fullest extent of the *Gītā*'s critique of the class structure and its suggestions for reform. As class function goes, the *brahmin*/intellectual class is responsible for sacred and educational work, whereas the *kshatriya*/warrior class is concerned with the administration and defence of the state. The *vaiśya*/ economic class undertakes agricultural, trades, and market-related work, and the service/*śudra* class for menial work in the service of the other three classes. Members of these classes are individuals/*dehas* and not just psychological agents or doers/*kartās*. But the thought seems to be that if things go in accordance with Providence, transmigrating subtle-bodied doers/*kartās* are born in the appropriate class in accordance with their predispositions/*ceṣṭas* that are then the blueprint for the gross body and its sense organs.

We need, therefore, to look at what constitutes the differences in the doer's predispositions (which we know are shaped by action) so that class categorization is possible, and which the *Gītā* tells us is a function of the configuration of basic constituents called strands/*guṇas*. While there are other schools that conceive the ultimate constituents of the material world in terms of atoms, most of the tradition follows the Saṁkhya in thinking of these constituents in terms of strands (or an ancient version of string theory). At root there is a metaphor at work (as there usually is when it comes to ultimacy of this sort) of combination. Invisible strands intertwine to give us invisible subtle elements (of air, water, earth, and fire), which in turn combine eventually to give us the visible gross versions of the same elements, and so on. Combination, therefore, allows us to explain how the different invisible, living strands become the tangible visible rope, and where the rope signifies how things are brought and held together.

5.4.1 *Guṇa* Theory in General and in the *Gītā* in Particular

There are thought to be three basic kinds of strands/*guṇas*—*sattva*, *rajas*, and *tamas*—that constitute material Nature (*Prakrati*), presumably because three is the minimum number necessary to explain the world's diversity, and simultaneously maintain the theory's simplicity and elegance (*BG* 14.5).[9] *Tamas* is the strand that is responsible for inertia (*BG* 14.13) and therefore perhaps for materiality. We might say that *tamas* is that which responds to gravity and makes for the tactility of matter. *Rajas* is the strand which provides motile energy parallel to the way in which electromagnetic energy does in atomic theory. There is clearly a creative tension between *tamas*'s tendency to resist motion and *rajas*'s drive to cause it, that is complemented by *sattva*. *Sattva*'s buoyant nature is at odds with *tamas*'s inertial character, even if it is different from *rajas*'s motile energy which drives rather than rises. *Sattva* is also described as illuminating, because it makes conscious activity and especially knowledge possible (*BG* 14.11). The theory tells us that the invisible strands are always found working cooperatively together and never apart, so that they are clearly a theoretical posit meant to explain phenomena. Yet what ultimately causes variation in Nature is the fact that one or other of the strands is predominant while suppressing the other two to varying degrees in subtle elements that further combine to give us gross ones. Thus, a flame has *sattva* predominant, its wick the matter which burns, *tamas*, and the oil that fuels it, *rajas*. Interestingly enough, all three strands working together are described later in the tradition in terms of wick, oil, and flame in a lamp.[10]

As suggested above, the transmigrating doers "program" the body, and now we can see how this might be so in terms of the *guṇas* (*BG* 14.15). For the view seems to be that they are of the same *guṇa*-based material nature, even if the doer is constituted by subtle elements and the body by gross versions of the same. Nor is there a problem here in terms of the distinction between organic and inorganic nature, since all Nature is conceived organically.[11] The variation in human nature that leads to class categorization, unsurprisingly enough, is a function of strand pre-eminence (*BG* 14.10). Unsurprising also is the isomorphism of *guṇa* nature in both the world and in humans.

If *tamas* is inertial by nature, then one would expect its predominance in humans to cause inactivity or indolence, as the *Gītā* repeatedly confirms (*BG* 14.13, 18.28, 18.35). The suppression effect on the other two strands is felt through indolence since *tamas*'s ascendency reduces activity, and hence the play of *rajas*, and dampens the buoyancy of *sattva* thereby encouraging dullness and ignorance (*BG* 14.17). Depending on the range of *tamas*'s pre-eminence, such ignorance is manifest in a variety of ways: carelessness and a lack of attention to detail, confusion, stubbornness, and inconsistency (*BG* 14.9, 14.8, 14.3, etc.). More worryingly for the central notion of detachment, being predominantly *tama*sic makes it difficult to know, let alone live up to, the nature of one's duty (*BG* 18.7, 18.32); or to understand the complexity of causal relations, be it in the form of the consequences of one's actions on others or their relation to the agent's overall ends (*BG* 18.22, 18.25). Unsurprisingly, the text tells us that the primarily *tama*sic persons are attached to neglect and sloth (*BG* 14.8–9, 18.39), and the fruit of their actions is ignorance (*BG* 14.6). It is important to note that the attachment to indolence here is clearly a desire that bears a certain kind of fruit. Such desire, therefore, can determine the mind-as-will/*manas* as much as desire for action can, as we will see below.

Rajas is responsible for motility and therefore for all the life processes in human nature, including nutrition, growth, perception, reproduction, etc. Yet, consistent with its practical character, the *Gītā* chooses to focus on *rajas*'s expression in overt, sense-driven human activity and therefore on the mechanism of desire which grounds action (*BG* 14.7).

Sense-driven desire has many dimensions, as we saw in our discussion of the mind/*manas*. First, it needs objects like food or wealth or position, and therefore takes more or less excessive forms such as lust, hunger, and greed (*BG* 14.7, 14.12). Second, as we saw in our discussions of sense-control, sense-driven desire presupposes ownership which like objects of desire require individuation. Thus, for instance, there has to be an individuated object that satisfies my hunger if I am to be moved to pursue it. This individuation of objects by the mind/*manas* we are told is ultimately the work of *rajas* both at the perceptual and conceptual levels (*BG* 18.27), perhaps because motility inherently presupposes separation. But *rajas* is also ultimately responsible for individuation on the subjective side, since the text repeatedly tells us that the desire for personal fruit in attached action is *rajas*ic (*BG* 17.12, 17.18, 18.24, 18.34, etc.). That is, while *rajas* is responsible for action in general, its relative ascendency and the resulting form of attachment to action (*BG* 14.9) ends up over-emphasizing the subjective so that the consequences are not impartially weighed. Thus, *rajas* seems to be ascendent in the constitution of the I-sense/*ahamkāra* as well.

Third, given that *rajas* is the basis of desire that originates in the *manas*, the text expectedly says that *rajas* is the basis of passion since this too, as we have seen, originates in the *manas*. After all, the passions (which, as Aristotle says, are what are pleasurable and painful) are the consequence of desire satisfied or unfulfilled. In fact, the text goes so far as to say that while *rajas* is what causes attachment to action, it is characterized by passion in the way in which *tamas* is characterized by sloth (*BG* 3.37, 14.16–17). Moreover, the fruit of *rajas*'s pre-eminence is pain as much as it is ignorance when *tamas* is predominant (*BG* 14.6). But since the satisfaction of desire—which occurs at least some of the time—is pleasurable as much as its disappointment is painful, it may seem puzzling that the text insists that the fruit of *rajas*'s primacy is essentially painful. But we should remember that in the discussion of sense-control, the *Gītā* tells us that while the short-term satisfaction of desire is pleasurable, in the long run it is poisonous and therefore painful (*BG* 18.38). The fullest justification for why the *Gītā* holds this view will hopefully become obvious before this chapter is done.

While *rajas*'s primacy over *tamas* means that lethargy is overcome, the resulting tension between them introduces a stutter in *rajas*ic action so that it is characterized as restless and unsteady (*BG* 17.18, 19.18). *Sattva*'s buoyancy that makes knowledge possible, on the other hand, is weighed down and overcome by passion. *Rajas*'s predominance over *sattva* results not only in the focus on personal consequences as we saw above, but in a misunderstanding therefore of what the right consequences may be (*BG* 17.12, 17.18, 17.21, 18.8).

Sattva as buoyant in nature translates into an effortless, bright kind of human energy when it is predominant in human nature (*BG* 14.11); but *sattva* is also described as illuminating, which may seem puzzling (*BG* 14.6). Given that *sattva* is associated with knowledge—as we will shortly explore more fully—one might think that the language of illumination might have to do with conscious, thinking activity. In fact, *sattva* is illuminating insofar as it is what carries out conscious thinking (and is likely also responsible for the conscious aspects of sensory activity) in humans, even if it is not the source of consciousness (which we saw above is the *Ātman*).[12]

If *sattva* makes conscious thinking activity and hence knowledge possible, its predominance in individuals should make them knowledge-seeking and attached to knowledge, as the text confirms (*BG* 14.6). The *Gītā* emphasizes that such knowledge in general is concerned with synthesis and unity, and therefore the focus is very much on the larger scheme of things (*BG* 18.20). That is, *sattva* is what makes it possible to grasp, for instance, that morality/*dharma* is concerned with general welfare; that *dharma* is not only continuous with cosmological law, but with the other human ends such as material well-being/*artha* and pleasure/*kāma* with which it has to harmonize. But this also translates into keeping such ends in mind when acting so that duty is fulfilled correctly and for the right kinds of reasons (*BG* 18.23, 18.26, 18.30). Detached action, where the right action is undertaken for the right reasons, therefore, presupposes a preponderance of *sattva* nature (*BG* 17.11, 17.20 18.10). It goes without saying that the distinction making capacity that we discussed above, originates in *rajas* and is crucial if subordinate here. Without *rajas*'s distinction making capacity, separating right from wrong action may not be possible; and even more fundamentally, neither would means to end thinking, for instance.

Getting back to *sattva*'s predominance, we might think that the attachment to knowledge, therefore, is compatible with, because it is necessary for, detached action. But in fact, the text is warning us that while knowledge is necessary for right action, attachment to it is not. This is especially clear since such attachment to knowledge is spoken of in the same breath as attachment to happiness (*BG* 14.6, 14.9). Since the latter is clearly a form of personal aggrandizement, and therefore not consistent with detachment, the implication is that so is the former. The pursuit of knowledge, after all, can also be a means to personal aggrandizement, for which we saw the *Gītā* explicitly criticize the *brahmin*-class in chapter 3. The important if unstated implication is that the desire for knowledge is the basis for attachment, even if such desire can be subverted. So, it would seem that, interestingly enough, the pre-eminence of all three strands/*guṇas* manifests as desire: for stasis (*tamas*), for action (*rajas*), and for knowledge and happiness (*sattva*). The mind-as-will/*manas*, therefore, is not stirred by reason per se and desire, for instance, as much as it is by different kinds of desire. This in turn confirms what is stated earlier in chapter 4: that the mind-as-will is determined by desire alone. Thus, an interesting parallel arises with Aristotle, despite the substantially different moral psychology of the *Gītā* and its *guṇa*-driven undergirding. For Aristotle also sees that what moves us to act is desire so that he thinks that there is such a thing as rational desire (or wish) that has to be in sync with deliberative desire (or choice). This will make for an interesting dialogue in the upcoming coda especially as we think about the differences in the nature of the psychological drives in each of the texts and their significance.

Returning to the issue at hand, the subordination of the other strands by *sattva* in human nature plays out in interesting ways. *Sattva*'s buoyancy overcomes *tamas*'s inertia so that predominantly *sattv*ic individuals are tireless, attentive, and thereby successful knowledge seekers. Increasing the predominance of *sattva* in a life translates into upward buoyant movement that we might implicitly take to be through the class system, even if it is explicitly used to speak of the final stage of such a movement to freedom/*mokṣa* (*BG* 14.14, 14.18). While *rajas* subordinated is still key to distinction making, *sattva*'s predominance means that unitive, knowledge-driven thinking and acting that is not driven by passion prevails in the final analysis (*BG* 18.10, 18.20, 18.23). *Sattva*'s buoyancy in conjunction with *rajas*'s motility is perhaps what allows such activity to be steady (*BG* 18.26, 18.33). Yet, depending on the extent of *sattva*'s predominance, such individuals and their activities are consistently described by the text as more or less tranquil, peaceful, and free of passion (*BG* 2.64–65, 6.27, 18.37, 18.42).

5.5 Personality Traits and Class Membership

One can now begin to see how *guṇa* predominance can be the basis of class distinctions (that clearly parallels the way in which Plato in the *Republic* speaks of class membership in terms of the predominance of reason, spirit, or appetite). After all, the predominance of one *guṇa* over others means the preponderance of a certain kind of desire-based activity; and such activity understood in terms of duty is in fact the basis of class distinctions, as we have seen in chapter 4 section 3, and as is confirmed by the text (*BG* 4.13). Roughly speaking, *sattva*'s predominance which is responsible for the desire for knowledge as we just saw, is the basis of the intellectual *brahmin* class; *rajas*'s primacy can be seen as key to passions involved in the courage of the *kshatriya* or warrior class (*BG* 18.41–45). But beyond that, things get murky, mainly because we have three *guṇas* and four classes. Would the economic classes, given their interests in material prosperity, not also be *rajas*ic? And if the fourth serving class is predominantly *tamas*ic and therefore prone to indolence, how might it actually do the work of servitude?

Śaṇkara, the great Indian commentator on the *Gītā*, suggests what may seem to be an obvious solution in hindsight because it seems right in the context of this explanatory framework. Class distinctions are not simply about *guṇa* priority, but ordinality as well. Thus, the difference between the predominance of *rajas* in the warrior and in the economic classes is that *sattva* is secondary in the former whereas *tamas* is secondary in the latter. This ideally translates not only into the brilliant heroism and majesty of the warrior's quest for power and glory, but also the pursuit of coarser natured sense-driven objects by the economic class.[13] *Rajas* is secondary to *tamas* in the serving class, which means that with direction (since *sattva* is tertiary) and encouragement, it can make it possible to overcome inertia more or less successfully. Śaṇkara's view here, therefore, provides the philosophical basis of subdividing the class structure further into castes and sub-castes (*jāti*), depending on the extent of *guṇa* priority and on ordinality. But we return now to our original purpose and ask how the *guṇa* analysis helps us understand detachment better.

5.6 Detachment: A Final Approach

In the previous chapter we undertook a preliminary analysis of detachment in terms of reason and desire, which we have now deepened in terms of the *guṇa* analysis. Thus, in recent sections of this chapter, we saw that detachment needs to be understood in terms of the predominance of *sattva* over *rajas* and *tamas*. We will attempt here to bring both together in what is hopefully a fuller understanding of detachment. Since Krishna's urgings are directed at Arjuna, we can focus on how the transformation from attachment to detachment might obtain for the great warrior—in ways that are fully obtained only in the descriptions of the sage. The possibility of such a transformation, it is important to emphasize, is not directed at the members of the highest *brahmin* or intellectual class. In fact, by articulating the key ideas in a text that is widely accessible (see the Introduction), Krishna makes the blueprint for detachment and hence freedom/*mokṣa* available to all. What this will require, as we shall see, is the possibility of *guṇa* reconfiguration to enable *sattva*'s predominance through detachment in this life for members of any and every class.

5.7 Arjuna's Transformation

Arjuna's standing as a warrior means that *rajas* should ideally dominate *sattva* in his character. The text warns us of the ever-present threat to the appropriate distribution of births by class based on *guṇa* configuration, if in fact the class structure breaks down (*BG* 2.40–43). It is to avert just these kinds of existential threats to the overall *dharm*ic order that the Divine incarnates in the world, in this instance as Krishna (*BG* 4.7–8). But matters have not reached such a dire stage, since the evidence in the text suggests that Arjuna is indeed true to type. Arjuna (and the narrator Sanjaya's) assessment of his response to the moral dilemma is that it is clearly emotional, which speaks to the predominance of *rajas* in his personality. He is described as saddened and sorrowful in the face of his dilemma (*BG* 1.28, 1.47); and himself admits to feeling extreme and paralyzing fear and confusion (*BG* 1.29, 2.7). Krishna reinforces this assessment since he chides Arjuna for being overwhelmed by pity and fear and urges him to overcome his emotions (*BG* 2.1–3). *Sattva*'s secondary status in Arjuna is expectedly less explicit even if it is the basis for his thinking in general; and in particular for the understanding of his ends, for the recognition of his duties, and of the broader dangers his potential actions pose for civil society. More interestingly, *sattva*'s presence is manifest in the penetrating questions he asks of Krishna at the beginning of many of the books of the *Gītā* (for example, *BG* 3.1–2, 4.4, 5.1, etc.); questions whose analytical acumen undoubtedly involve *rajas*'s recently discussed divisive role in the workings of thought. For instance, it is Arjuna's recognition of the moral dilemma confronting him that creates the text's narrative momentum.

The problem is that *rajas* also adversely affects the workings of thought especially in relation to ends, as becomes obvious when we consider the *Gītā*'s discussion of faith (*shraddha*). While faith often speaks to one's relation to the Divine in the text as in the Christian tradition, it covers ground beyond that as well. Faith tells us who people are, what their outlook might be and what is important to them. Faith, therefore, is a function of *guṇa* configuration (*BG* 17.2–4). Those within the orthodox fold are considered broadly *sattv*ic not just because they believe in various approximations of the Divine, but because they are interested in, and capable of, eventually becoming *sattv*ic and obtaining their freedom/*mokṣa*. As we will soon see, freedom's realization is delayed by more or less subtle variations in the *guṇa* configuration that make an eventual progression to *sattv*ic predominance possible. The faithful are therefore themselves characterized as divine, as opposed to the demonic who presumably fall outside the orthodox fold because they are atheists. The demonic outlook values the satisfaction of desire above all else and where the desires are broadly sense-driven, grounded in ignorance, and confused. The text suggests that the primacy of sensual desire—which is either *rajas*ic or *tāms*ic—is such that it makes even an eventual progression to *sāttv*ic predominance implausible. This unlikelihood is perhaps being flagged when the text characterizes the demonic as atheists (such as the hedonistic Charvāka school)—whose deep investment in desire denies the possibility of an alternative world view (*BG* 16.6–12).

Within the orthodox fold, the impact especially of *rajas* on ends inhibits *sattva*'s ascendency in a variety of ways that shed light on Arjuna's character. Orthodox faith in the Divine is characterized by four kinds of worshippers, which speaks to their broader outlook in general: those who are distressed and therefore seek the Divine's help to mitigate their suffering, those who pray for wealth, those who seek knowledge, as well as the wise who have it (*BG* 7.16–19). The first two kinds of faith display strongly *rajas*ic strains since they are concerned with sense-related pleasures and pains. Knowledge and wisdom, on the other hand, are clearly *sattv*ic, even if the latter distinguishes the sage's stasis from the knowledge seeker's transitive state. Arjuna's is clearly an intermediate faith since his pursuit of knowledge is on display with his consistent and acute questioning of Krishna (discussed above). But the dominant, passionate dimensions of his broader outlook are quite clearly evident in his distress and his assessment of his options in terms of power, wealth, and possessions. The overweening force of the passions is such that it clouds his judgement concerning his duties and his understanding of his ends within the orthodox worldview.

Detachment, we would therefore expect, would ideally help reconfigure Arjuna from being *rajas* over *sattva* to being primarily *sattva* over *rajas*. Detachment, as we saw in chapter 3, has a rational and a non-rational component. The rational component asks us to carefully consider how we undertake duty since it is possible to do so for a variety of reasons. Arjuna seems to see the rational dimension of his problem in terms of how the consequences of his actions affect him and therefore in terms of personal fruit. He is concerned with losing his extended family members, his former teachers, and his friends. Arjuna wonders how he will be able to enjoy the fruits of his (potential) blood-stained victory especially if it results in the destruction of civil society. Whereas Krishna thinks that duty must be undertaken precisely because it is one's duty and not because of how its consequences might affect the agent. His point is not that this will magically clear the way for Arjuna to see what he must do. Rather, had Arjuna consistently undertaken his duty with the right intention, then perhaps the dilemma would not have arisen in the first place. This shift away from thinking about duty in terms of personal aggrandizement is *sattva*'s contribution to reducing the primacy of *rajas*. After all, *rajas* is responsible for the I-sense and for the desire for the objects that aggrandize the I, both of which are clearly affected by undertaking duty with the right intention. But the rational component of detachment is not always enough to reorder *guṇa* priority for which sense-control, which is concerned with the non-rational component, comes into play.

Since *rajas* is responsible for much of the workings of the mind-as-sense/*manas* that perceives objects per se, sense-control would seem to hold the key to detachment in Arjuna's *rajas*ic personality. But sense-control does more than that since it affects the emotions that are a function of desire, and the I-sense/*ahamkāra*, both of which we saw are *rajas*ic in nature. Eventually, these affections will have a profound effect on the mind-as-will/*manas* as well, as we will soon see.

Sense-control, we saw in the previous chapter, is essential for the agent not to be driven by considerations of personal fruit. This is so because the agent trains herself not to dwell on sense objects which is how personal fruit is understood (be it in terms of wealth, position, or power). Sense-control, especially in the case of those like Arjuna who live the life of action (*karma yoga*), is made more plausible by a process of substitution of sense objects with the notion of a moral exemplar or sage. The many descriptions of the sage in the *Gītā*, therefore, are partially meant to help make the substitution. This substitution, where the exemplar is an object to be emulated rather than possessed, further weakens *rajas*'s manifestation as desire for sense objects. The weakening of *rajas*ic desire through sense-control not only makes right-intentioned *sattv*ic action possible, but gradually makes *sattva* and hence the ascendence of knowledge a reality.

The simultaneous strengthening of *sattva* and weakening of *rajas* has a cascading effect on the agent over time. The satisfaction or lack thereof of *rajas*ic desire we know causes passions like relief, happiness, anger, and frustration, which cloud judgement and inhibit knowledge. Ripening detachment means passions have less play in clouding knowledge as sensory desire is curtailed, and the *sattv*ic desire for knowledge gains pre-eminence. Such knowledge is not simply external, such as a clearer sense of what is to be done in light of the four ends, etc.; but is internal as well, as the internal springs of action become more obvious to the agent, more specifically to the doer/*kartā*.

The I-sense/*ahamkāra*, which along with the intellect/*buddhi* and mind/*manas* constitutes the doer/*kartā*, is *rajas*ic in nature since it is what individuates on the subjective side of action. The waning of *rajas* means a weakening at this level as well, abetted by a waxing *sattv*ic awareness that the "I" arises from this compartmentalized faculty of I-sense that in turn is ultimately constituted by strands/*guṇa*s. *Sattva*'s pre-eminence (manifest as a desire for knowledge) means that such internal insight is not simply of the I-sense but applies to the workings of the mind and of the intellect (which after all is what seeks knowledge) as well. The workings of the mind-as-will are, we have seen, anchored in the I-sense; after all, it is the "I" that wills. Such willing is increasingly swayed by *sattv*ic (as opposed to *rajas*ic) desire for knowledge in this process of *guṇa* reconfiguration, even as the authority of the I is being called into question. Thus, one would expect that the intellect—which is where the increasing internal understanding of the inner workings of the doer take place—becomes gradually transparent to itself.[14]

Much of what I say above about the gradual transformation of Arjuna's *rajas*ic personality is not always obvious in the *Gītā*. After all, such a transformation is yet to take place, if at all. But what we do get in the text are multiple descriptions of the sage, which constitutes descriptions of the transformation after the fact—even if none of these are of Arjuna as much as they are stated for his edification. To these descriptions we turn next, not only to understand how the transformation resolves, but to confirm the plausibility of the process of metamorphosis I have been describing.

5.8 The Sage

Given that the *Gītā* discusses different paths/*yoga*s to freedom/*mokṣa*, the multiple discussions of the sage in it are unsurprising. The paths of devotion or contemplation traverse very different ground from that of action. Yet the convergence of these paths on freedom means that at their core, the descriptions of the detached sage are substantially the same (*BG* 13.24). We will focus here on the descriptions of the sage devoted to the life of action, since the path of *karma* is Arjuna's path. But we will range beyond the active sage as well, to see what additional insight we might glean from these other descriptions, and from more general ones where the sage is only briefly referenced.

Detachment, we are coming to see, has to do with more than the rational and the non-rational dimensions of the human psyche, even if we think of it in terms of the doer/*kartā* rather than the lower self/*deha* with which the doer is continuous. But even the doer—understood in terms of the intellect, mind, and I-sense—is amenable to further analysis in terms of the *guṇas*. This analysis is expressed in the *Gītā* as having both a theoretical dimension that we can intellectually grasp and a phenomenological one that we can only dimly imagine. Let us begin—if only because it is exegetically convenient—with what the *Gītā* says about desire and emotion in the detached sage, which as we have seen in chapter 4 section 5, originates in the mind-as-sense.

The detached sage—understood here as the lower self/*deha*—is repeatedly described as being free of desire and hence from emotion (*BG* 2.55, 4.19). Thus, it would seem that the trajectory of sense-control as part of the practice of detachment leads to the complete falling away of desire. Now this clearly applies, first and foremost, to a desire for sense objects (*BG* 6.4, 5.21, 4.21), which is likely the culmination of the process of substituting the external objects for internal ones. But the text's insistence must be taken to mean that even the desire to be like the perfect active sage and therefore to promote world welfare—which are the substituted internal objects—falls away once one is an active sage. This is at best a stopgap explanation since one could object that there should persist a desire to continue to be such a person, the response to which will be obvious in a moment. For now, assuming all desire does fall away, the implications for the emotions are obvious; for we have seen the *Gītā* thinks that the emotions are the direct result of the satisfaction or the lack thereof of desire. Without desire, therefore, the emotions too fall away. Hence the sage is described as having transcended the duality of pleasure and pain, as being indifferent to fortune and misfortune, and in whom passion, fear, and anger are absent (*BG* 4.22, 2.56–57).

The falling away of desire and emotion completes the ascendency of *sattva* and hence of knowledge, for the text thinks that the intellect is obscured by passion just as fire is obscured by smoke (*BG* 3.38). The imagery is telling since it speaks to the inherently revealing nature of the intellect as light. Even so, we need to remember that the *sattv*ic intellect is at best the purveyor of light rather than its source (which, as we saw in chapter 4 section 2, is the Higher Self/*Ātman*). Moreover, the intellectual dimensions of becoming detached (which involve the appropriate intentionality and assessment of consequences) purify the intellect thereby increasing the *sattv*ic predominance to the point of complete self-transparency in detachment. The ensuing self-understanding plays out in a variety of ways when it comes to the doer/*kartā* and lower self/*deha*, and to the *Ātman*. We will focus here on the former and leave consideration of the latter to a later chapter.

One key insight is into the nature of the I-sense, that is now clearly seen in terms of its constitutive strands/*guṇa*s, rather than as an indivisible cornerstone of agency. Such insight is undoubtedly aided by two things: first, the weakening of *rajas* whose predominance is key in the constitution of the I-sense/*ahamkāra* as much as it is to that of the mind/*manas*. Second, the reduction in the activity of the mind-as-sense; after all, it is the latter that is home to desire and emotion, and which mediates the relation between the I-sense and its objects. All of this has implications for the rest of the lower self as well since desire and emotion are manifest through the body. The upshot is that there is insight that action is a function of the *guṇa*s acting (*BG* 14.23). If so, it means that this insight itself can at best only be spoken of as belonging to the detached sage in some loose sense; for knowledge itself is no longer anchored in the I-sense.[15]

Full detachment's impact on the mind-as-will/*manas* is also substantial. Not only is the mind-as-sense which drives so much of the willing in ordinary life quiescent, but the undermining of agency means that the willing itself becomes pointless. Hence the text repeatedly tells us that there is no longer a need for the detached sage to act, and that he undertakes no purposive action (*BG* 3.17–18, 4.20–21, 5.8, 5.13, 6.4). This is said presumably because there is no longer a person that acts in the usual sense, even if the actions continue because of residual *karma*, as we will see below. The fact that the sage is no longer a doer/*kartā* in the usual sense also responds to the possible objection as to why there is no desire—even desire for knowledge as such—to persist as a sage.[16]

Yet detached action persists in light of impersonal knowledge, and we need to understand what this means before we close out this chapter. Recall that the world is conceived organically in terms of the constant interaction of *guṇa*s. This world cannot be discontinuous with the detached sage since his person and action we saw is also conceived in terms of *guṇa*s acting on *guṇa*s. The continuity between the sage and the world is frictionless since the insight here is not only impersonal but synoptic because of *sattva*'s high predominance. In fact, one might say that the whole point of detachment is to align seamlessly with nature by detaching from the personal point of view. This alignment makes sense if we remember that the *Gītā*'s outlook is monistic, even if we are restricting ourselves to what happens at the level of Nature/*Prakrati*. Broadly speaking, therefore, the point seems to be that the personal perspective can be out of sync with the workings of Nature (which is why the long-term pursuit of personal pleasure is painful).[17] Thus the impersonal perspective is not only more in sync with everything else but is also representative of how things actually are. The full significance of this cannot be seen until we complete our understanding of the *Gītā*'s moral position in chapter 7. There, we will see how our concern with the form or intentional dimension of moral action fits with the principle that is the basis of its content: the maintenance of world-welfare.

Finally, we can see here a blueprint for all within the orthodox fold to obtain their freedom/*mokṣa* is on view here. For clearly what applies to Arjuna applies to all the believers who are characterized as divine, even if they do not belong to the higher classes. Undoubtedly, the challenges will differ by class and path, as might the level of difficulty. From the internal point of view of an agent, it is harder to move from a predominantly *tamas*ic rather than *rajas*ic configuration to a *sattv*ic one, which is presumably why we have a class-hierarchy in the first place. But the text insists that the recourse is there for all who fall within the orthodox fold and are therefore broadly *sattv*ic: women, *śudras*, and even outcastes, a recourse that seemingly makes freedom possible in this life (*BG* 9.32).[18] After all, from the external point of view at least, the ultimate reduction of all activity to *guṇa*s acting of *guṇa*s is the great equalizer, as is detachment, which through *karma* (and as we will see, *bhakti*) *yoga*, is available to all. This is particularly clear to the impersonal wisdom of the sage, who sees all humans, animals, and inanimate objects as indifferently equal (*BG* 5.18, 6.8).

The sage's activities persist, I have suggested, so long as the sage persists. But the text is clear that at the death of the body, the sage does not return, by which it clearly means that the subtle body/*kartā*'s configuration is dissolved (*BG* 8.16, 8.21, 15.4). Thus, the ultimate position of the text seems to be that while insight is clearly an epistemological change, it eventually leads to a substantive ontological one for the *kartā* that has, up to this point, persisted across lifetimes. Such a possibility is explained in terms of actions no longer generating future actions/*karma* (*BG* 2.39, 2.51, 4.19). After all, it is attachment to the fruit of action that creates the further fruit (of persistence) by generating more action/*karma* for the agent/*kartā*.

Notes

1 Though it should be said that "*Ātman*" often refers to the person, as becomes clear in context, as in, for instance, *BG* 4.7, 4.35, and 4.40. It should therefore be emphasized that intentionality is a feature not of *Ātman qua* Higher Self but of the

intellect, *contra* George Teschner, "Anxiety, Anger and the Concept of Agency and Action in the 'Bhagavad Gita,'" *Asian Philosophy* 2, no. 1 (1992): 61–77. "*Puruṣa*" is associated with the later Saṁkhya school where it refers to a limited and multiple spiritual entities in relation to Nature/*Prakrati* so that we have a multi-substance dualism. Whereas in the proto-Saṁkhya there are a range of possibilities so that the term may refer to a single *Puruṣa* that is related to material nature resulting in a single substance dualism (see Mikel Burley, *Classical Saṁkhya and Yoga: An Indian Metaphysics of Experience* (London: Routledge, 2006), 15–17). Since the *Gītā* is not attempting to reconcile monism with multiple substance dualism, but a monism with a single substance dualism, the issue is not whether *Ātman/Puruṣa* is one or many, but whether Nature/*Prakrati* is separate from it (see Gerald James Larson, Ram Shankar Bhattacharya, and Karl H. Potter, *The Encyclopedia of Indian Philosophies*, vol. 4, *Saṁkhya, A Dualist Tradition in Indian Philosophy* (Princeton: Princeton University Press, 2014), 3–5).

2 One would think that, *qua* World Principle, the Higher Self would have to act as the text confirms (*BG* 3.10), but even on this front Krishna denies this is so at the ultimate level (*BG* 4.14, 5.14). We will address some of the reasons for why he might think this in chapter 8.

3 But Bal Gangadhar Tilak and S. B. Sukthankar, *Śrīmad Bhagavadgīta Rahasya, or, Karma-Yoga-Śāstra* (New Delhi: Asian Educational Services, 2007), 1181–2, translates "*daivām*" as "destiny" which then is based in part on one's past *karma* and does the work that I have suggested is done by the *ceṣṭas*, and in part on the Divine's plan. But this is not supported by either Śaṇkara or Rāmānuja.

4 For more on early Buddhism's discussions on causality, see Appendix 2.

5 Both Śaṇkara and Rāmānuja take "*ceṣṭas*" to mean functions of the body even if "*saṃskāras*" which is used later in the tradition to mean "predispositions" is absent here.

6 See Chakravarthi Ram-Prasad, *Divine Self, Human Self: The Philosophy of Being in Two Gita Commentaries* (London: Continuum, 2013), 82–5.

7 The picture in Rāmānuja is complicated by the fact that knowledge of the world arises as a result of the relation between the *Ātman* and what the *Gītā* calls the *kartā*, which is distinct from the changeless knowledge that *Ātman* has of itself (see Rāmānuja, *Sri Rāmānuja Gita Bhasya: With Text and English Translation*, trans. Swami Adidevananda (Madras: Sri Ramakrishna Math, 2007), 3.27, 13.6, 13.14; Bimal Krishna Matilal, "Caste, Karma and the Gita," in *Philosophy, Culture, and Religion: The Collected Essays of Bimal Krishna Matilal. Volume 2: Ethics and Epics*, 136–44 (Oxford; New York: Oxford University Press, 2001).

8 My views here (though more detailed) are in broad agreement with A. Herman, "Ethical Theory in the Bhagavad-Gītā: Teleological Attitude Liberationism and Its Implications," *Journal of Vaishnava Studies* 3, no. 2 (1995): 47–70, on how the relationship between *guṇa* configuration, class participation, and duty are

related. But see Stephen Philips who thinks personality is limited to this life and individuality is what transmigrates for him; both influence each other insofar as the former impacts the long run individual which in turn maintains continuity over lifetimes (Stephen Phillips, *Yoga, Karma, and Rebirth: A Brief History and Philosophy* (New York: Columbia University Press, 2009), 172–74). But it is unclear what this individuality might be if it is not personality. Matilal, "Caste, Karma and the Gita," 136–44 suggests the hereditary-based class hierarchy is anti-rational and unfair, and the theodicy that emphasizes the merit based nature of the social order is therefore a rationalization rather than a rational order. But this presupposes a particular (and especially) naturalistic hermeneutic rather than one that frames the text as part of the *smriti*/remembered tradition that follows *śruti*/heard texts (more on which in the upcoming sections of this chapter).

9 The Sanskrit names for the strands/*guṇas* are left untranslated to avoid misleading the reader, since English translations are heavily contextual and not always obviously continuous with each other. The reasons for why this is so will become obvious shortly.

10 See Vacaspati Misra's ninth-century commentary on verse 13 of the *Samkya Karika*, for instance.

11 I follow Alladi Mahadeva Śastry, *The Bhagavad Gita: With Commentary of Sri Sankaracharya* (Madras: Samata Books/Lotus Light Publications, 1992), 108, and David White, "The Bhagavadgītā's Conception of Human Freedom," *Philosophy East and West* 34, no. 3 (1984), in suggesting that the *guṇas* constitute all of nature and not just living entities, *contra* Ellen Briggs Stansell, "The Guna Theory of the Bhagavad Gita," *Journal of Indian Council of Philosophical Research* 25, no. 4 (2008): 61–80, who follows Rāmānuja. Even if Briggs Stansell is right in suggesting that the *guṇas* only constitute living entities (though I am not convinced, see, for instance *BG* 7.14), the world can still be conceived in terms of *guṇas* since the Gītā conceives the world as a living organism more than once (see, for instance, *BG* 14.3–4, 15.1–3).

12 While it is true that Rāmānuja thinks that consciousness is a feature of the Self but not its essence, he does suggest that the highest form insight (*kaivalya*) is essentially luminous (see *RGB* 8.21, 285–86).

13 See *BGB* 125–26; Bimal Motilal, "Caste, Karma and the Gita," in *Indian Philosophy of Religion*, ed. Roy W. Perrett (Dordrecht; Boston: Kluwer Academic Publishers, 1989), 51–56, suggests that the discussions in *BG* 18.41ff concerning the constitutive properties of Brahmanhood, etc. are a significant and original contribution of the text insofar as it made it possible to separate class status as the basis of nature rather than birth, even if this is at best suggestive. The author acknowledges that the *karma* doctrine which suggests predestination (at least of class membership if not of action, as I suggest) as the basis of the constitutive properties of character is the most plausible reading of the text.

14 See Ram-Prasad, *Divine Self, Human Self*, 100, who rightly points out that Śaṇkara is unwilling to grant anything more than a penultimate role to agency, which follows from his views on the nature of the self in terms of *māyā* (as we will see). Whereas I part ways with Śaṇkara because of my views on the nature of the self, based on what I call aspect-dualism in chapter 8.

15 See *BGB* 139.

16 See Christopher G. Framarin, "The Desire You Are Required to Get Rid of: A Functionalist Analysis of Desire in the Bhagavadgita," *Philosophy East and West* 56, no. 4 (2006): 604, who insists that intentional action entails desire, and who therefore thinks desireless action is not possible. Whereas I think that is true prior to insight but not after. In addition, I think the point here is not that the sage has the power over another, or everything else for that matter, as suggested by Franklin Edgerton, *The Bhagavad Gita* (Cambridge, MA: Harvard University Press, 1997), 13, or that it means that the individual and divine wills coincide (see Purushottama Bilimoria, "Protestant Ethic and Hindu Dharma: With Reference to Kant and Gandhi," in *The Contemporary Essays on the Bhagavad Gita*, ed. Sinha (New Delhi: Siddharth Publications, 1995), 90), mainly because this is to fundamentally misconstrue the sage's nature as an agent in some sense.

17 See David Appelbaum, "Tangible Action: Non-Attached Action in the Bhagavadgıta," in *Sanskrit and Related Studies: Contemporary Researches and Reflections* (New Delhi: SRI Satguru Publications, 1990), 99–111; and Simon Brodbeck, "Calling Krsna's Bluff: Non-Attached Action in the Bhagavadgītā," *Journal of Indian Philosophy* 32, no. 1 (February 1, 2004): 91, whose understanding of the workings of nature, at the very least, I agree with here. One of the implications of my view, therefore, is that I take the possibility of Arjuna's choice seriously so that he can either go to war or act otherwise, even if his choice is eventually undermined by the coming conflagration. Such a choice, then, while based on rational considerations, is ultimately based on ignorance of one's true nature but allows for a limited sense of freewill. I will say more on this issue later, in chapter 10.

18 But see Roy Perrett, *Hindu Ethics: A Philosophical Study* (Honolulu: University of Hawaii Press, 1998), 41, who thinks that *mokṣa* is an ideal for all to honor but not necessarily to pursue or else we have the undermining of the social structures that support the sage. But this, as we have seen, is precisely the problem that the text circumvents in response to the Buddhists, since it consistently suggests that renunciation is not of action but of its fruit.

Coda 1 (to Chapters 2–5)

It would be reasonable to say that the substantial overlap and disconnects in our discussion of the two texts so far should make for an interesting dialogue, which I propose to organize around three themes: intentionality, tripartition, and personality. What will hopefully become evident is that there is a common core of ideas concerning what is essential to ethical action that will allow us to reflect on their importance in general. But significant differences arise that will throw light on the different framing considerations of the texts; differences that ultimately lead to divergences in the traditions that are inspired by, or at the very least exemplified in, these influential texts.

Moral Intentionality

It is not inappropriate to start with moral intentionality since we began our discussions with it in chapter 2. By moral intentionality we mean the form of an action as opposed to the content (and its basis), or why an action is undertaken rather than the nature of the action or its principles. We started here because the "why" of an action can affect the nature of the action itself, regardless of the principled basis of the action. Thus, if X loans money to Y because the Golden Rule requires it of her, it makes the act very different from doing so as a political favor. But intentionality, it turns out, does more than shape the action since it is crucial in shaping character and personality in both texts.

Key to both positions on intentionality is the rational removal of a certain kind of self-interest from intention. In Aristotle this begins with a discussion of how a virtuous choice is made, i.e., for its own sake and therefore as virtuous. Such choice instantiates the virtuous wish for the real good since choice in this context speaks to the end/*telos* rather than the aim/*skopos* it is concerned with, as we saw in chapter 2. But to make an end that is wished for or chosen for its own sake is the work of rational love. In the case of virtuous wish, the desiderative origin of the end is reason which is perceived as good; whereas in the case of virtuous choice it is the action that is loved as an end that simultaneously instantiates wish. Such love of virtue that expresses Aristotle's views on the moral intentionality is not distinct from what he calls the right kind of self-love. For the activity is nothing but the personality or character actualized as excellent or virtuous, in contrast with the wrong kind of self-lover who we would call "selfish."

In the *Gītā*, the removal of the wrong kind of self-interest is more direct even if it is conceived negatively. Thus, the agent is asked not to pursue the personal fruit of their duty/*dharma*, even as they attempt to determine the appropriate way in which duty can be instantiated in a particular situation. This is not unlike Aristotle's suggestion that an action be chosen for its own sake, since the point in the *Gītā* is that one should undertake one's duty because it is one's duty and not because of what might accrue to the agent from it. Even so, Aristotle might insist that nobility does accrue to the agent and, *qua* virtuous activity, constitutes happiness or flourishing for the properly configured agent or self-lover. Here then we begin to see the emergence of a divide that will pervade our discussions; for it is not that there is no such thing as a properly configured personality in the *Gītā*, even if tripartition here is discussed in terms of strands/*guṇas*. Nor is it the case that the *Gītā* will deny that undertaking duty is good or noble. The difference arises because the proper configuration of personality is in the service of construction of a flourishing agency in Aristotle, whereas in the *Gītā* proper *guṇa* configuration is a means to the eventual deconstructing of agency. To think through the implications of this divergence will require us to consider their respective discussions of tripartition, since this will allow us to include the non-rational dimensions of personality.

Tripartition

Desire is central to understanding tripartition in both texts, and not just because we are including the non-rational in our considerations; for the rational is also conceived in terms of desire in both. In Aristotle, this is so with virtuous wish *qua* rational desire, which works with the non-rational desire in choice along with deliberation. Despite the fact that the *Gītā* speaks of the will that decides, it is either determined by rational desire (for knowledge) or by desire for sense objects. Broadly speaking, therefore, the rational/non-rational dichotomy applies to both as does the importance of cultivation of desire in terms of upbringing (in Aristotle) or in terms of the stage-and-station scheme in the *Gītā*.

Even so, their moral psychology differs in important ways, though the reasons why are not obvious. It may seem that the *Gita*'s *guṇa*-based views are drive-focused, whereas Aristotle seems to emphasize faculties. But this is misleading since the predominance of a particular *guṇa* such as *rajas* is simultaneously conceived in terms of the pre-eminence of the corresponding faculty which in this instance is mind-as-sense/*manas*. Similarly, Aristotle's faculties of thinking and appetition represent distinct drives. It is true that Aristotle's complex of reason/spirit/appetite looks very different from the intellect/mind/I-sense construct in the *Gītā*. The latter folds appetitive and spirited elements into the mind and speaks of them together in terms of their respective desired sense objects, while also bringing the notion of the will into play. Whereas Aristotle seems to think that decisions are determined purely by the priority of the drive/faculty in an individual's life. Still, both realize that choice is an important fulcrum in the philosophy of action, even if they disagree on the nature of its mechanism.

Tamas represents a real difference between the two texts since it speaks of inertia and therefore what seems like an absence of drive. There is no parallel discussion in Aristotle except perhaps the paralysis brought on from being torn by weakness of will broadly construed, but this does not seem to be all that the *Gītā* is attempting to explain. For the text, following tradition, seems to think that the desire for inactivity is real and not simply reducible to the absence of other drives or the immobility resulting from their being at odds. Thus, insofar as it thinks that *tamas* inherently promotes ignorance and sloth, the *Gītā* gives additional reasons why ignorance is difficult to overcome. For it is not just that the senses (or the appetites and emotions in Aristotle's language) beguile and distract us, but that there is a kind of desire within our nature that can hold us back.

This brings us back to desire per se and the very different approaches to it that we see in the two texts. Aristotle thinks that rational and non-rational desires are to be rationally cultivated so that they are broadly in line with each other in the virtuous person. But while cultivated desires are equals in virtue, Aristotle is quite clear that it is rational desire that has primacy, which seems consistent with his view that all virtuous desire is cultivated rationally. The satisfaction of rational desire is good because it constitutes right or virtuous action for Aristotle, which he speaks of in terms of the love of virtue. But because such love of virtue is also simultaneously a form of the right kind of self-love, Aristotle is clearly suggesting that virtue is not just good per se but good for the virtuous person and constitutes their well-being (as the function argument discussed in chapter 6 will confirm). In other words, to act well is also to live well or to flourish, a qualification that applies to the person or substance, and is the result of the rational configuration of desires.

Whereas the *Gītā* is centrally concerned with the eventual dissolution of desire. Detachment initially asks us to shift focus away from a certain kind of consequence, and sense control asks us to do the same with sense objects, both of which involve a substantial rational component. But reason here is not the end in itself as it is in Aristotle; rather, the whole purpose of detachment is to bring about *sattva*'s ascendency by reconfiguring desire away from the sensible. While it is true that the eventual result of *sattva*'s rise is knowledge, such knowledge does not enhance the sage's happiness since it consists of the insight that the sage is nothing but "strands/*guṇa*s acting on strands." Such insight, then, seals the fate of rational and non-rational desire since desire by its very nature connects a subject to its object. This view raises the question of how the text might allow for the legitimate satisfaction of at least some of our desires prior to insight, and to which we will see the *Gita*'s response in chapter 7.

Personhood and Personality

Personality or character is an attribute of the person, and this distinction clarifies important ideas in both texts. In Aristotle, a rational personality is the mark of virtue that characterizes the flourishing person or substance. Substances are fundamental building blocks of the world for Aristotle, so that everything in the world is a substance, an attribute of it, or said of it (as in the case of universals). While Aristotle does not address the persistence of human substances beyond this life, in other places, he is quite clear that the human substance does not persist beyond this one (*DA* 3.5 430a10–26). Thus, the construction of character, which is constituted by the formation of desire as a harmony, is very much in the service of the full life here and now.

The story is complicated in the *Gītā* since it does think that there is persistence across lifetimes of the doer/*kartā*. The doer, as we have seen, is constituted by the lower self without the body and therefore of the subtle elements in the form of the intellect, mind, and I-sense. The subtle elements themselves are conceived in terms of the configuration of their constituent strands, though the text seems non-committal as to whether the ever-active strands themselves persist in a particular configuration or whether it is just the configuration that does.[1] Even if the former is true, the text does not take recourse to the language of substance (*dravya*) which is available to it, and is a key notion in other orthodox schools like the Vaisheshika. If the latter is true, then continuity would have to be the basis of identity. In important ways, though, the issue is moot since the text seems focused on the dissolution of identity based on *guṇa*-reconfiguration rather than on its persistence. This is so because persistence is not conceived as a good in itself, but rather the cost of misperceiving the unity of nature that is only overcome with insight. While such insight perfects the transition of the sage's activity to being seamless with that of nature, it marks the beginning of the end of the persistence of the sage—and specifically of the transmigration of the reconfigured doer/*kartā*—at the end of that life.

Despite their divergent views on the importance of the individual, it is clear that for both texts the stability of the personality is important. Stability for them seems to be a matter of internal configuration be it of drives or *guṇa*s. Not only does the configuration of reason/spirit/appetite make for a flourishing, stable, moral, and political life for Aristotle, it also provides the foundation for the high-functioning life of the philosopher (as we will see). Such stability is not hegemonic but rather the result of an internal harmony that is grounded in self-love. Whereas the stability of the sage in the *Gītā*, which is the end result of *sattva*'s ascendancy in the process of *guṇa*-reconfiguration, seems ultimately concerned with harmony with the world. Thus, the *Gita*'s holism (i.e., its emphasis on the whole rather than the part) might be contrasted with Aristotle's atomism (i.e., its emphasis on the individual), since it gives us a sense of their priorities. These priorities will shape their views on the remaining matters we discuss here, starting with a shift from the form to the content of ethical action in Aristotle.

Notes

1 This noncommittal nature of the *Gītā*'s position on (a) whether the same strands persist in the doer and (b) whether the strands themselves are static or in flux make it difficult to accept the insightful reading of Antonio T. de Nicolás, "The Problem of the Self-Body in the Bhagavadgītā: The Problem of Meaning," *Philosophy East and West* 29, no. 2 (1979): 167, who thinks that the Gītā clearly affirms a theory of universal flux.

6

Ethical Content in the *Nicomachean Ethics*

6.0 Introduction

If the earlier chapters discussed the "why" (or form) of virtuous action, it is time to focus on its "what" (or content). In Aristotle, we saw that why we act virtuously is central to the action's ethical status, for the very same action can be undertaken for a variety of reasons. The rational capacity must be educated to choose the right reason to act (which Aristotle describes in terms of "choosing the action for its own sake" or "for the sake of virtue") and has to do with the *telos*/end of action about which we will complete our discussion in terms of wish here. Moreover, as we saw, for truly virtuous action, the non-rational capacities of emotion and appetite must harmoniously align themselves with reason in ways that involve the love of virtue across the board. The "what" of virtuous action, on the other hand, grounds the "why" by giving it specific content understood in terms of obtaining the goal/*skopos* of action. In chapters 2 and 3, we discussed the contextual nature of acting virtuously for the right reasons. But now our focus shifts to the broader considerations of what constitutes virtue that then is the basis of such detailed deliberations. Thus, for instance, we need to know that being able to face a noble death is constitutive of courage before we can determine how this is instantiated in a particular action and circumstance for a specific agent.

It is not unusual to think that the content generation of ethical action is a function of a rule or principle.[1] For instance, the content of ethical action can be determined by the so-called Golden Rule, versions of which can be found in Egyptian, Chinese, Indian, and Greek traditions and which asks us to treat others as we would like to be treated ourselves; or versions of the utilitarian principle that ask us to pursue actions that would maximize general welfare.[2] We can very easily see how these principles might work and work well. The golden rule tells us, for example, that we should not steal from others as we would not want to be subject to theft ourselves. Such a rule can help us determine the course of action in a variety of circumstances involving courage, temperance, kindness, honesty, decency, generosity, etc. precisely because we can put ourselves at the receiving end of our own actions. The utilitarian principle, on the other hand, seems less focused on the agent since it asks us to prioritize general welfare. We should pay our taxes not mainly because it benefits us (for it clearly sometimes may not) but because it promotes the general good. Both principles, in their own way, have the advantage of being able to consistently guide human action in a clear and practical fashion. This is not to say that dilemmas such as the one that Arjuna faces can be easily resolved by principles of this sort, since dilemmas are by definition intractable; yet their proponents argue that the usual ethical situations we are faced with are easier to navigate with the help of such principles.

Despite the obvious advantages, ethical theories that generate content based on principles face challenges precisely because they are rule driven. For instance, we may not think it acceptable if a masochist tried to live by the Golden Rule for many would not appreciate being at the receiving end of the resultant pain. Similarly, the utilitarian pursuit of general welfare can come at the expense of minorities or even individuals (as in the case of a tax on religious minorities). On the former view, the problem seems to be that the origin of the rule focuses too much on the interests of the agent, and in the latter, because it does not consider the needs of some agents enough. More generally, therefore, the problem with rule-driven ethical theories is the other side of the coin of their strong suit of consistency: they tend to be inflexible because their priorities limit their scope. Nor is it simply a matter of trying to combine the rules in a single ethical theory to cover all our bases, for such an attempt brings up any number of problems. For instance, given that these theories have different priorities (i.e., on the individual as opposed to the group), there are bound to be difficulties in application. Moreover, it is unclear which would get priority and when, nor is it apparent that even two or more rules would help navigate our complex ethical lives adequately.

Aristotle seems to take a very different approach, since he emphasizes that the standard of measure for virtuous action is the person rather than the rule:

> … the good man judges each class of things rightly, and in each the truth appears to him … For each state of character has its own ideas of the noble and the pleasant, and perhaps the good man differs from others most by seeing the truth in each class of things, being as it were the norm and measure of them.
>
> (*NE* 3.4 1113a32–35)[3]

We have seen this passage before and now we consider it not only from the point of view of the person as standard, but in terms of how this is so. In other words, the content of virtuous activity in any and every context is generated by what the good person "sees" needs to be done, for the good person is an expert in ethical matters as a master batsman like Tendulkar is in cricket. Tendulkar knows what shot to play and when, knows how to build momentum within an innings and over a series of matches in a World Cup, and how to handle pressure in high stakes games, etc. Similarly, the good person grasps situations accurately, deliberates on the options, determines the likelihood of success, and chooses the right action accordingly. Having the good person instead of the rule as the standard of measure ensures that action fits the often-intricate ethical scenarios in ways that the mechanical application of a rule might not always allow. Tendulkar might know that an unorthodox stroke will work better in a high-pressure situation precisely because the fielders are in orthodox positions and has the skills to pull it off. Thus, the good person, as we saw, not only perceives the situation well, but intuitively knows what needs to be done.

The danger here is thinking that there are no rules at all since Aristotle says that the good person is the standard.[4] That Tendulkar has no regard for the rules nor has his development as a player have anything to do with them. Yet this is only eventually true, as we will see, for the good person is ultimately the basis of the rule (and eventually the law) in ways that will allow a place for latitude that is grounded in Aristotle's ethical naturalism. In the interim, we can note that without a place for rules and laws, and not just in her development, the good person's actions run the risk of simply being arbitrary and out of sync with those of other good people. Or, to continue the cricketing metaphor, it makes it difficult to distinguish between the orthodox and unorthodox shot. While rules and laws also make it possible to maintain consistency across different situations for the same agent, Aristotle may be understood to be saying here that the ethical life is too complex to be navigable by rules. Rather, it takes a full-fledged virtuoso (i.e., the virtuous person) to make the right call so that knowing when and how to act, and in relation to whom and to what extent, is a complex matter that is not itself reducible to rules. The good person then is often the basis of determining when to apply a rule or even to bend it, and in some circumstances, whether it is necessary to eventually change it.

6.1 On Human Function

Aristotle thinks if we understand what human well-functioning (*ergon*) is, we will grasp what is good for humans which is what constitutes their happiness (*NE* 1.7 1097b22–25). More interestingly, he suggests that what the good is for humans (that is, their happiness) is also what the good human does, ethically speaking (*NE* 2.6 1106a14–23). This congruity is why Aristotle thinks that the good person comes to see the good in every situation because it is available in their nature if such nature is cultivated and educated appropriately. Thinking through Aristotle's so-called "function argument" will help us understand how he thinks this equation might work.

Aristotle describes the good (or happy) person as a well-functioning human being, which may sound odd to our ears (*NE* 1.7 1097b21–1098a18). While we might see how a well-functioning machine fulfills what it means to be that machine, it is unclear if this works as well for humans since we no longer think that humans have a function or purpose in the way in which machines do. But suppose we start with thinking about function/*ergon* not in turns of "purpose" but in terms of "work" (which is the literal meaning of "*ergon*"). Then we can perhaps see Aristotle means that a well-functioning human being is analogous to a healthy, working human being. If we push the analogy with health, it becomes obvious that a healthy human being is one in whom all the body parts are functioning well as a harmonious whole. Being sick, on the other hand, is precisely when the body is not functioning as a harmonious whole be it because of an organ malfunction, or a cancer, etc. Even so, there has to be more to being a well-functioning human being (as opposed to, say, a well-functioning mollusk) than physical health. We might say that psychological (or what Aristotle calls psychic) health must also be involved since we are more than merely instinctive creatures. Individuals have personalities or characters, which not only dominate the rest of human nature, but also range over a number of possibilities. A person can be an optimist or pessimist, excessively rational or too emotional, and these personality traits mark out who we are as human beings. So, if there are well-functioning human beings they must, by extension, have a deeply integrated and hierarchical psychology and physiology of a special sort.

This well-functioning personality for Aristotle, unsurprisingly enough, turns out to be rational. Much of the story about the well-functioning kind of personality we have already seen in chapter 2's discussion of the right kind of teleology of desire. There, it became clear that the soul/*psyche* (hence "psychology") has three drives or kinds of desire: that of reason, of spirit, and of appetite. These desires are educated and cultivated such that there is deep integration on the intentional front led by reason, and which Aristotle articulates in terms of the love of virtue. But the story of the cultivation of rationality we saw in chapter 2 section 7 is complicated by the fact that rationality's desire is either its own *qua* wish or works in conjunction with non-rational desire in deliberative choice. Yet the cultivation of rational and non-rational desire occurs at the same time on the back of individual actions that are encouraged with normative language that foster a broader perspective in turn. Hence eating moderately is encouraged as good when the tutee regularly eats reasonable amounts of healthy food until they increasingly come to see such eating as good. I think Aristotle's point is that such apprehension of the good is essentially related to our functioning well—as something that is available to us if we are working properly, so to speak. After all, apprehension of the end is simply a way of speaking of how our nature is actualized when we function well, a potentiality that must be within us to be actualized in the first place.[5] Of course different things may appear good to us depending on how we are brought up, but the difference between the apparent and real good we saw has to do with whether or not their origin is in reason (on which more below).

Aristotle has two additional reasons for making rationality central to human function. First, rationality is inherently capable of organizing itself and its pursuits. It is, after all, reason that determines whether one becomes a doctor or a politician in light of how one might instantiate the higher end of acting well in one's circumstances, given one's interests and capabilities. Such determining of higher, intermediate ends is not deliberative but something that becomes apparent with experimentation and time (*NE* 3.3 1112b12–16).[6] In addition, reason can set priorities for the various basic drives (for food and sex) and emotional responses (such as anger and jealousy and the desires that these motivate) so that it is capable of integrating all aspects of human nature (in ways that we have already seen in chapter 2). This is not to deny that, say, the appetite for bodily pleasure cannot be the dominant force in human life and use reason's organizing power to obtain its ends (as is often the case in tyrants, for instance). But Aristotle thinks that such integration is at best provisional since such people end up being at odds with themselves as their actions often cause them remorse. Remorse is not just a sign of disharmony at the peripheries of human nature, since it characterizes the majority of lives in which the different drives often take priority over time (*NE* 9.4 1166b5–24). Whereas Aristotle thinks that rational integration of personality is more enduring and not prone to remorse, presumably since remorse is an intellectual response that is unlikely when reason consistently gets its way.

Second, the way in which rationality manifests itself in human life is distinctive enough that in separating us from other species it defines us. At the broadest level, what distinguishes one species from another is difference, whether it is in physiological or functional terms. It is true that humans share the nutritive and reproductive capacities with plant and animal life, and perceptual and locomotive capacities with animals. But, for Aristotle, what separates us from them is our rationality. We may object that there are animals that clearly display rationality in their ability to problem solve (dolphins, for instance), and for Aristotle at least, there is the Unmoved Mover who is nothing but pure, theoretical mind (*Metaphysics*[7] 12.7 1072b18–29; *NE* 10.8 1178b7–23). But Aristotle is more interested here in the distinctive way in which rationality is manifest in human life, especially if I am right about the importance to him of the deeply integrated personality in this context—even if such integration is also essentially related to the way in which humans come to emulate the Divine. Not only are we capable of being just theoretically minded, therefore, but also that we are adept at using reason in the practical life. Thus, as we saw in chapter 2, we have non-rational capacities of emotion and appetite that are capable of heeding reason in one way or the other.[8] Humans are therefore at the crossroads of the continuum of life between the divine on the one hand and the animal on the other, a distinctive position that we hold surely because of the way in which it is possible for our life to be shot through with reason.[9] (I will say more about what is good for humans or for their complete happiness, understood in terms of the excellent activities of (especially theoretical) reason, in chapter 9.[10])

So, it would seem that well-functioning human beings are integrated in such a way that prioritizes reason as this gives them the best chance to live fulfilled flourishing and happy lives, or what we might say is their highest good. Yet, this may not be enough, for Aristotle has still to show that rationality is inherently ethical; that is, why should we agree with him that what is good for humans end up being what the good human does? For even if he could argue that the tyrant's life is not rational because appetite subverts reason for its own ends, it is unclear how an undiverted rationality gives us virtue.

In response, it is worth reminding ourselves of what was said earlier in chapter 2: that on the intentional front, Aristotle thinks that to undertake an action for the sake of virtue is to act, not from considerations primarily of utility or pleasure, but as the situation impartially demands (or what he calls "in accordance with the fine or noble"). In chapter 3, we saw that the language of self in the discussions of self-friendship really refers to the personality rather than the person. Thus, a personality or character that is shaped by appetitive priorities is, for Aristotle, the bad personality precisely because such a person is selfish or what he takes to be the wrong kind of self-lover. That is, this kind of self emphasizes *it*self because he is moved by considerations that originate from his body (after all it is hard to make sense of an excessive appetite for sex without a body; or a cowardly person who prioritizes his personal safety over those of others in the battlefield). Again, this is not to deny that such appetitive personalities use rationality in a subordinate fashion. Whereas the self that prioritizes rationality is what the Christian tradition might call "selfless" just because she does not prioritize the body (though Aristotle himself calls such a person the right kind of self-lover, *NE* 9.8 1168b28–1169a7); for Aristotle seems to rightly imply that rationality is inherently concerned with the general and the universal, since it is what seeks and acquires knowledge. So, in the ethical context one would expect that such a person would act from impersonal considerations of what is fitting and appropriate to the situation, or what we have seen Aristotle describe as "acting in accordance with the fine or noble" (*to kalon*) (e.g., *NE* 2.3 1104b29–1105a1; 3.7 1115b11–15). While this emphasis on circumstances is in keeping with Aristotle's emphasis on the good person as the criterion of right action, what should not be forgotten here is the connection to generality and universality that are the hallmarks of knowledge.[11] This connection, as we will soon see, will be articulated in terms of the law.

Aristotle speaks of the separation of the use of reason by the appetitive individual—in contrast to when it has primacy in human life—in terms of mere functioning as opposed to functioning well. The difference between the two selves is like the difference between two knives both of which have edges (comparable to rationality) but only one is sharp enough to cut well or excellently. Interestingly enough, "well" or "excellence" translates "*aretē*" which also means "virtue" (and even though we would not usually speak of a virtuous knife, we would easily understand what is meant by it). This in turn allows Aristotle to complete making his case by taking recourse to ordinary language: the well-functioning person is in fact virtuous or ethical, so that what the good (or ethical) person does, is also what is good or fulfilling for them.

But if Aristotle is right and to be virtuous is to fulfill human nature, we have to come to grips with how this is consistent with the fact that virtue in the fullest or complete sense, even for him, is rare and laudable. The rarity of such fulfillment is a concern for, by contrast, animals come to fulfill their nature instinctively if conditions are favorable. After all, it is natural for a cub to grow into a lion in the jungle (as opposed to in the Arctic), for things in nature happen in a certain way for the most part (*Physics* 2.8 199b15–25). To complicate matters, virtue's rarity might explain why it is laudable, yet if it is laudable, it is unclear how it is natural and not something earned with difficulty. A response on Aristotle's behalf, as readers will expect by this point, will have to do with the centrality of rationality to his views. Rationality allows us the choice to pursue the aims of reason or not, such that if our development is to be earned, as moral development is thought to be, something must depend on us (*NE* 3.5 1114b16–17). What depends on the agent, we saw in chapter 3, has to do with what we do in that transitional period between being tutored and becoming the person one decides to be, for better or for worse. Moreover, complete virtue, as we will see in chapter 9, involves not just practical but the fullest actualization in contemplation of theoretical virtue. Such completeness is even more challenging to obtain and not just because of the inherent difficulties of pursuing knowledge, but because such pursuits are more susceptible to ill fortune thus making virtue in the fullest sense a rare beast.[12]

6.2 Virtue and the Rule of Law

Even so, we should note that just because Aristotle thinks something is up to us does not mean everything is; since ideally, a significant familial, social, political, and cultural investment needs to be in place for moral (or dispositional/character) development, in addition to the role of choice, which might also go some distance in explaining virtue's rarity. If bee development from the larval stage presupposes a hive in an appropriate climate and habitat, the parallel context for human moral development for Aristotle is the city-state/polis (*Politics* 1.2 1252b27–1253a18). That is, a city-state is a natural phenomenon even if it is a human construct, in much the same way in which a hive is a natural phenomenon; for Aristotle famously thinks that humans are essentially political animals and cannot flourish (though they might merely survive) in isolation (*Politics* 1.2 1252b27–1253a7). Unsurprisingly, then, the city is not just a physical construct and at its heart are the institutions that administer justice and make it possible for its citizens to do more than simply live, and in fact live well (or virtuously).

This connection between a state that is ideally just, and the virtuous individual, is made by the laws of the state in ways that will help us work through the issues of consistency and extreme particularism that are often thought to plague Aristotle's virtue-centric ethics.

First, the law is key in the development of virtue in individuals, for the wise politician not only organizes the activities of the state, but also promotes moral virtue through good habituation fixed by the law. Hence Aristotle says " … legislators make the citizens good by forming habits in them, and this is the wish of every legislator … " (*NE* 2.1 1103b3ff) And again " … it is difficult to get from youth up a right training for virtue if one has not been brought up under right laws; for to live temperately and hardily is not pleasant to most people, especially when they are young. For this reason, their nurture and occupations should be fixed by law … " (*NE* 10.9 1179b31–35). Education, whether it is administered by the state or privately, clearly has a strong ethical dimension that not only has a place for social restraints (as is the case in a liberal democracy) but also actively promotes ethical excellence. Hence, we saw how courage is developed in the context of martial training in chapter 3, for instance. Similarly, encouraging the consumption of healthy food is as, if not more, important than discouraging a harmful diet in the development of temperance. A musical education is essential for the appreciation of the fine and the good, and so on. Even for those who do not have the background that allows them the luxury of an extensive education, the law is a touchstone the ignorance of which is inadequate to justify vice and avoid reprimand (*NE* 3.5 1113b35–1114a3).

Second, the connection between the law and full-fledged virtue is even more substantial for Aristotle, as is evident in his discussion of the relation of political and practical wisdom in Book 6 of the *Ethics* (1140a24–1140b30) and of the wider sense of justice in Book 5 (1129a1–1130a14). Practical and political wisdom are the same disposition (*hexis*) but their definition is not the same, thinks Aristotle. That is, if a person *qua* (or as) citizen is practically wise and therefore able to self-legislate and act on what promotes the good life for him, then, *qua* ruler, he should be capable of legislating and acting on behalf of the city as well. After all, what a good (and therefore practically wise) person chooses to do should be coincident with the law in every instance, if in fact the law, as in Aristotle's ideal state, is responsible for making him good in the first place and is also what constitutes their flourishing as we saw. Since practical wisdom is the acme of virtue for Aristotle, the equation with political wisdom in this context is significant.

This substantive convergence between the law and virtue is confirmed in Aristotle's discussion of justice. For him "justice" has two senses, the lawful and the fair, and much of Book V is spent in discussing the latter, narrower, sense of the term that is concerned with the fair distribution of natural goods such as wealth, honor, power, etc. But the former sense of lawful is virtually identified with virtue:

> … for practically the majority of the acts commanded by the law are those which are prescribed from the point of view of virtue taken as a whole; for the law bids us practice every virtue and forbids us to practice any vice. And the things that tend to produce virtue taken as a whole are those of the acts prescribed by the law which have been prescribed with a view to education for the common good.
>
> (*NE* 5.2 1130b22–26)

Thus, it would seem that everything that is lawful is virtuous for Aristotle, presumably in an ideally just society (even if, as will see towards the end of this chapter, Aristotle's views on this matter are complicated). Yet since this wider sense of justice, as it is traditionally conceived, has to do with our relations to others and not our relations to ourselves in addition (contrary to what Plato thinks in the *Republic*), it is not all there is to virtue, though it assumes virtue (1129b13–1130a13). Interestingly enough, therefore, Aristotle seems to exclude some actions here such as temperate eating that may only affect the agent but not temperate sexual relations since these involve others (even if the habituation involved in temperance in general is endorsed through the law). Included in this understanding of justice is the category of what we would call supererogatory actions; for example, courageous and generous actions that do not usually fall under the purview of the law even if they are consistent with it.

If, therefore, virtuous actions are related to the law, as these texts suggest, then there does seem to be a place for rules and principles in Aristotle's ethics since he relates much of the life of virtue to the law. If this is true, the problem with Aristotle's ethics might be the opposite of what was originally supposed: the life of virtue is so rule-bound (because it is law-governed in every aspect) that there is little or no character-based latitude here rather than too much! Moreover, while it is one thing to have a principle-driven ethic, it is quite another to have the law cover all aspects of the ethical life since the latter is often thought to be beyond the scope of the former. Hence, supererogatory acts (such as endangering one's life to save another's) are thought to be discretionary rather than strictly required by the law. So let us return to the issue of latitude to see where it originates in Aristotle and how it relates to our problem here.

6.3 The Doctrine of the Mean

The usual way in which latitude is discussed in the *Ethics* is in terms of the Doctrine of the Mean in the context of action in accordance with virtue (*NE* 2.6 1106a14–1107a25). Perhaps by starting here, we can begin to understand the nuances of Aristotle's response to problems outlined in the previous paragraph. "Nothing in Excess," one of the famous inscriptions in the Temple of Apollo at Delphi, deeply permeates Aristotle's views on this matter. Based on considerations of nature, Aristotle points out that excess and defect in general are both bad. For instance, all things being equal, too much or too little water, excess or defect, can destroy a plant whereas the Mean amount maintains its health. This Mean or optimal amount obviously falls within a range of quantities—depending on things like the plant species, size, placement, etc.—that are more or less favorable with the extremes being least salubrious. Similarly, then, for humans too there is a Mean amount of food between excess and deficiency that is optimal for health. The point, of course, is that the Mean is absolute; for any given plant or human in a particular context, there is only one Mean amount that is truly optimal, though the approximations to and fallings away from it are interminable.

In the case of humans, just as in plants, the Mean amount could be widely different depending on the person and the context. Six pounds of food a day for a Sumo wrestler would be too little but perhaps just right for me, though this too could vary depending on my age, physical state, etc. But what is good for the person (in terms of not just their physical but also their psychical health, as we saw above) is also what the good (or virtuous) person will do. Translating this into actions that are in the realm of value, we can see that in some instances, Hector's standing his ground against or even attacking the Greeks despite the Trojans being in retreat is courageous. Hector's actions are brave since he is capable of single-handedly turning the tide of battle or dying gloriously in the process, whereas such action might be utter foolishness, even rashness, for a lesser warrior like Socrates. Moreover, what constitutes courage for Socrates could be—as was the case in the battle at Delium that Alcibiades describes in the *Symposium* (221a–221c)—an intimidating (to others) and orderly retreat so he can live to fight another day, which is not necessarily inconsistent with our intuitions about the matter. After all, it might have been sheer foolishness in those circumstances for him to fight if nothing was to be gained by it. The upshot is that the Mean responses not only differ for the same person depending on the circumstances, but that they can be different—even contradictory—in the same circumstances for different individuals.

Now while we can see that different circumstances and agents may call for different responses in the realm of value, it is not clear how these are, as Aristotle says, actions that hit the Mean. The short response is that such actions hit the mean (and are therefore in accordance with virtue) precisely because they originate in moral dispositions that are intermediate (*NE* 2.6 1106b16–28). Since, as we saw in chapter 2, moral dispositions are developed on the back of cultivated action, it is unsurprising that such dispositions are the basis in turn of similar action themselves. Of course, such action, as we saw, is distinct from its habit-based forbear in that it arises from a fully moral disposition that is in tune with reason out of a love of virtue—which is why it is called action in accordance with virtue. These dispositions themselves are so-called because of how one is disposed to feel, or stand with regard to one's feelings, such as fear and confidence in the case of courage, since how strongly these are felt determines (and restricts) the choice of possible actions available to the virtuous agent on the battlefield (*NE* 2.7 1107a34–1107b4). Too much or too little fear is either paralyzing spinelessness or results in a lack of caution; too much or too little confidence results in rashness or cowardice so that courage seeks to find a balanced (but not mathematical) intermediate between the extremes on both continuums of fear and confidence. Thus, it is plausible to see how Hector's ethical education, which is closely intertwined with his training (and ability) as a warrior, leads to a very different choice of action than Socrates'. For what constitutes the intermediate disposition of courage for Socrates takes into consideration that, unlike Hector, he is a citizen-soldier, has a certain physique, etc. These differences between Hector and Socrates are widened if one considers the circumstances of their acts of courage which impact how their courageous dispositions react to them.[13] Thus, for instance, the fact that Hector is defending his home whereas Socrates is not, impacts his choice, as do many other things which are often singular in circumstance and hence depend on perception (*NE* 4.5 1126b2–9).[14] For as we have seen, how one sees a situation affects the way in which they perceive the end or what is to be done (see chapter 2 section 3).

Now let us see what implications this view on the Mean has for actions that usually fall under legal purview, and then for those that are thought to fall in the ethical domain. Aristotle thinks that there are certain kinds of actions that are wrong simpliciter, i.e., they are not wrong because they are the excess or defect of some continuum for which there is a Mean. For instance, while cowardice is wrong because it is a deficiency of confidence and an excess of fear, murder, theft, and adultery are simply wrong by definition and punishable by law (*NE* 2.6 1107a9–18). Whereas murder is wrongful killing, adultery is wrongful sex, and theft is wrongful acquisition of property. It should be emphasized that part of the inflexibility here arises because we are assessing *actions* rather than character. While courageous action can depend on character, strength, and circumstance, the thought seems to be that certain kinds of action are absolutely proscribed by the law regardless of circumstance, motive, or character. Justification for proscriptions of such actions might implicitly be derived from the fact that such actions undermine the autonomy of those at whom they are directed (and eventually, threatens one's own autonomy), autonomy being necessary for virtue and hence happiness as we discussed in chapter 3. More interestingly, such proscriptions are likely the negative if not the comprehensive aspects of what

Aristotle calls "natural justice" which he thinks has the same force everywhere, unlike legal justice which is variable and conventional (*NE* 5.7 1134b18–24). While all this might be true, it does not mean that there is no latitude here, as I think we would all expect; for it could be argued that in order to assess whether an action is murder or self-defence, for instance, we still need to include discussions of character, intention, and circumstance (a proper assessment of which depend on the doctrine of the Mean).[15] Thus we see that legal proscription hinges on the proper description of the action, in ways that are not necessarily the case for actions that lie on a continuum like generosity and temperance do, for instance, and where the *agent* is essentially being assessed. Hence Aristotle is more forceful in emphasizing the inflexibility with regard to such actions, even while acknowledging the possibility of latitude when it comes to thinking about them as naturally just (*NE* 5.7 1134b30–35), which we will discuss in greater detail below.

Aristotle implicitly makes at least two different responses to actions that fall within the ethical rather than legal realm, both of which involve the doctrine of the Mean. First, many kinds of virtuous actions such as generosity, courage, magnificence, etc. are lauded or honored by the state and praised in general as a way of encouraging them in society (*NE* 3.1 1109b30–34; 3.7 1115a29–32; 4.6 1126b4–10; 7.11 1152b1–3; 10.9 1180a6–8). True, here too specific actions are picked out; a particular stand in battle is feted or an act of magnificence, but this is usually because such a Mean action is representative of a series of similar actions. Hence, Aristotle thinks we are less inclined to honor one-off actions, as we are non-representative ones. The upshot then is that consistent with Aristotle's ethics of character, it is the agent that is honored by the state, which means that latitude is available in the assessment here. Second, legal penalties are enforced on actions that are contrary to some of the virtues. Thus, cowardice is penalized, as is drunkenness, slander, and physical violence against fellow-citizens, etc., as a way of moving people away from these extremes and towards the relevant Means of courage, civility, etc. (*NE* 3.5 1113b31; 3.8 1116a17–20; 10.9 1180a8–13). But here, it is even more difficult to determine whether an action is cowardly than it is to determine whether it is murder, for instance, precisely because such action is based on continuums of fear and confidence that are sensitive to context, and because again we are not just assessing the action but the agent as well. Moreover, as we saw in the case of Hector and Socrates, the continuums differ from person to person in ways that further complicate the assessment.

6.4 The Mean, the Right Rule, and the Law

If it is the Mean that makes accommodation to the law possible, then we need to show that Aristotle makes the connection between them more broadly; and indeed, he does, in terms of what he calls the "right rule" (*orthos logos*). Hector's plunging into battle and Socrates' calculated retreat as described above are courageous because these actions are Means between rash and cowardly responses on two different continuums of action. If these actions were just that, we would be unable to reconcile their seeming contradiction. Hence Aristotle insists that the Mean is determined by a rational principle or rule as a way of categorizing them as courageous (*NE* 2.2 1103b32–1104a1; 2.6 1106b35–1107a2). Many contemporary readers who insist that there are no rules in Aristotle's character-based ethics are uncomfortable with translating "*orthos logos*" as "right rule" and prefer the alternative "right reason" instead, since "*logos*" can legitimately be translated as both.[16] After all, the distinctiveness of Aristotle's ethics in contrast to more modern theories for them relies precisely on its character-based nature. But if all that has been said above regarding the relation of law and virtue is true, then "right rule" may not be an implausible translation, especially if it can be shown that there is a connection between rule and law (or *logos* and *nomos*). To begin, let us look more closely at the most important passage on the right rule in the *NE*.

> Since we have previously said that one ought to choose that which is intermediate, not the excess nor the defect, and that the intermediate is determined by the dictates of the right rule (*ho orthos ho logos*), let us discuss the nature of these dictates. In all the states of character we have mentioned, as in all other matters, there is a mark (*horos*) to which the man who has the rule (*logon*) looks, and heightens and relaxes his activities accordingly, and there is a standard (*mesotētōn*) which determines the mean states which we say are intermediate between excess and defect, being in accordance with the right rule (*NE* 6.1 1138b18–24).[17]

The person who has the virtuous states of character discussed in this introductory passage of Book 6 turns out to be the practically wise person, who remains at the center of discussion for much of the Book. Such a person is one in whom all the virtues that pursue the good in specific spheres are brought together in terms of what is good for the agent's life as a whole. Practical wisdom therefore presupposes and is the culmination of the excellences of both practical reason and moral dispositions (*NE* 6.11 1143a25–29; 6.13 1144b20–45a1). So it would seem that Aristotle is suggesting here that the practically wise person determines the Mean by looking at the right rule, which in turn has a mark (*horos*) of some sort as its guiding principle. But let us begin with right rule before we can see what Aristotle means by the mark.

So in the context of determining the Mean action of courage, I suggest that the right rule is a law regarding courage; something like "Dauntlessness in the face of a noble death in war" (*NE* 3.6 1115a33–35). Clearly, Hector and Socrates are guided by such a rule, even if their actions are very different. Alcibiades tells us that no one dared attack Socrates for he was formidable even in retreat; whereas Hector's charge into battle with Achilles is more obviously dauntless in the face of death. In defence of this equation between rule and law, it should be said that Aristotle himself makes it when he says that the law is a rule that proceeds from practical wisdom (10.9 1108a20–22). His claim is unsurprising since we have already seen him say that the law is key to the development of virtue in individuals since the practically wise politicians promote good habituation through the law (*NE* 2.1 1103b3ff; X.9 1179b31–35). That is, the reason the law that habituates the young proceeds from practical wisdom is precisely because it comes from practically wise legislators (*Politics*[18] 1325b7–10; 1329a2–17). Second, we saw in the discussion of general justice that there is a deep consonance between the acts commanded by the law and those prescribed by virtue. Now we see both these reasons show *how* the connection is developed by good habituation and maintained by practical wisdom. Still, Aristotle is very careful to insist that the state from which such action issues " … is not merely in accordance with the right rule, but that the state implies the presence of the right rule, that is virtue; and practical wisdom is a right rule about such matters" (*NE* 6.13 1144b23–25). The novice's rule-following is in accordance with the right rule, because the rule is not yet her own. Whereas the practically wise person becomes the practically wise *when* she makes the rule her own, after the process of integration we discussed in chapter 3. Even so, this is not merely a transfer of ownership, so to speak, but implies the capacity to generate the right rule. After all, in a polity where the practically wise person *qua* politician determines the nature of the law in deliberation with other practically wise people (*Politics* 7.14 1332b25–27), we can see *why* this equation is the case. Of course, how the law is translated in particular circumstances will depend not only on the perceived particulars of the situation but also on the virtuous agent in question, as we saw in the case of what constitutes a courageous response for Socrates as opposed to Hector. Thus, choice not only is about how the action is undertaken (i.e., for its own sake) but also presupposes a deliberative exercise in the context of the right rule or law to determine the nature of the action that will obtain its goal.

The rule of law, in turn, promotes the larger goals of a society, and this is what the mark (*horos*) represents in section 1 of this chapter. In a tyranny, this goal is the pleasure of the tyrant; in an oligopoly it is the economic agenda of the wealthy few, and so on. For Aristotle, the highest goal for his ideal city is one in which the human good (or happiness) is obtained for all its citizens (*NE* 1.2 1094b5–12), which he later specifies as one in which practical wisdom (presumably *qua* political wisdom) makes the life of philosophy possible for its citizens. Hence, he says " … it [i.e., practical wisdom] is not supreme over philosophical wisdom … anymore than the art of medicine is over health; for it does not use it but provide for its coming into being, it issues orders, then, for its sake, but not to it" (*NE* 6.13 1145a6–9; cf. *Politics* 7.14 1334a22–36).

In chapter 9 we will see that possessing philosophical wisdom/*Sophia* is the basis of contemplation/*theoria*, and why this is the highest human activity of happiness and how contemplation completes the practically virtuous activities of happiness. This is not to say that everyone can pursue such a life, just that it is the high water mark of amounts to individual flourishing by which the city sets its laws. Thus, the universality of the law mediates between the particular, practically good action on the one hand, and the highest, theoretical aspects of the human good on the other. Of course, we might ask how acting ethically promotes philosophical contemplation since Aristotle thinks ethical action is undertaken as an end in itself. But perhaps since such action has outcomes, we might speak to how these are related to philosophy (and for many the life of culture broadly construed). Thus, for instance, moderation in the pursuit of our appetites makes it easier to pursue the life of mind; courage defends the city or helps it procure resources that make the life of leisure (and hence culture) possible, etc. But the story is more complicated than I can tell here, as I hope will become obvious in chapter 9. For now, let us consider the implications of Aristotle's views on the evolution and development of the law.

If the Mean helps us understand how latitude is possible within the confines of the law, then equity (*NE* 5.10 1137b10–31) and judgment (*NE* 6.11 1143a19–33) show us how latitude is achieved beyond it such that these become the possible basis of the eventual evolution of the law. The law's universal nature means that there will always be exceptions to the rule. After all, we are not working with the laws of physics, but those that govern human beings whose doings are concerned with particulars that are indefinite, and therefore intractable to the law.[19] Such a correction requires a great deal of experience of the world (which is another way of speaking about the particulars) in combination with sympathetic judgment (*NE* 6.11 1143a32–35), which discerns the equitable. In fact, it may not be inappropriate to say that such discernment is a way of speaking to how perceiving the moral particular and the ensuing wish is out of sync with the law. Hence the equitable is a correction of legislated justice, not just by anyone but as the practically wise legislator would have it; or else it becomes too easy to subvert the law in general.[20] It would not be unreasonable to extend Aristotle's point here to suggest that regular exceptionalism in relation to any law may be the eventual basis for its change and hence its evolution. After all, the practically wise citizen, who ultimately judges whether the exception is warranted, is also the politically wise citizen *qua* legislator.[21] Aristotle also makes place here for exceptions that do not fall under any rule for which a very particular act based on a decree is needed. For example, the legislature decrees that because of Nicias's great contributions to the city, he is exempt from paying this year's taxes. Here we finally have the articulation that some have thought to be the basis of Aristotle's ethical particularism in which there is no place for rules, when in fact all Aristotle is speaking to are some instances that are so particular that it would not be appropriate to lay down a law to cover them with anything but a decree (*NE* 5.11 1137b26–31; 6.8 1141b27).[22]

It might be useful to consider an important objection regarding the possible evolution of the law in an ideally just society before closing the chapter. If we have an ideally just society (as we have presumed the context to be in much of the discussions above, based on what Aristotle himself says) it is hard to see why such perfection needs to evolve. After all, Aristotle himself says that natural justice is like fire in that it has the same force everywhere (*NE* 5.7 1134b18–20), presumably because an ideally just society instantiates natural justice. In response, it might be said that political (or complete) justice involves both natural and legal (or conventional) justice, the latter being defined as that which is capable of being otherwise since it is conventional (*NE* 5.7 1134b20–24). So, for instance, weights and measures are set by law but can differ from country to country and can evolve so as to be standardized across regions of the world without suggesting that such standardization is final. Second, Aristotle suggests that even natural justice is changeable albeit in a different fashion. Thus, while right-handedness is the norm (and thereby analogous to natural justice insofar as it is pervasive), it is still possible for all of us to become ambidextrous (*NE* 5.7 1134b30–35). The suggestion, at the very least, seems to be that *some* kind of evolution is plausible here, perhaps to accommodate changing circumstances. For instance, we become ambidextrous from a very young age to handle new weapons or technology.[23] Since an ideally just society involves both natural and legal justice for Aristotle, both of which are changeable albeit in different ways, it is plausible to see how the law might evolve for him. Third, the evolution of political justice is even more plausible in less than ideally just societies, because experience tells us that good people who are the products of imperfect institutions can bring about their progress.

In sum, the good person does not become good in a vacuum but rather is the product of a good city-state with good laws (ideally speaking) that are essential to her education. The good person in turn is responsible for adapting the law to her circumstances and even modifying it (*qua* judge) either because of a particular circumstance or more generally (*qua* legislator). It is in the movement forward of the law that it becomes clear how Aristotle maintains the primacy of the good person (within the constraints placed by human nature and function) without sacrificing the place of rules and laws in his ethics.[24] Such a position garners the advantages of rule-driven ethics (such as consistency and clarity) and avoids some of the latter's short-comings (such as rigidity and the myopia that can occur with over-reliance on a single rule). The deep connection between virtue and the law is also not open to dangers of extreme ethical particularism and subjectivism that would be the case for a purely virtue-centric ethics. Moreover, the dichotomy that we started concerning the good of the whole vs the good of the individual is for Aristotle a false one; for the good of the whole is to be understood in terms of the good of good individuals, even if what it means to be a good person cannot be realized except in the context of the whole.

Notes

1 In general, I use "ethical" as opposed to "moral" when speaking of value theory broadly construed (of which virtue ethics is a part) since Aristotle uses "moral" to speak of dispositions of character, as we saw in chapters 2 and 3.

2 John Stuart Mill, *Utilitarianism* (Indianapolis, IN: Hackett Publishing Co., 1979), 6, 11.

3 This is not an isolated instance in the *NE* where he says this; other instances include: 1.8 1099a13–24; 2.3 1104b30–5a1; 9.4 1166a10–13; X.5 1176a7–29; 9.9 1170a14–16; 6.12 1144a29–35.

4 Indeed there are those who read him this way. See for instance, Martha Nussbaum, "The Discernment of Perception: An Aristotelian Conception of Private and Public Rationality," *Proceedings of the Boston Area Colloquium in Ancient Philosophy* 1 (1985), 151–201; and Julia Annas, *The Morality of Happiness* (New York: Oxford University Press, 1993), 93–94.

5 For more details, see Roopen N. Majithia, "Function, Intuition and Ends in Aristotle's Ethics," *Ethical Theory and Moral Practice* 9, no. 2 (April 1, 2006): 187–200.

6 For more details, see my "Function, Intuition and Ends in Aristotle's Ethics," 195–97.

7 Jonathan Barnes, ed., "Metaphysics," in *The Complete Works of Aristotle: The Revised Oxford Translation*, by Aristotle, trans. W. D. Ross, vol. 2, Bollingen Series 71 (Princeton, NJ: Princeton University Press, 1984), 1552–728.

8 See Richard Kraut, "The Peculiar Function of Human Beings," *Canadian Journal of Philosophy* 9 (1979): 473, who disagrees since if it were hypothetically possible that we can become like the Unmoved Mover, we could not be urged to do so since such activity would no longer be peculiar to us. But it is unclear why we should be convinced by such a hypothetical especially if Aristotle means, as I suggest, the total life of reason that is both theoretical and practical.

9 Compare, for instance, with Plato's *metaxu* in the *Symposium* (201e ff).

10 See Rachel Barney, "Aristotle's Argument for a Human Function," *Oxford Studies in Ancient Philosophy* 35 (2008): 293–322. Barney insightfully points out that there may be varying levels of what we might call practical rationality involved in the life of an artisan's creative activity (say, as opposed to a citizen-legislator) so that there may be varying levels of completeness when it comes to happiness for Aristotle. But the point is wider, I think, since it is not just rationality in general but activities in accordance with virtue in particular that potentially permeate all aspects of human life (such as the pursuits of leisure and creativity) and not just those of citizens and craftsmen.

11 See Alfonso Gomez-Lobo, "The Ergon Inference," *Phronesis* 34, no. 1–3 (1989): 170–84, who I think is right in suggesting that much of the detailed argument for showing that that what is good for humans is also what the good human does comes after the function argument in the discussion of the virtues. But I do also think that the suggestion that the rational is inherently ethical because of its concern for the universal is implicit in the function argument.

12 See the "best case scenario" argument in Samuel H. Baker, "A Monistic Conclusion to Aristotle's Ergon Argument: The Human Good as the Best Achievement of a Human," *Archiv für Geschichte der Philosophie* 103, no. 3 (September 1, 2021): 373–403.

13 Thus it should be clear that what Aristotle means by a Mean disposition is not the same as a disposition that is predisposed to express moderate emotions, as Urmson worries about in "Aristotle's Doctrine of the Mean" in Amélie Rorty, *Essays on Aristotle's Ethics*, Major Thinkers Series 2 (Berkeley: University of California Press, 1980), 160–61. See also Sarah Broadie, *Ethics with Aristotle* (New York; Toronto: Oxford University Press, 1991), 100–03, and Annas, *The Morality of Happiness*, 60–61.

14 I have attempted to walk a fine line here between two kinds of reading as represented by Hursthouse in Stephen L. Darwall, *Virtue Ethics*, Blackwell Readings in Philosophy 10 (Malden, MA: Blackwell, 2003), 194–98, and Lesley Brown, "What Is the Mean Relative to Us in Aristotle's Ethics," *Phronesis: A Journal of Ancient Philosophy* 42, no. 1 (1997): 80–81. For while the former thinks a virtue theory should be flexible enough to allow for differences in virtuous action but only because, unlike scientific knowledge, there is no universal, consistent, and complete ethical knowledge; whereas the latter thinks that preserving such a possibility requires seeing that the Mean is the same for all mainly on the grounds that when Aristotle says that the Mean is relative to us, he means not that it is relative to the individual but to human beings. My reading, while maintaining that the Mean is relative to the individual, will show how it is connected to the law (and hence is universal) in ways that avoid the problem that Brown fears.

15 In fact Kevin L. Flannery, *Moral Taxonomy and Moral Absolutes* (Washington, DC: Catholic University of America Press, 2007), 255–56 argues that the laws determining the nature of self-defence, for instance, are themselves exceptions derived from absolute prohibitions against murder.

16 Thus, for instance, see Aristotle, W. D. Ross, and Lesley Brown, *The Nicomachean Ethics*, Oxford World's Classics (Oxford: Oxford University Press, 2009), 1138b24, 1107a1, 1103b31, and 1114b29, etc., where Brown revises Ross's original translation of "right rule" to "correct reason." Similarly, Broadie, *Ethics with Aristotle*, 74–78, esp. 76.

17 The original, unrevised Ross translation is used here and in the remainder of this section.

18 Jonathan Barnes, ed., "Politics," in *The Complete Works of Aristotle: The Revised Oxford Translation*, by Aristotle, trans. B. Jowett, vol. 2, Bollingen Series 71 (Princeton, NJ: Princeton University Press, 1984), 1986–2129.

19 See, for instance, Roger Shiner, "Ethical Perception in Aristotle," *Apeiron: A Journal for Ancient Philosophy and Science* 13 (1979): 79–85, who makes this point forcefully.

20 See Allan Beever, "Aristotle on Equity, Law, and Justice," *Legal Theory* 10, no. 1 (March 2004): 33–50.

21 See Steven C. Skultety, "Disputes of the Phronimoi: Can Aristotle's Best Citizens Disagree?," *Ancient Philosophy* 32, no. 1 (2012): 105–24, who shows how the wise can disagree and yet make laws based on a majority in the legislature. Interestingly enough, Annas, *The Morality of Happiness*, 114, agrees that the good person's views are in a relation of reflective equilibrium with those of other citizens in the city, even if she doesn't think that this is mediated by the law as I do. Finally, see P. A. Vander Waerdt, "Kingship and Philosophy in Aristotle's Best Regime," *Phronesis: A Journal of Ancient Philosophy* 30 (1985): 249–73 for an interesting

argument for why Aristotle might have ended up preferring kingship over the rule of the best citizens despite acknowledging that their way of life and scheme of education are compatible with either.

22 Thus Nussbaum, "Discernment of Perception," 158–60. But see Steve Wexler and Andrew Irvine, "Aristotle on the Rule of Law," *Polis: The Journal of the Society for the Study of Greek Political Thought* 23, no. 1 (2006): 116–38 for an interesting contrast to Nussbaum since they emphasize the importance of law in Aristotle in ways that are consistent with my reading.

23 But see Annie Hewitt, "Universal Justice and Epieikeia in Aristotle," *Polis: The Journal of the Society for the Study of Greek Political Thought* 25, no. 1 (2008): 115–30, who disagrees that such an evolution of what she calls "universal justice" is possible.

24 That is, since "good" in Aristotle is understood within the context of human function, the good actions are not simply whatever a good person might do. See Michael Slote, "Law in Virtue Ethics," *Law and Philosophy: An International Journal for Jurisprudence and Legal Philosophy* 14, no. 1 (1995): 91–93.

7

Ethical Content in the *Bhagavad Gītā*

7.0 Introduction

It might be useful to remember that we began by dividing our discussion of ethical action into a discussion of its form and its content. The form, we saw, is the intention that significantly shapes the content of action even while the latter is mainly determined on different grounds. This ground, in Aristotle at least, is based on the law, which is ideally the product of the collective deliberations of good people (*qua* legislators), and therefore broadly coincident with their actions. What emerges for Aristotle is the centrality of the human being as the basis of right action, a human being that is connected with the ideal *polis* or state through the law. The law itself is an expression of the cultural, political, and moral traditions of Greek culture, so that the law's evolution represents the aspirations of the *polis* itself on all of these fronts.

When it comes to the *Gītā*, we have only part of the story that concerns form. Here too intentionality plays a key role, for a shift in its focus from personal to impersonal considerations (not unlike in Aristotle) makes it obvious that agency and desire detract from right action (quite unlike in Aristotle). It is time, therefore, to turn our attention to the content of moral action in the *Gītā*, which is based on the broad notion of *dharma*. *Dharma* in the *Gītā*, as we have seen already, has deep continuities with the texts of the orthodox tradition, both early (like the *Vedas*) and late (like the *Manusmṛiti*). But there are also revolutionary aspects to the *Gītā* that become obvious when we bring its discussion of form and content of morality together. Specifically, when the core idea behind the change in moral intentionality brought about by the notion of detachment is applied to the moral content supplied by *dharm*ic law, it brings about a proper alignment between the two as well as a broadening transformation of *dharma*. This transformation allows us to see the place of latitude—in a moral and political tradition notorious for its rigid hierarchy—that is especially a response to a regnant Buddhism. More importantly, the transformation shows how the *Gītā* articulates and develops a basis for supererogatory actions that ultimately ground class distinctions in moral rather than social and economic considerations.

7.1 *Śruti* and *Smṛiti*

In chapter 4 and in Appendix 2, a great deal has been said about the meaning of "*dharma*," its content (in terms of the *varṇāśramadharma* scheme), its relation to other ends, and the continuities between the usage of the term in the *Gītā* and in the preceding tradition. It is appropriate now to say more about the preceding tradition if only to have a deeper sense of the *Gītā*'s relation to, and transformation of, this tradition. The tradition is rooted in the *Vedas* (and associated texts such as the *Brahmanas* that include the *Āranyakas* and the *Upaniṣads*) that are said to have originally been heard (*śruti*) by the earliest sages of the tradition; and the tradition develops on the back of later, derivative texts that are explicitly labeled "remembered" (*smṛiti*), either because they have a known author or because they represent custom. This latter group includes texts that deal with *dharma* in general called the *dharmaśastras* (including the preeminent *Manusmṛiti*[1]); texts that discuss the other ends of life (*Arthaśastras* and *kāma* texts); purported history (as found in the epic texts of the *Mahābhārata and Rāmāyana*); and much more.

The issue of authorship, especially of the *śruti* texts, is vexed. For some theistic strains of the tradition, the authorship is divine even if revealed to the original sages of the tradition (hence "revelation" is one translation of *śruti*). For atheistic schools like the Purva Mimamsa, the texts are authorless[2] and are the veritable blueprints of the universe that the disciplined austerity (*tapas*) of the original sages allows them to literally perceive. The authorship of *smṛiti* texts, on the other hand, is usually attributed in the tradition to historical individuals even if the texts themselves are found in various versions and with many accretions. Thus, Vyāsa, a legendary sage, is the author of the *Mahābhārata* and hence of the *Gītā*, Vatsayana of the *Kamasutra*, Manu of the *Manusmṛiti*, and so on.

Authorship in turn has implications for the relations between *śruti* and *smṛiti*, and especially for the latter's authority. *Śruti*'s authority within the orthodox tradition is undisputed, regardless of whether or not it is thought to have a divine author. (In fact, what makes a tradition heterodox in the subcontinent is its non-acceptance of *śruti*, as in the case of Buddhism and Jainism.) The human authorship usually attributed to *smṛiti* texts is consistent with its accepted purpose of explaining *śruti*. The problem is that *smṛiti* also often expands on *śruti*, and especially when it comes to matters regarding *dharma* on which discussions in the *śruti* are at best sketchy.[3] For example, while it is the *Ṛg Veda* that originally presents us with the class system that we see in the tradition (*Ṛg Veda* 10.90), it is the *Manusmṛiti* that expands on it by first presenting the *varṇāśramadharma*/stage-and-station scheme in conjunction with it (*MS* 1.36–50, 1.92–101 and Books 2–4 and 6), a move that we have seen the *Gītā* affirms. The expansion makes a great deal of sense if we see that these texts are often trying to respond to external pressures, or make current practices seem consistent with the past. Thus, making house-holding and monasticism stages in a life rather than as alternative lives (as in Buddhism) is an attempt to respond to the rising popularity of heterodoxy.[4]

Yet how can humanly authored *smṛiti* expand on *śruti* without exceeding its brief? Without straying too far from our concern with the *Gītā*, the following might be said: the way in which the *Gītā* implicitly attempts to justify its expansion on *śruti* is precisely in terms of authorship. Vyāsa, in the tradition at least, is the accepted author of the *Mahābhārata* within which the *Gītā* is ensconced. Whereas the de facto author might as well be Krishna, whose views are clearly and repeatedly reinforced by his self-proclamations of divinity in the text (*BG* 4.1–4; much of Book 7; 8.4–34; etc.).[5] It is perhaps this divinity that justifies the *Gītā*'s expansion on *śruti* since the *Gītā* clearly belongs to a strain of the tradition that attributes divine authorship to *śruti* and thereby moves them to the same level. Hence Śaṇkara's Advaita Vedanta will put the *Gītā*'s authority on par with the *Upaniṣads*. A similar move in the *Manusmṛiti* is made by Manu as author of the universe (*MS* 1.33), which as we just saw, also expands on *śruti*. This is not to deny that other *smṛiti* texts are expansionist, but just how the *Gītā* and the *Manusmṛiti*'s versions might have gained their pre-eminence.[6]

7.2 The *Gītā*'s Continuities with the Tradition

Given the *Gītā*'s continuities with *śruti* mentioned above and discussed in chapter 4, it is unsurprising that Krishna directs Arjuna to fight based on scriptural injunction. Recall that the *Gītā* begins by showing Arjuna as torn between his commitment to his duty as a warrior (his *svadharma*) and his duty to his family (*kuladharma*) or to humanity (*sāmānya dharma*). The key directives to fight based on scriptural injunction bookend the *Gītā*, with the first coming almost immediately after Arjuna expresses his anguished bewilderment

(*BG* 2.31–33); and second, towards the end (*BG* 18.5–9). In the first, Krishna specifically speaks to Arjuna's duties as a warrior (or his *svadharma*). He says that every warrior welcomes a legitimate battle like the one that faces Arjuna, and that to try and avoid it is to commit evil (*pāpa*). The second affirmation of *śruti*-based duty/*dharma* is broader, since Krishna urges us to undertake all our duties (and especially the key ones of charity (*dāna*), austerity (*tapas*), and ritual (*yajña*)) with detachment. This second affirmation in Book 18 is important not only because it comes at the end of the text where Krishna goes out of his way to tell us that it is his "decided and final view" (*BG* 18.6), but because it is the culmination of a long argument beginning in Book 16. It is worth our while, I think, to rehearse the not always obvious steps of this argument.

Book 16 itself concludes with Krishna's injunction to Arjuna to comply with scriptural law (*śastravidhim*), as opposed to action based on what Arjuna hopes or desires (*BG* 16.23–24). This follows from a distinction made early in the chapter between those who are divine and demonic (*BG* 16.5), which we have looked at in detail in chapter 5. For our purposes here, it is enough to remind ourselves that those who have a divine nature as Krishna says Arjuna has—have faith that the world originates in the Divine, and hence should follow the Divine's articulated injunctions in scripture. The demonic—likely the hedonist Charvāka school is being referred to here—believe that the world is the product of the free play of desire in nature (since they deny the existence of God), and hence simply follow their desire (*BG* 16.8–18).

Arjuna's question at the beginning of Book 17 is therefore interesting as it asks of those who don't quite fit in either the divine or demonic category: what of those, like him, who wish to act with faith in the Divine but whose actions are not in accordance with scripture (*BG* 17.1)? The problem is that the question is at once narrower (since it asks specifically of ritual activity that is not in accordance with scripture) and broader (since it asks Krishna to class the agents of such action in terms of their *guṇa*/strand configurations). Krishna's response compounds the problem since, first, it speaks in terms of the divine/demonic dichotomy and its implications for the *guṇa* configurations of the individuals (*BG* 17.2–6). Second, it addresses not only actions that fall under the duty of *yajña* (ritual), but those that fall under the category of *dāna* (charity) and *tapas* (austerity) as well. To keep things simple, I will mainly discuss the question relevant to us at the beginning of this paragraph: is it possible to have faith in the Divine and act contrary to scripture?

Krishna's answer to this question is a resounding "No!" The first articulation is of those who perform passion-driven, violent (i.e., *rajas*ic) austerity (and by implication other activity that would fall within the purview of *dharma*) that has no scriptural sanction and is clearly termed demonic (*BG* 17.5–6). This fits Arjuna's case especially if he does not fight. So important is scriptural injunction that we are told here (*BG* 17.12) that it is better to do your duty even if it is for the wrong desire-driven or *rajas*ic motivation (for example, fighting because it will make you a rich, world-renowned warrior), than not. The second articulation of Krishna's negative response to the question refers to those who do not follow scriptural injunction out of ignorance rather than passion, and hence because of *tamas* (*BG* 17.13). Interestingly, so important is it to follow scriptural injunction that Krishna does not rank the culpability of the defaulters, even though one would think that it is much worse to knowingly disobey one's *dharma*. Scriptural injunction's importance as the basis of every duty is affirmed at the end of Book 17 (*BG* 17.24), and again as the argument concludes when Krishna tells us that it is his "final and considered view" at the beginning of Book 18 (*BG* 18.6).

But Book 18 will also take us back to the heart of the *Gītā*'s innovations on the tradition by specifically addressing problems with Arjuna's approach to his situation. We are told again that disregard for all duty, because of ignorance (and hence *tamas*) or pain and fear (and hence *rajas*) is unacceptable (*BG* 18.7–8). Now it is obvious that the ignorant do not perform duty because they lack knowledge of its requirements, but an important insight is added here as to how passion leads to its non-performance. We have seen how passion can divide us internally so that we are paralyzed and/or confused, as is clearly the case with Arjuna. Here, as we have seen in detail in chapter 4, we are told that passion separates us from each other, emphasizes the world's multiplicity rather than its unified Being, and is therefore responsible for our misapprehending the larger scheme of things (*BG* 18.20–21). Tracing back this line of argument, then, will take us to the core of the *Gītā*'s revolution.

7.3 The *Gītā*'s Discontinuities with the Tradition

Krishna expects Arjuna to act in accordance with scripture (a broad justification for which we have seen already and will shortly see again). But it is unclear how doing so requires Arjuna to follow his duty as a warrior rather than his universal duty as a human being. One line of thought suggests that Krishna is asking Arjuna and everybody else to always follow their *svadharma*. Yet in the two important places where he suggests this, the text can be read quite differently.

In the first, Krishna asks Arjuna to fight not simply because he is a warrior, but because this is a lawful battle (*BG* 2.31–33). In the second, Krishna asks Arjuna to follow his *svadharma* (as a warrior) over that of other people's *svadharma* (*BG* 3.35). Yet this does not mean that when it comes to a choice between his duties (*BG* 2.7) that he should always follow his *svadharma* or duty as a warrior over his *sāmānya dharma* or his duty as a human being. Moreover, to always follow one's *svadharma* seems inconsistent with Krishna's instructions to Arjuna's brothers on other occasions during the war.[7] Nor does such a reading seem consistent with some important texts in the *Gītā* itself, to which we now turn.

In his discussion of the origin and importance of ritual (*yajña*) in Book 4, Krishna is at pains to emphasize that all *dharm*ic activity can be ritualized (if undertaken with detachment). More interestingly, that, ritual activity, and by implication all *dharma*, is key to keeping the world's wheel turning since ritual action summons the rains, which grows the food that makes life and hence ritual activity possible (*BG* 3.8–16).[8] This makes a great deal of sense, given that we have seen "*dharma*" is derived from "*dṛ*," which means "to uphold or sustain." The whole point of *dharma*, Krishna is saying, is that it upholds and sustains the world by organizing and correlating its activities in an orderly fashion. The detached sage, like Krishna, always acts without personal expectation and with the welfare of the world in mind (*loksamgraha*), for to stop such activity is to bring the world to ruin (*BG* 3.22–24).

So, if the priority is acting with world-welfare in mind, then you are not required to follow *svadharma* every time, though you are required to follow *dharma*.[9] What causes one to think that one should always follow one's *svadharma* is Krishna's insistence that Arjuna should do so in this instance. If the looming war with his cousins were not a just war as Krishna decrees, for example, Arjuna's reluctance to fight would be more plausible.

It is important to remember from chapter 5 that Arjuna's befuddlement arises because he is unable to act with detachment, even though this is not the same as being a detached sage. We saw there that it is *rajas* that impedes Arjuna's ability to see through the dilemma. In fact, he sees that world-welfare is the key to determining the right action in his situation, though he thinks world-welfare requires him not to fight (*BG* 1.38–44). He does not rightly see what is to be done, I suggested, because he does not have the sage's perspective, and he does not have the sage's perspective because he is not detached. But part of what it means to act with detachment is to set aside personal considerations, which we have explored already; here we begin to see how world-welfare plays a role in intentionality. In contrast to the sage, who always acts from considerations of world-welfare without desire because s/he is already detached, Arjuna is asked to act without attachment (for what are clearly personal considerations) and "with the desire to maintain the world's order" (*chikīrṣur loksaṁgraham BG* 3.25).

It cannot be emphasized enough that to act with detachment is to act with desire (as opposed to being a detached sage who is without desire); and not just any desire, but the desire to maintain the world's welfare. This may seem circular since to do so is to act in accordance with *dharma* which is after all about world-welfare—but in fact is not. Krishna here is asking Arjuna to bring his intentions for undertaking *dharma* (which are internal and align well with Aristotle's language of *telos*), in line with the explicit goals of *dharma* (which are external[10] and line up with Aristotle's sense of *skopos*). After all, we have seen it is very easy to undertake *dharma* for all kinds of reasons or intentions. Acting with detachment—that is, acting without concern for personal fruit and with concern for world-welfare—makes the agent's intentions utterly consistent with the purported goals of *dharma*, which is world-welfare. Thus, not only does a misalignment between intention and action distort moral action, as we saw in chapter 4, but it can make it difficult to see what one's duty might be in circumstances like Arjuna's. A proper alignment of the two takes time, since to follow *dharma* for any reason is no easy thing, let alone undertaking it consistently with detachment.

Hence Krishna is not offering up a magic bullet here, but a prescription for a world where *dharma* is in decline (*BG* 4.7–8) precisely because of this misalignment between intention and action. For too long, the misalignment has led to the distortion of *dharma* since it has meant an emphasis on the letter of the law by the *brahmin* (and, by extension, by others as well) for the attainment of pleasure and power (*BG* 2.42–43). It is no wonder that the *Gītā* is thought to include a considered response to Buddhism.[11] It not only affirms the priority of scriptural injunction as denied by all the heterodox traditions, confirms innovations in the *varṇa* scheme offered by the *Manusmṛiti*, and finds a way of addressing the tradition's shortcomings by primarily addressing our attitude towards the actions. But this change in attitude has important implications for the content of *dharm*ic action as well, as we see next.

7.4 *Dharma* and Supererogatory Action

Dharma, which covers much of what falls under value theory, is discussed in great detail in the *Manusmṛiti* and more broadly in the *Gītā*. The *Manusmṛiti*'s purview is vast indeed, since it covers religious activities such as when, where, and by whom ritual and restorative activity should be undertaken (*MS* 5 and 11); it also discusses class and caste obligations of the various stages of life (as mentioned above), including acceptable kinds of work (*MS* 4.1–12; 9.3–36), appropriate types of food that may and may not be eaten (*MS* 5.1–44), pollution and purification regimes (*MS* 5), relations between the sexes and family members (*MS* 9), etc. Finally, the *Manusmṛiti* considers the entire arena of statecraft including civil and criminal law, the implementations of which are obligations of the king (*MS* 7–8).

The *Gītā*'s more general view divides action into that which produces desirable results for us and action that is obligatory (*BG* 18.2). But it seems unclear whether the text is classifying action broadly construed or *dharm*ic action, since there are *dharm*ic rituals that produce desirable results for the agent (for instance, a place in heaven or male offspring). Since, as we have just seen, all *dharm*ic action can be undertaken to produce desirable results for the agent, it is more likely that Krishna is classifying action broadly construed. If so, we are faced with the daunting prospect of giving up all actions (and not just *dharm*ic ones) that produce desirable results. But how is it possible to even subsist since such a prohibition restricts us to obligatory actions which would then seem to exclude even those actions that promote our basic well-being?

The answer must be that promotion of our well-being must fall under obligatory action (whose scope is quite extensive as we just saw from the rough outline of the *Manusmṛiti*'s contents); but we have to understand how this is so. If all *dharm*ic action can be undertaken for desirable results for the agent, as Krishna has complained is the case above, it is quite reasonable to see how that might be true of all our actions; after all, this would simply be a matter of intending all the agent's actions for her own purposes, which, *in extremis*, is exactly the position of ethical egoism. It must be remembered, then, that the converse is also true; all the agent's actions can be transformed if undertaken with detachment. For all detached action promotes world-welfare, which is the point of obligatory action in the first place. Thus, an agent undertakes the promotion of her own well-being as necessary to undertake her function in the larger scheme of things. Indeed, much of this is expressly prescribed in the *Manusmṛiti*, especially when it comes to the kinds of food one can eat, how to stay clean, etc.

Yet it is simply not possible for all human actions to be covered by *dharm*ic law so that there is a gap between all the agent's actions that are capable of being undertaken with detachment, and the actions that are explicitly obligatory in *śruti* and *smṛiti*. This space is filled by what we may call discretionary or supererogatory action. These actions are broadly consistent with *dharma*, whether they give it specific content, or when they go beyond its scope (as in the case of adjudicating dilemmas). Even if the requirements of charity (*dāna*) are specific in time, place, and relation, there are always opportunities (for example, to someone the agent fleetingly crosses paths with on a journey and who is facing hardship) that fall outside of such specificity. Or when we may say that an agent has gone above and beyond the call of duty by patiently withstanding wrongful abuse (patience being a universal duty broadly prescribed by both the *Manusmṛiti* (*MS* 5.107, 6.92) and the *Gītā* (*BG* 10.4, 13.7)). Even more broadly, the attitude of detachment can be brought to bear on all secular activity, such as the pursuit of trades, thereby bringing about a *dharm*ic transformation of all human action.[12] Such action is still being driven by desire, a desire that Krishna says is not contrary to *dharma* (*BG* 7.11), for it is a desire to act without concern for personal fruit and with concern for world-welfare. Of course, the desireless sage is the limit to the supererogatory since her actions are perfectly consistent with both the letter and spirit of *dharma* and hence with world-welfare.

Yet, increasingly, detachment opens up the supererogatory to those who are not quite sages in a way that makes it very much a part of the everyday moral life, as one would expect. Now one's life in the *varṇa* scheme is defined by work (for example, a warrior's by his defence of the realm, the priest's by his pursuit of knowledge and its dissemination, etc.). What is interesting is that each of these lives is marked by the predominant virtues such as courage and vigor in the warrior and impartiality and wisdom in the priest, to the point where the class is defined in terms of its virtues rather than its activities (*BG* 18.43–44).[13] Yet there is more virtue in any life than those manifest in the activities that preoccupy it and are prescribed to it, as is clear from the broad list of virtues that are repeatedly presented in the *Gītā* for each of the classes. Undertaking one's class obligations with detachment, therefore, explains how this happens: for detachment decenters the agent in ways that translate into all areas of his life, and not simply the ones explicitly covered by *dharm*ic law.

We are now in a position to reconcile two seemingly inconsistent views in the *Gītā*; for it tells us not only that we must obey scriptural injunction as we saw in Books 16 through 18, but that the good person (or sage) is the standard of right action (*BG* 3.21). Since this latter claim is made in the context of the discussion of world-welfare, it is all the more relevant to our discussion here. The point, I think, is not that *śruti* and *smṛiti* can be upended; rather it is that moral dilemmas like Arjuna's, as Matilal has pointed out, require the application of the good person's judgement to determine which duty has priority.[14] But to extend the point, there is a whole area of supererogatory action, as discussed above, that is not covered explicitly by *dharmic* law, where the sage's discretion comes into play. The sage is a standard, then, not only because her actions are consistent with the letter of the law, but its spirit as well, so that her actions are a beacon for the rest of us to follow.

A similar point is made in the *Manusmṛiti*, but much more explicitly (*MS* 2.12). The basis of *dharma*, the text says, is the *Vedas* (*śruti*) first, then tradition (i.e., that which is encompassed in *smṛiti*), then the conduct of virtuous people (i.e., the sages), and finally what seems appropriate to the agent in light of the above (and who is presumably one of the many to whom *dharmic* law applies). There is a place for discretion here, therefore, but there is reason why it appears in the latter half of the list; for it is not meant to supplant as much as to complement *śruti* and *smṛiti*. Interestingly enough, towards the end of the text, we also get a fascinating discussion of the evolution of the tradition (*MS* 108–13). Many of the issues not discussed in the tradition clearly fall within the purview of discretion. But others may require new laws that are specifically not mentioned in the tradition. In such cases, the text gives the details for the requisite number of members for the "review committee" and their appropriate qualifications. Given that the emphasis is on a consistent evolution of *śruti* in *smṛiti* (even if it is expansive), it is unsurprising that priority is given to the qualification of having a deep knowledge of the *Vedas*. Furthermore, the divine status of the *Manusmṛiti*'s author helps in establishing the orthodoxy of the process by which this evolution is undertaken.

The *Gītā*, therefore, presents us with a full-fledged moral theory.[15] First, it tells us how human society and its activities fit into the larger cosmological scheme (i.e., by being continuous with it, in ways that are reminiscent of Heraclitus and Plato). Second, its position is prescriptive for it tells us what we ought to do and how we are to undertake such action, while also allowing for individual discretion. Moreover, it does not simply ask us to blindly follow our *svadharma* but provides the principle of world-welfare as a basis for adjudicating between duties. True, it does not give us the freedom to pick our own *dharma*, but it is not clear that we are entirely free to do so in any moral theory. After all, for instance, we all have obligations to our families, at the very least, that cannot be otherwise. Furthermore, the availability of detachment to all, regardless of class and sex within the orthodox worldview (*BG* 9.32), clearly shows ways in which the *Gītā*'s views can be universalized beyond it. Not only has this application been attempted in the scholarship,[16] but it can plausibly be considered the basis for the *Gītā*'s perennial and global popularity.

7.5 Assessing the *Gītā*'s Emerging Consequentialism

The moral view emerging from the *Gītā*, in western philosophical parlance, is called "consequentialism."[17] It is true that our job here is to lead up to a discussion about the *Gītā* in relation to the *Nicomachean Ethics* on moral content. But I think it would be useful to undertake a preliminary (if diverting) comparative exercise with John Stuart Mill's influential version of western consequentialism.[18] Such a comparison will allow us to assess the strengths of the *Gītā*'s consequentialism, and to see if in fact it can respond to crucial problems that face its western counterparts.

Consequentialism is often defined as the view that conceives right and wrong actions in terms of whether or not they promote some distinct conception of the good. In Mill's case, the good is pleasure (or happiness) together with the absence of pain, based on what he takes to be self-evident, presumably in nature (*Utilitarianism* 4–5). So right actions are right, not simply if they promote the agent's pleasure and the absence of pain (or else this would be an egoistic hedonism). Rather, actions are right insofar as they maximize the happiness of all who are potentially affected by the action (which can range widely in number), or what Mill calls "happiness altogether" (*Utilitarianism* 7–11). Clearly, Mill's conception of happiness altogether as pleasure can easily be understood in terms of a calibrated version of world-welfare, even if the *Gītā* might differ on what world-welfare means exactly (as we will soon see). Yet, the consequentialist parallels are clear enough since both theories determine the nature of right action on the basis of the good promoted.

The problem with this kind of moral perfectionism, as has been noted, is that it leaves little or no room for what is inherently valuable to the agent, as opposed to the kind of perfectionism on offer in Aristotle which is after all agent-focused.[19] In Mill's case, one is always supposed to pursue the maximal overall good, even if it sometimes comes at the detriment of the agent; for the agent is to be strictly neutral when it comes to choosing between her happiness and that of others (*Utilitarianism* 11). Since Mill grounds his view in what he takes to be the self-evident claim that agents pursue their own happiness (*Utilitarianism* 2–5), he cannot deny that the agent's deliberations do take her own welfare into consideration especially when her actions do not affect others. But since it is always possible to act in a way to promote happiness altogether (even if it is to mitigate overall suffering), it would seem that promoting one's own welfare is acceptable only if it is a means to promoting general welfare. For example, suppose I have resources to devote to a project that is of great value to me. On Mill's view such an expenditure could be hard to justify unless it allows me to act in ways that would promote even greater general welfare than, say, a donation to a cause that effectively relieves immense suffering, might otherwise make possible.

The problem of constraining the agent's actions in this manner also arises in the *Gītā*, as we have already seen, but it seems to impact Mill's position more substantially. This is partly because Mill's liberalism takes the primacy of the individual's happiness seriously, even if this happiness is aggregated. For the problem suggests that the agent cannot directly promote her own well-being without constraints and has in fact to rely on others to do that for her when they promote happiness altogether.[20]

Whereas the *Gītā* can and does consistently focus on world-welfare especially since, in the final analysis, as seen from the sage's ultimately cosmological perspective (and as discussed in chapters 4 and 5), the empirical agent is nothing but strands/*guṇa*s acting on *guṇa*s. Thus, giving primacy to the agent's needs—and by extension her projects—makes much less sense here unless it promotes world-welfare, as we have already seen. Yet the class-system can be seen as a way of mitigating the excesses of consequential perfectionism precisely because it anchors the agent's projects and commitments and gives a plausible stability and structure to her life.

If what is said above is true it might explain why *mokṣa*, understood as liberation in and from this world, becomes an attractive proposition within this version of the orthodox worldview. For life in this world for the *Gītā* seems to be about the satisfaction of desire or the pursuit of duty. But to satisfy desire is to be ensnared by it since such activity only inflames and enhances the desire (and hence the inaccurate sense of agency that is its basis) that then leads to suffering in this and future lives (*BG* 16.10–20). Whereas the strict pursuit of duty is clearly an onerous burden even if it is so for an agent who misconstrues the nature of her agency. Freedom from either burden is only possible in this world when one has the sage's insight, which in turn eventually leads to freedom from it (*BG* 18.49). So, the burden of duty is eventually relieved, and is perhaps what makes it worth bearing. The question of whether or not there is an eventual beneficiary of this, even a transcendental one, is something we will leave for the next chapter. To see if in fact a consequentialist reading of the *Gītā* can be held, it is time now to consider some of its implications.

7.6 The *Gītā* on *Dharma* and *Mokṣa*

One key issue is the relation between *dharma* and *mokṣa*.[21] Recall that in chapter 4, it was suggested that *dharma* is traditionally conceived as subsidiary to *mokṣa*. That is, in the traditional hierarchy of the four ends of *artha*, *kāma*, *dharma*, and *mokṣa*, the first two are subordinate to the third and the third to the fourth. For material goods and pleasure are to be pursued in an orderly fashion and hence for the sake of, and in accordance with, *dharma*, which as we saw is about world order and hence world-welfare. But it is hard to see how *dharma* in turn is not a means to *mokṣa* since it leads to it, as we just saw. If so, we are led to the conclusion that *dharma*, which is about maintaining the world order, is a means to *mokṣa*, which is a release from it! In response, we might begin by reminding ourselves that from the point of view of why we pursue *dharma*, Krishna seems to be suggesting that we do so precisely because it is our *dharma*/duty. From the point of view of the "what" of *dharma*, we can say that this is based on world-welfare which is compatible (*qua* outcomes) with its "why." But then, herein lies the rub; for *dharma*'s outcomes seem to be about world-welfare, whereas *mokṣa* is concerned with freedom from it. How might we reconcile the two?

The answer I think is that world-welfare is ultimately about making *mokṣa* possible for all and thereby indirectly for the agent. If, as we just saw, the world is conceived as a place that is either blighted by desire or burdened by obligation, then it makes sense to seek release from it for everyone. Indeed, the whole point of world-welfare is to make it possible for everyone to find an orderly path through it and from it.[22] That is, world-welfare is not an end in itself, as it might be for someone like Mill who gives the highest value to pleasure for all in this life. Rather, the world may be conceived as a quagmire without *dharma* so that *dharma* is the basis of a carefully engineered passage through it. But this is not an escape route one can or should build for oneself. Rather, this exit is one that requires the concerted effort of others acting in tandem so that everyone, including oneself, may pass through, which, after all, is quite consistent with the text's emphasis on making *mokṣa* directly available to all in Book 5. Release for oneself then is not the direct object of the agent's intention, which makes sense given the ultimately misconstrued nature of one's agency, even if it is the eventual indirect result.[23]

It may be objected that there are several suggestions in the *Gītā* that release for oneself is in fact the direct object of the agent's intention, and if so, this may cause a problem to the reading I suggest above. For instance, Krishna says of the world-renouncer who spends his time in meditation, that he is intent on his own liberation through sense control, and a constant focus on the Divine (*BG* 5.26–28), understood abstractly as That (*BG* 5.17) and explained elsewhere as unmanifest or beyond form (*BG* 12.5). Contrastingly, after revealing his true, terrifyingly manifest form as creator, maintainer, and ground of the world in

BG 11, Krishna confirms that such a vision is only available to those who are devoted to him, intent on him, and who long for him as the goal (a parallel for which can be seen in many traditional forms of theism). What makes this objection seem so powerful is that it deflates the all-consuming altruism that I have suggested so far and finds a place for the individual's goals even if *mokṣa* is austere in the extreme.

In response, it may be said that our focus so far has been on the *Gītā*'s moral theory, and hence on *karma yoga*/the path of action. After all, we have not only been speaking of world-welfare as the goal of action but doing so in relation to one's *dharma*/duty in the context of one's stage and station in life. But the *Gītā* also mentions (*BG* 13.24–25) and discusses the path of renunciation and meditation/*dhyāna yoga* and that of devotion/*bhakti yoga*, with which the above references are consistent. The pursuit of the Divine as unmanifest is by the world-renouncer or mendicant who clearly follows the path of meditation/*dhyāna yoga*. Those, on the other hand, who long to unite with the Divine understood as having a manifest form, clearly pursue the path of devotion/*bhakti yoga*.

Such a response is not meant to suggest that *mokṣa* is not the goal of every *yoga*, because it clearly is (*BG* 13.24–25); just that personal salvation is not the direct goal of *karma yoga*. Yet even the direct concern for one's own *mokṣa* in the case of the other *yoga*s is mitigated by several important considerations. In the case of the path of meditation/*dhyāna yoga*, the concern for personal salvation is problematized to some extent by the impersonal nature of the unmanifest Divinity that is the goal of meditation; for the impersonal nature of the goal undermines how it can be personal in any way (especially if the empirical self is itself "strands/*guṇa*s acting on strands," as we have seen earlier in chapter 5). Moreover, even in the context in which the text speaks of the mendicant who pursues his own *mokṣa (BG* 5.26–28), the text also goes out of its way to tell us that such a person is also concerned with the welfare of all. This claim makes sense, given that earlier in the same Book (*BG* 5.6), the text emphasizes that the renunciation of action is necessary for meditation/*dhyāna yoga* which is much easier to obtain on the back of *karma yoga*, presumably because it presupposes renunciation in action (or detachment). Which is why Krishna says in 3.4 that renunciation alone is not enough for knowledge and hence *mokṣa*. Now this temporal priority of action to renunciation is not surprising, given that it is enshrined in the stage-and-station/*varṇāśramadharma* framework we have seen previously. But it is endorsed here also as a way of responding to Buddhism, which openly affirms walking away from worldly life to take up a monastic one. The *Gītā*, in other words, remains broadly committed to this world and hence to *dharma* and morality, even when it speaks to those who wish to leave it. More on this issue, though, in the next chapter.

It is not correspondingly easy to mitigate the sense that the path of devotion/*bhakti yoga* is focused on the moral agent's *mokṣa*. One way to try might be to see that *bhakti yoga* simply makes detachment less impersonal. Instead of acting dispassionately for the sake of world-welfare, one acts for Krishna's sake (which is what I take being intent on him and doing everything for him in BG 18.57–58 means). But if what I suggested earlier is true, and acting for the sake of world-welfare means to act for everyone's eventual *mokṣa*, then the problem still persists; since to act for Krishna's sake is eventually about the agent's *mokṣa* (as Krishna explicitly says in *BG* 12.55) and not everyone else's. Yet to the extent that in acting for Krishna's sake the agents still undertake their duties, then to this extent they are still acting for the sake of world-welfare, even if this is oblique to the agents' intentions (in the way in which *mokṣa* is for the agent in *karma yoga*).

Perhaps for this reason we can say, following Śankara the first great commentator on the *Gītā*, that *bhakti yoga* has not the same status as *dhyāna yoga* (which is described as of highest difficulty, as we saw). Nor is it on par with *karma yoga*, which is described as the best path (*BG* 12.12, 18.6). But unlike Śankara, who thinks only the path of knowledge leads to *mokṣa*, we follow the *Gītā*'s explicit articulation that every path leads to knowledge and hence to *mokṣa* (*BG* 4.33). The difference, as we have just seen, has to do with whose *mokṣa* is pursued by a *bhakti yogin* as opposed to the other seekers. Another reason for its reduced status might be that if the pursuit of one's own *mokṣa* is paramount, why not simply set aside one's duties (which are after all about world-welfare) and devote oneself to God whole-heartedly?[24] The *Gītā* only eventually mentions this world-abnegating possibility (*BG* 18.66), which is then fully realized in the later, more fuller developments of the *bhakti* tradition.[25] I will say more about the role of *bhakti yoga* and its limitations in the next chapter when we discuss the *Ātman-Brahman* relation.

Karma yoga, then, represents a novel middle path between the extremes that eventually seem to deny the world, be it because the Divine is unmanifest (*dhyāna yoga)* or not (*bhakti yoga*). For *karma yoga* is the only path that emphasizes the importance of the world even as it seeks freedom for the individual perspective from it. It is a middle path that is different from the Buddha's, which conceives of itself as a mean between the extremes of austerity and hedonism. Yet in its own way *karma yoga* constitutes the heart of the *Gītā*'s response to the Buddha's middle path precisely because it asks us not to renounce the world but to take it seriously by performing our duties with detachment.[26] But we must not forget that our comparative effort is aimed not at the Buddha but at another proponent of the Mean: Aristotle, and specifically to the *Nicomachean Ethics*. It is to this comparative evaluation, restricted to the content of moral virtue in both the *Gītā* and the *Ethics* that we have investigated in these last two chapters, that we now turn.

Notes

1 *The Laws of Manu*, Penguin Classics (London; New York: Penguin, 1991).

2 But see J. N. Mohanty, "Dharma, Imperatives, and Tradition: Toward an Indian Theory of Moral Action," in *Indian Ethics: Classical Traditions and Contemporary Challenges*, vol. I, ed. Purushottama Bilimoria, Joseph Prabhu, and Renuka Sharma (London; New York: Routledge, 2017), 57–78. Mohanty interprets "authorless" to mean that the author's intentions are not relevant for the understanding of the text, which seems a rather anachronistic suggestion.

3 Thus Olivelle in *Dharmasharstra* in Knut A. Jacobsen et al., *Brill's Encyclopedia of Hinduism*, Handbuch Der Orientalistik. Zweite Abteilung, Indien 22 (Leiden; Boston: Brill, 2009), 57–60, speculates about the minimal presence of "*dharma*" in the *Vedas*. He suggests its origins in royal rather than in ritual vocabulary, with its rising prominence attributable to its usage in early Buddhism and in the imperial theology of Ashoka in the third century BCE. Whereas Wilhelm Halbfass, *Tradition and Reflection: Explorations in Indian Thought* (Albany, NY: State University of New York Press, 1991): 14–16, thinks that while there is a diversity of usages of the term "*dharma*," there is no doubt that all of these reinterpretations originate in the *Vedas*, and "reflects the elusive, yet undeniable coherence of Hinduism itself, its peculiar unity-in-diversity." I am inclined to follow Halbfass on this.

4 See K. N. Upadhyaya, "The Impact of Early Buddhism on Hindu Thought: With Special Reference to the Bhagavadgita," *Philosophy East and West* 18 (1968): 163–73.

5 See J. A. B. van Buitenen, *The Bhagavadgītā in the Mahābhārata: Text and Translation* (Chicago: University of Chicago Press, 1981), 7.

6 Bilimoria, on the other hand, thinks that the *Gītā* represents a new sort of text that confirms a new kind of revelation: personal, historic, and original. See Purushottama Bilimoria, "Varieties of Interpretation of the Bhagavadgītā," in *The Gītā in World Literature* (New Delhi: Sterling Publishers, 1990), 1–15.

7 For instance, when Krishna instructs Arjuna's brother Bheema in the Gada-yuddha Parva of the *Mahābhārata* to break the rules of combat to defeat his cousin and arch enemy, Duryodhana, the eldest of the Kauravas.

8 This is amongst the earliest occurring language concerning the wheel in orthodox Hinduism, though earlier Buddhist references (notably to the Buddha's *First Sermon* where he sets the wheel of *dharma* in motion) and later Hindu ones are pervasive. This is therefore perhaps another indicator of the *Gītā*'s interest in responding to and co-opting aspects of early Buddhism.

9 Thus, there is a single, overarching principle that, if properly contextualized within the stage-and-station framework, is the basis of all duty. But see Bina Gupta, "Bhagavad Gita as Duty and Virtue Ethics: Some Reflections," *Journal of Religious Ethics* 34, no. 3 (2006): 381–82, who disagrees, mainly because she thinks the text is not consequentialist in nature.

10 See S. Gopalan in Arvind Sharma, *New Essays in the Bhagavadgītā: Philosophical, Methodological, and Cultural Approaches* (New Delhi: Books & Books, 1987), 7–10, who makes a similar point. But he may not agree on how the subjective is brought in line with the objective (i.e., in terms of losing the sense of self as is the case for the sage on my reading).

11 See Purshottama Billimoria, "Protestant Ethic and Hindu Dharma: With Reference to Kant and Gandhi," in *The Contemporary Essays on the Bhagavad Gita*, ed. Sinha (New Delhi: Siddharth Publications, 1995), 79–80.

12 See Wilhelm Halbfass, *India and Europe: An Essay in Understanding* (Albany, NY: State University of New York Press, 1988), 326.

13 As Aurobindo points out and as noted by Tara Chatterjea, *Knowledge and Freedom in Indian Philosophy* (Lanham, MD: Lexington Books, 2003), 114; Bimal Krishna Matilal, "Caste, Karma and the Gītā," in *Philosophy, Culture, and Religion: The Collected Essays of Bimal Krishna Matilal*, vol. 2, *Ethics and Epics*, ed. Jonardon Ganeri (Oxford; New York: Oxford University Press, 2001), 53, interestingly enough, takes this to be an indicator that the class and caste system originated on the basis of ability but eventually became about heredity.

14 See Bimal Krishna Matilal, "Dharma and Rationality," in *The Collected Essays of Bimal Krishna Matilal: Ethics and Epics*, ed. Jonardon Ganeri (New Delhi: Oxford University Press, 2002), 56–60. Though I do not agree with him (and others) who think that the discussions of *dharma* are implicit in traditional wisdom and not evolved from the *śruti* texts. See J. N. Mohanty, *Classical Indian Philosophy* (Lanham, MD: Rowman & Littlefield, 2000), 98–99.

15 This is contra Austin Creel, "'Dharma' as an Ethical Category Relating to Freedom and Responsibility," *Philosophy East and West* 22 (1972): 163–65.

16 See, for instance, Chatterjea, *Knowledge and Freedom in Indian Philosophy*, 114–18.

17 On the *Gita*'s consequentialism, see Bilimoria, "Protestant Ethic and Hindu Dharma," 80; Sandeep Sreekumar, "An Analysis of Consequentialism and Deontology in the Normative Ethics of the Bhagavadgita," *Journal of Indian Philosophy* 40, no. 3 (2012): 277–315; Joseph Dowd, "Maximizing Dharma: Krsna's Consequentialism in the Mahābhārata," *Praxis* 3, no. 1 (2011): 33–50; Joshua

Anderson, "Sen and the Bhagavad Gita: Lessons for a Theory of Justice," *Asian Philosophy* 22, no. 1 (February 1, 2012): 63–74.

18 John Stuart Mill, *Utilitarianism* (Indianapolis, IN: Hackett Publishing Co., 2001).

19 See, for instance, J. J. C. Smart and Bernard Williams, *Utilitarianism: For and Against* (Cambridge: Cambridge University Press, 1973), ch. 2.

20 This problem also affects those who use Kant as their preferred western prism through which to think about the *Gītā*. Thus Arindam Chakrabarti, "The End of Life: A Nyāya-Kantian Approach to the 'Bhagavadgītā,'" *Journal of Indian Philosophy* 16, no. 4 (1988): 331–32, thinks that detachment is an acceptable means to the end of *mokṣa* precisely because detachment is the meaning of *mokṣa*.

21 Many think that there is no doubt that *dharma* is a means to *mokṣa*, even if they disagree on the nature of this relation. Important contributions to this discussion include: Daniel Ingalls, "Dharma and Moksa," *Philosophy East and West* 7 (1957): 41–48; J. A. B. Van Buitenen, "Dharma and Moksa," *Philosophy East and West* 7 (1957): 33–41; Karl Potter, "Dharma and Moksa from a Conversational Point of View," *Philosophy East and West* 8 (1958): 49–64. Roy Perrett, *Hindu Ethics: A Philosophical Study* (Honolulu: University of Hawaii Press, 1998), 60, suggests a parallel to many western theories where the right is about acting well and the good about living well, so that *dharma* is about the former and *mokṣa* about the latter. Here I suggest another option.

22 This perhaps may be a way to think about why the highest value attributed to freedom/*mokṣa* that some think should not have been the case if in fact the tradition focuses on the individual's freedom. See Rajendra Prasad, *Karma, Causation and Retributive Morality: Conceptual Essays in Ethics and Metaethics* (New Delhi: Indian Council of Philosophical Research in association with Munshiram Manoharlal Publ., 1989), 320–21.

23 Prasad, *Karma, Causation and Retributive Morality*, 221–22 thinks freedom concerns the lower self, to which I respond more fully below. But see Sreekumar, "An Analysis of Consequentialism," 302–306, who thinks that freedom here is directly about the agent's higher self so that the *Gita*'s consequentialism involves agent relative considerations. In chapter 8, I will address why I think it may be implausible to speak of liberating the higher self. Nor am I convinced by Charkrabarti's deontological sounding reading in which he distinguishes the hope from the desire for *mokṣa* (as Kant does for happiness). This allows the agent to hope for *mokṣa* which is then understood in terms of desirelessness (presumably of the agent). I am not convinced, first, because it is unclear to me that hoping is not a form of desiring, at least for the *Gītā*, and second, because it assumes a form of agency that is important to Kant but seems to be missing in the *Gītā* on my reading. See Chakrabarti, "The End of Life," 331–32 for more details.

24 There are interesting parallels here to Buddhism where one could devote oneself to one's own salvation as one might in *bhakti*. But there is also the possibility

of devoting oneself to the salvation of others in later Buddhism to forestall the problems of just devoting oneself to one's own salvation, something that might be credited to the *Gītā*.

25 For a sense of the *Gītā*'s role in the later developments in the *bhakti* movement, see Richard H. Davis, *The Bhagavad Gita: A Biography* (Princeton, NJ: Princeton University Press, 2014), 43ff. Indeed, important commentators in the tradition have prioritized *bhakti yoga* in the *Gītā*. Thus, for instance, *Sri Rāmānuja Gita Bhasya: with Text and English Translation*, trans. Swami Adidevananda (Madras: Sri Ramakrishna Math, 2007). We will have occasion to evaluate the metaphysical basis of this path in some detail in the next chapter.

26 See Upadhyaya, "The Impact of Early Buddhism on Hindu Thought," 163–73. I say this because of the centrality of *karma yoga* for Arjuna, the protagonist of the text. But see Van Buitenen, "Dharma and Moksa," 39–40, who thinks *karma yoga* remains a makeshift and tentative solution in the *Gītā* despite its revolutionary nature. But, given that the text begins with a moral dilemma and Krishna's response has to do with right action, important commentators have taken *karma yoga* to be the main focus of the text. In so doing, I follow Bal Gangadhar Tilak and S. B. Sukthankar, *Śrīmad Bhagavadgīta Rahasya, or, Karma-Yoga-Śāstra* (New Delhi: Asian Educational Services, 2007).

Coda 2 (to Chapters 6–7)

It might be useful to quickly review our recent findings as we attempt to consider them together here. In Coda 1 we synthesized our initial focus on the form rather than the content of ethical action from chapters 2 through 4. We saw that both texts emphasize the right kind of ethical intentionality that attempts to remove the wrong kind of self-interest. This self-interest is ultimately understood in terms of inappropriate desires so that the seemingly different tripartitions of faculties and drives attempt an ordinality that shapes the good or practically wise person (*phronimos*) in Aristotle and the sage in the *Gītā*. But while such ordinality of desire prioritizes the rational and the *sattv*ic, substantial differences appear. In Aristotle the organization of all desire by the rational personality is in the service of that person's flourishing so that flourishing is to be understood in terms of the satisfaction of desire. In the *Gītā*, *sattva*'s priority is commensurate with the rise of knowledge which in turn is ultimately about overcoming desire and undermining the self. As we turn our attention to reviewing the content of ethical action in chapters 5 and 6, we need to consider the implications of this divergence not only on rationality and desire but on the relation of the ethical and political, of the role of rationality, latitude and of the social context in both.

The Relation of the Ethical and Political

The importance of individual happiness in Aristotle is at the very least consistent with his view that it is the happy (or good) person who is the standard of right action, essentially because what the good person does is also what is good for that person. This doesn't mean that the community is not important for determining the law since it is precisely good people *qua* politicians who legislate. While the focus therefore remains on individual flourishing, it is also clear that the political is therefore very much in the service of the ethical even if it is continuous with it. Still, it is not that the social can be subverted to serve the individual's desires at least on Aristotle's views because of what flourishing requires (in terms of the conditions necessary for its very possibility) and what it entails (in terms of its normative commitments).

On the other hand, *dharma*'s tenuous origins in *śruti* is conceived as continuous with its development in the hands of a mostly anonymous tradition with its focus on world welfare. Krishna's divine voice brings renewed authority to this position in the *Gītā*, so that the text's consequentialism is consistent with the various paths/*yoga*s being traversed by individuals without focusing on individuality, given the text's view of the latter's ultimately inconsequential nature. *Dharma*, therefore, is fundamentally social and political upon which the ethical is dependent.[1] If this is correct, then *dharma* as world-welfare is, in an important sense, about engineering a cultural context that is a passage to freedom/*mokṣa* for all, so that doing one's duty promotes this end. Yet in pursuing world-welfare, one also fulfills the basic needs of life as well as the more complex obligations of stage and station while still being able to consistently deny the ultimate reality and value of the self. Nevertheless, this is not to say that the priority of the social and political is only possible on such a view of the self (or lack thereof) even if it may be hard to see how such a denial is possible without the usual complaints of fascism arising.

Rationality and Latitude

Aristotle's focus on the agent's happiness also seems consistent with his particularism wherein good action (which is a manifestation of the agent's happiness) is dependent on context and agency. Yet for any agent and circumstance, there is only one Mean which is determined by reason (*qua* deliberation and wish) in relation to the right rule or law. Thus, as one would expect, it is rationality that mediates between Aristotle's ethical particularism and the universal (understood in terms of the law), a rationality that is central to what happiness means for him. The centrality and universality of reason—a theme which Aristotle inherits from Plato—saves him from what might otherwise be a subjectivism of the individual. Yet ironically it is the importance of the individual that best explains the challenges of acting ethically and with the right kind of self-love. And the language of love signals the importance of the emotions and desires in Aristotle, which again is consistent with his emphasis on human flourishing.

It is not that rationality is unimportant in the *Gītā*, given the role of the intellect/*buddhi* in individual decisions regarding the nature of one's duty and that of the tradition in the evolution of *smriti*, as we have seen. Rationality also plays an important role in the alignment of intention and the specific actions entailed by duty/*dharma* so that the universal obtains on the back of the *Gītā*'s holism. Thus, latitude here is not determined by individual rationality but by the requirements of stage-and-station so that agents from different classes, for instance, would be called to act in different ways by their *dharma*. Since the use of reason is cultivated on all paths/*yoga*s albeit in slightly different ways, it is unsurprising that the *Gītā* thinks the sage's wisdom is available to all, especially within the orthodox fold. Such detached wisdom is constituted by an impersonal synoptic knowledge of the world that is immediately intuitive and makes for actions that are in sync with Nature/*Prakrati*, so that the rationality at work here is not discursive but intuitive and is made possible by *sattva*'s high predominance. This wide accessibility to the highest good in the *Gītā* emerges as another important difference from Aristotle, whose version ends up being available only to a few, as we will see in chapter 9. This despite the seeming lack of emphasis on desire and its satisfaction in the *Gītā* that makes it seem less accessible rather than more. We will therefore have to see how the text addresses this seeming lacuna in chapter 8.

When it comes to latitude in ethical activity, then, it would seem that Aristotle focuses on the latitude available to individual agents, whereas the *Gītā* is more interested in having it expressed in a range of social activity even if individual action is much more circumscribed. By relating ethical activity to the law, the *Ethics* seems not only to avoid the excesses of subjectivity but those of objectivity as well. Thus, a nuanced assessment of ethical disagreement, for instance, is plausible in theory even though such assessment does not always resolve into a single right answer. Whereas while ethical action is more tightly bound up in the scheme of duties in the *Gītā*, it would seem that a kind of latitude is on offer from a social perspective here because of the different obligations for different agents depending on their stage and station (in ways that seem consistent with the text's holism). It follows, then, that latitude is on offer as the individual perspective broadens as a result of deepening detachment and the increasing clarity of perspective that it brings. This latitude is especially on offer in instances where one's *dharma* is not obvious because of competing considerations or because of the unusual nature of the circumstance. Both texts therefore recognize that right action is contextual and especially dependent on the nature of the agent, even if they have very different ways of accommodating such difference.

Priority and Circumscription of *Dharma* and Virtue

Regardless of emphasis, both texts think that *dharma* and virtue have the highest priority in life and are therefore all-encompassing. Note that priority does not entail inclusivity since something can be more important and exclusive at the same time, as in the case, say, of a sybarite's preference for bodily pleasure over all else. Whereas *dharma* is inclusive precisely because it is a way of pursuing personal, social, political, and economic activities so that it has suzerainty over *artha* and *kāma*. Hence the central question of the text on whether to fight or not to fight is about *dharma* first. But it also becomes clear that detachment broadens *dharma*'s reach so that all action falls under its purview, which when taken together with its circumscriptive nature, explains how freedom/*mokṣa* is plausibly accessible to all in this lifetime. Yet the text does not fall into the trap of making *dharma* a mere means to the agent's freedom/*mokṣa,* as we saw, since *dharma*—when thought about in such terms—is always about everyone's freedom, even when it is undertaken as the agent's highest priority and is therefore only indirectly about the agent's freedom.

Virtue is the good person's highest priority not only because it constitutes human happiness, but because it determines the mode and extent of the pursuit of external goods. This in turn means that the occupations we undertake, the relations we have with others, and the way in which we satisfy our desires are all ideally to be in accordance with virtue. Yet since it is the possibility of theoretical virtue (and specifically philosophy) that is the standard for the law and hence for ethical activity, there is a seeming divergence in the *telos* or intentionality of virtue as an end in itself, as opposed to its outcome or *skopos*. But as we will see in chapter 9, Aristotle finds a way to unite the practical and theoretical since they are, after all, manifestations of virtue, nonetheless. It would seem therefore that both texts concern themselves with making practical ethical activity the highest priority even if it doesn't have the highest value in both; and both therefore have to consider how to avoid making the ethical a mere means to that which has the highest value, even if they are essentially at odds about what that might be. A fuller discussion on this matter will follow in our closing considerations.

Given that *dharma* and virtue are the highest priority and are essentially social, it follows that the social context is essential for both. For Aristotle not just because others are necessary to act well in accordance with our function, but because we are social animals, and a great deal of social, political, cultural, and familial infrastructure is necessary for us to become humans who are capable of flourishing. So much so that the standards of ethical action are the basis of, and are in turn governed by, the law. Similarly, the stage-and-station setup presupposed and developed in the *Gītā* confirms the importance of the cultural infrastructure necessary to learn to fulfill what are essentially social obligations that are then politically enforced while being construed as continuous with cosmological law. Thus, despite their differences, both seem to affirm the value of the world in their different ways.

The Status of the World

Despite the *Gītā*'s efforts to counter Buddhist notions of the renouncing of action by focusing on renunciation in action, it agrees with Buddhism in finding its ultimate value in freedom from the world for the individual perspective (even if it is clearly not about doing away with the world altogether). This is not to say therefore that the individual's duty is not to be undertaken or that the persistence of the sage is denied post-insight; but if I am right, then the value of the world and its *dharm*ic organization is not because the world is valuable in itself for the individual. If it were, then the text would not speak of *mokṣa*/freedom in terms of the individual's freedom (by eventual extinction) from suffering and from *dharm*ic obligation. But it should also be clear that such abnegation is from the individual perspective and is very different from versions that ask you to deny this world so that you can get to another one. Some have therefore questioned how the loss of oneself as a goal is attractive and have therefore emphasized the goal in terms of obtaining the sage's cosmological perspective.[2] But since the sage's perspective ends at death, it is hard to see how it can be worth the culmination of what is conceived as many lifetimes worth of effort. Moreover, if I am right, then for the most part, the pursuit of freedom is a social rather than an individual goal so that it is not a direct motivator for the individual. We may still ask why freedom as a social goal is worthy of pursuit, to which I think the *Gītā*'s response is at least consistent: because it attempts to ideally align and transform all the misguided individual perspectives with the cosmological one. And even just theoretically speaking, the rationale for doing so is based on the metaphysical unity of nature that grounds the cosmological perspective. More importantly, if the *Gītā*'s view of nature is right, then it explains why we might be inclined to act for the welfare of all since we are all related parts of a whole. Such a view has interesting implications for the world as a totality; for we have seen that the *Gītā* is committed to the maintenance of the world and its order even while *dharma* is about undermining the individual perspective. Still, it could be argued that the whole point of the order (and hence of the world) is to make *mokṣa* from the individual perspective possible, and nothing more. But I think on this matter the *Gītā* is at odds with the early Buddhists who want nothing to do with the world because it is the source of suffering. After all, the *Gītā* sees the world as an aspect of *Brahman,* who is also much more than the world,[3] so that *dharma* is continuous with the law that governs the cosmos. It would therefore not be implausible to say that *dharma* organizes the human sphere and is concerned with freeing us from the individual perspective while maintaining the human sphere so that it is continuous with the cosmological one.

Aristotle's views on the basis of ethics and of the world as a whole are also optimistic but for very different reasons. Contrary to the populist views of his time and more considered ones from the later Christian tradition (among others), virtue is not a burden. Not only does virtue constitute human flourishing but its fruit is easily shared and often augmented as a result, at least in terms of honor if not always in terms of outcome. If the *Gītā*'s views obtain altruistic outcomes by subverting the self/other dichotomy, Aristotle undermines the altruism/egoism dichotomy by suggesting that ethics is not a zero-sum game. His view that human happiness is the same as human well-functioning is not just optimistic about human nature, but about the ideal social and political context of the best kind of city-state/*polis*. The best city-state is a natural construct whose framework of law is focused on nurturing, promoting, and celebrating the flourishing activity of its citizenry. The city-state is a natural construct in the way in which a beehive is natural since both are necessary for their respective denizens to function well and flourish, even if the latter's focus is on the whole hive and the former's is on the individual.

Thus, contrary to what we might expect, a denial of the individual self's ultimate value does not lead to a denial of the world, or to the denial of the needs of the individual. For the *Gītā* is careful to emphasize the importance of the world as an aspect of *Brahman* wherein *dharma* ensures that the parts not only play their role and have their needs taken care of in the process. Nor does the emphasis on the individual's happiness in Aristotle lead to neglect of the social and of the world; for happiness is essentially relational because it is ethical and political. Yet this human affirmation of the world in both does not lead to the affirmation of humanity per se for both our texts, and for very different reasons as we will see in our final chapter. But before we do so, we turn now to our consideration of the highest good and how it relates to the practical life in both texts, starting with the *Gītā*.

Notes

1 The social dimensions of the enforcement of *dharma* were very much in the hands of the priestly classes reinforced by kings (members of the warrior class) in the political context, even if the political entities themselves were not always stable. See Paul Hacker and Donald Davis, "Dharma in Hinduism," *Journal of Indian Philosophy* 34, no. 5 (2006): 483; and Patrick Olivelle, *Dharma: Studies in its Semantic, Cultural and Religious History* (New Delhi: Motilal Banarsidass, 2009), 81.

2 See Tara Chatterjea, *Knowledge and Freedom* (Lanham, MD: Lexington Books, 2003), 105–106.

3 See Purshottama Billimoria and Raphael Lataster, "Panentheism(s): What It Is and Is Not," *Journal of World Philosophies* 3, no. 2 (2018): 49–64.

8

Karma and *Sanyāsa Yoga* in the *Bhagavad Gītā*

8.0 Introduction

It is time now to turn our attention to the nature of knowledge/*jñāna* in the *Gītā*. We saw in our discussion of the path of action/*karma yoga* in chapters 5 and 7 that such knowledge partially involves knowledge of the doer/*kartā* and of world-welfare, and partly of the Self/*Ātman* and its relation to the Universal Self/*Brahman*. It is this latter relation, then, which will give us a fuller sense of what knowledge means in the *Gītā*. While the *karma yogin* has knowledge in this full sense, it seems appropriate to study the nature of knowledge in the context of the path of knowledge/*jñāna yoga*, hence the postponement in chapter 5. After all, as we have seen the *Gītā* says that all paths end in knowledge (*BG* 4.33), so that the issue is more about focus on the nature of knowledge that the path of knowledge inspires than anything else.

Now since knowledge is the ground of freedom/*mokṣa* (*BG* 7.2, 9.1), and since the *Gītā* insists that all paths/*yoga*s lead to knowledge (*BG* 4.33), the question is: what can all the paths have in common so that they lead to knowledge and hence to freedom? The answer I will show has to do with the *Gītā*'s insistence, following early Buddhism, that action and activity in the world is ceaseless so that it is action that is the common denominator of the paths. After all, paths must be traversed by—as we saw in the context of *karma yoga*—a doer/*kartā* who is an embodied being or agent/*deha* in the world such as Arjuna. Yet knowledge leads to freedom precisely because it partly involves seeing that the actor is an aggregate that ultimately reduces to strands/*guṇa*s acting on *guṇa*s; so that acting with freedom is to act with selfless detachment. But beyond that knowledge leads to freedom precisely because selfless detached action does not generate additional *karma*, so that the end of life also means an end to the futurity of that configuration of the enlightened doer/*kartā* and their actions. That is, while activity may be incessant so that the components of *kartā* and even the *deha* are unceasingly active, this activity no longer constitutes the unified action of the enlightened doer since they are not reborn as that configuration. So at least part of the answer here will have to involve showing what it is about coming to know the Self that effectively undermines the futurity of the enlightened doer.

It would therefore seem that "knowledge" is meant in more than one sense in the *Gītā*. This sense is what we have discussed above: the knowledge, even if it is impersonal, which is had at the level of the doer/*kartā*'s intellect/*buddhi*, and therefore involves action. Such active, doer-or-self-knowledge involves knowledge of the Self/*Ātman* and which I call knowledge in the second sense since it is not primary. What is in fact knowledge that is primary or knowledge in the first sense is the knowledge the Self/*Ātman* unchangingly has of itself and which essentially characterizes it and is therefore not an action. Distinguishing knowledge in the first and second sense, it is hoped, will help us understand the nature of the relation between Self/*Ātman* and Universal Self/*Brahman*; and will in turn shed some light on the path of devotion/*bhakti yoga* and explain what it is about the self-knowledge of *Ātman* that leads to freedom.

8.1 The Challenges of Interpretation

In chapter 5, we saw that the relation between the Individual Self/*Ātman* and Universal Self/*Brahman* is traditionally controversial and important commentators such as Śaṇkara and Rāmānuja disagree on it. But this relationship in turn impacts the nature of the *Ātman*'s Self-Knowledge and the *kartā*'s knowledge of such Self-Knowledge (or "self-knowledge" in short). So, we need to consider our presumption in attempting to resolve the problem, for which we will need to recall some of the issues discussed in chapter 1 section 1.

Attempting to find a consistent philosophical position in a poetic text like the *Gītā* is challenging. Poetry is often allusive and non-literal, and consistency is not always its primary concern in the way it might be for articulating a careful philosophical position. Also, it is often the case that the requirements of meter impose a greater necessity on its expression than does the logic of argument. For instance, even the key language of *Ātman*/Self, which is usually taken to be unchanging and unaffected in both the text (*BG* 9.18, 12.3) and the Vedanta tradition, is sometimes used to refer to the person or even the doer/*kartā*[1] (*BG* 6.5–7). Thus, the challenge is to determine the considered position of the text so that we can plausibly make the case for reading some of its parts non-literally, but how?

Part of the answer is already implicit above: by prioritizing what is repeatedly stated in the text and perhaps in the tradition such as the claim that *Ātman* is unchanging—so that any text that suggests otherwise must be read non-literally. But relying on emphasis is inadequate in this situation because the text does not obviously favor one reading over another when it comes to the relation of *Ātman* and *Brahman* (as we saw in chapter 5). For the *Gītā* seems to suggest that *Ātman* is identical with *Brahman* (which is Śaṇkara's position) as much as that it is only an aspect of it (which is Rāmānuja's).[2] Nor is the reliance on just tradition the solution since what is at stake is precisely what divides these schools within the Vedanta tradition.

An additional component to the answer, therefore, might be to remind ourselves of what the text is responding to in its context. In Appendix 2 we see that the *Gītā* is responding to the threat of Buddhism, while at the same time trying to synthesize the growing schism within the orthodox tradition between the *Upaniṣads* and the proto-Saṁkhya. Chapter 5, for instance, details the response to the Buddhist call to renounce action in terms of the revolutionary possibility of renouncing the fruit of action instead so as to keep the wheel of the world turning. In so doing the text equalizes the theoretical (Saṁkhya) and practical (Yoga) approaches. In this chapter's context, wherein our approach is clearly more theoretical, the *Gītā*'s response to Buddhism is two pronged. While accepting that change is incessant, it insists that change is a function of the combination and separation of persistent strands/*guṇa*s that constitute Nature/*Prakrati* (*BG* 3.27–29). This view of Nature/*Prakrati* is distinctly material and likely originates in the proto-Saṁkhya about whom we know very little, though it is plausible to say that their *guṇa*-based matter/spirit dualism is what essentially characterizes them.[3]

More importantly, the *Gītā* maintains that there is a Self even while agreeing with Buddhism (and the *Upaniṣads*) on the ultimate impermanence of the empirical self or doer/*kartā*. Whereas early Buddhism either denies or is determinedly non-committal on the existence of the Self. The *Gītā*'s substantialism is not just limited to the Higher Self/*Ātman* since in following the tradition of the *Upaniṣads* it is committed to the existence of the Universal Self/*Brahman*, so that we have a monism of some kind that involves both of them as well as Nature/*Prakrati*, as we have seen (*BG* 9.7–10). This means that however the relation between the Universal Self/*Brahman* and Higher Self/*Ātman* is conceived, it does not seem to be akin to the later Saṁkhya's view on the pluralism of the Spirit/*Puruṣa*. Whereas the language of "*Puruṣa*" is adopted in the *Gītā*, and usually refers to *Brahman* or to Krishna understood as the sole *Puruṣa* (*BG* 3.19, 8.8), or to *Ātman* (*BG* 9.4, 9.12) and even to the individual person, as we saw. Given the *Gītā*'s overriding monism, therefore, *Ātman* can be an aspect or part of *Brahman* at best if not identical to it in the text; while the *Gītā* seems to adapt the Saṁkhya view that the world evolves from a primordial Nature, even as it denies its separation from Spirit understood as *Brahman* as we just saw (*BG* 9.7–10). Such a consolidation of Nature and Spirit makes sense, given the *Gītā*'s commitment to the broad-ranging monism of the *Upaniṣads*, even if this commitment is at odds with the dualism (of matter and spirit) of the Saṁkhya school. In so assimilating the proto-Saṁkhya views on matter as *guṇa*-based, the *Gītā* seems ultimately to deny early Buddhism's pure anti-substantialism on the empirical front as well since the *guṇa*s are persistent constituents of matter. The upshot therefore is that the *Gītā* takes as much as it rejects from early Buddhism and the proto-Saṁkhya, while trying to defend Upanishadic monism. One of the interesting implications of these various compromises it makes along the way, as we will soon see, is that these make the *Gītā*'s devotional theism (*bhakti*) more plausible (even if not ultimately viable).

8.2 Saṁkhya (Theory) and Yoga (Practice)

To see how the *Gītā* effects its vast reconciliations clearly, we need to understand and relate its discussions of the various kinds of paths/*yoga*s. This in turn will help us get a fuller understanding of its revolutionary claim that all paths lead to knowledge/*jñāna*, especially since the goal of knowledge itself was traditionally thought to be the exclusive purview of the path of knowledge/*jñāna yoga*. Finally, since the path is traveled by an embodied agent/*deha*, we will be able to understand what it means to have self-knowledge.

Since the *Gītā*'s focus is on helping Arjuna determine what he should do, and hence on the practical dimensions of life, it is not unreasonable to think that it primarily conceives the highest good of human freedom in practical terms. But the text does discuss the theoretical approach extensively, even if such an approach is sometimes denigrated because of the text's emphasis on the practical one. In fact (as we have seen in chapter 4 section 3) Krishna's earliest response is from a theoretical perspective (what he calls the intellectual method of the Saṁkhya), which he distinguishes from the practical approach of Yoga (*BG* 2.39), both of which are explicitly equated later as leading to freedom/*mokṣa* (*BG* 5.5). The traditional path of knowledge (as we saw in chapter 4 section 4) is discussed in the context of the stage-and-station/*varṇāśramadharma* discussion. The knowledge/*jñāna* of the theoretical blueprint for such a life is acquired in the student stage and is progressively put into practice over the consequent stages of life, culminating ideally in the withdrawn, ascetic/*sannyāsa* life of meditation/*dhyāna*. Broadly speaking, therefore, the text will indifferently refer to this approach as *jñāna yoga* or, when it wants to emphasize the latter stage of life which can be directly undertaken by circumventing the prior stages, the renunciant path/*sannyāsa yoga* (*BG* 6.1, 18.1) or meditative path/*dhyāna yoga* (*BG* 6.10–15). Whereas the practical approach usually applies to duty-bound action in the world that we have seen called *karma yoga*, so it is not inappropriate to include within it *bhakti yoga* since this approach is essentially about action as well. After all, in addition to devotional activity like singing, praying, etc. that is taken to be central to this path, devotees also undertake their duty/*dharma* for Krishna's sake as we saw in chapter 7 section 5.

Another important reason that the *Gītā* seems to emphasize the practical life even at the expense of the one of renunciation is because, as we have seen, it is responding to early Buddhism's overriding emphasis on the latter. While there is a place for the lay person in early Buddhism, it is quite clear that freedom/*nirvana* as it conceives it is reserved for those who renounce the world. In some sense, therefore, this position matches that of traditional Brahmanism which reserves such direct access to freedom/*mokṣa* to the *brahmins*/priests via the path of knowledge/*jñāna yoga* except that Buddhism encourages everyone to renounce the world. The *Gītā*'s response, therefore, takes this opening up of access to freedom for everyone seriously, but suggests that this can happen without necessarily renouncing the world but by renouncing the personal fruit of action, and as we will see, thereby making a place for love in *bhakti*.

Yet the reasons for this emphasis on the practical life and hence on action are manifold, and it is worth our while to work through them. First, as we have seen in chapter 7 section 6, the *Gītā* does think that there is a place for the satisfaction of human desires so long as they are in accordance with *dharma* undertaken with detachment. This is not because, unlike Aristotle, the human being *qua* empirical self is of ultimate import since in the final analysis it is simply strands/*guṇa*s acting on *guṇa*s; rather, such *dharm*ic activity keeps the wheel of the world turning in a regulated fashion (*BG* 3.16). The language of "wheel" here is interesting because in early Buddhism the *dharma chakra*/wheel is symbolic of the Buddha's teachings of the Four Noble Truths, the Eightfold Path, and Dependent Origination, upon which the case for the renunciation of the world rests. Whereas in the *Gītā* the context of this usage makes clear that *dharma* is very much concerned with action undertaken for the world's welfare, so that it not only expresses Divine nature optimally (*BG* 4.7–8), but allows for a carefully engineered passage to freedom, as we saw in chapter 7 section 6. So, wholesale renunciation is a problem because if the many were to follow the Buddha in undertaking it, the world would fall into a state of disrepair (*BG* 3.22–24).

Now the above considerations apply to the path of devotion/*bhakti yoga* as much as they apply to the path of action/*karma yoga* since both fall under the purview of the broadly conceived practical approach—and will in fact broaden the practical approach in a way that makes it as universal as the Buddhist one (and perhaps even broadens it further, as I will suggest below). Hence the *Gītā* speaks to the specific advantages of the *bhakti* approach as well, which explains why the text comes to emphasize it in the first place.

First, though, some background to this important discussion in the *Gītā* from the *Upaniṣads*. In an effort to express a version of monism in the early *Upaniṣads*, we see an important distinction drawn there between *Saguna Brahman* as having name and form (*nāmarupā*) constituting the world, and the same but formless *Nirguna Brahman* as higher precisely because it is beyond name and form (*Bṛahadāraṇyaka Up.* 2.3.1–3). Similarly, we see an epistemological distinction between lower and higher knowledge of *Brahman* based on its two states of being (*Muṇḍaka Up.* 1.1.4–5). The implicit suggestion (made explicit in the later *Katha Upaniṣad*) seems to be that knowledge of *Brahman* as world is constituted by the objects of the world and is therefore limited and ephemeral; whereas knowledge of the higher, featureless *Brahman*—even if it does not fit the norms of what we might call knowledge since it seems to be of the non-conceptual—is higher precisely because it is of *Brahman* understood as beyond change (cf. *Katha Up.* 1.26–29).

The *Gītā* uses the language of "unmanifest" (*avyakta*) when it refers to this highest, formless *Brahman* as part of its effort to reconcile its views with those of the early Saṁkhya and the *Upaniṣads*. The early Saṁkhya are dualists about the kind of substance but monists about the number of instances of both substances; and it is in the later, more worked out version of the *Saṁkhya Karika*, that the distinction between material Nature/*Prakrati* and Spirit/*Puruṣa* is explored more fully (see Appendix 2 for details). In its original, unevolved state, Nature is called "unmanifest" from which the manifest world emerges in the presence of multiple, unchanging Spirits (though multiplicity of Spirit is likely a later development in the school). The process of differentiation is the result of the way in which the three *guṇa*s are related to each other so that we have a world of what the *Upaniṣads* might call "name and form." The difference of course is that the unmanifest in the *Saṁkhya Karika* is purely material whereas in the

Gītā we are told that there is a lower (and likely material) unmanifest that is subordinate to a higher, unchanging spiritual unmanifest precisely because it is eternal and indestructible (*BG* 8.20–22)—a view that seems continuous with that of the *Upaniṣads* on the priority of higher over lower *Brahman*. Nor is this simply the only instance where the highest spiritual principle is discussed as unmanifest, for this language is present in the very first discussion of *Brahman* in the *Gītā* and beyond (*BG* 2.18, 2.27, 9.4, 13.5). Thus, the *Gītā* seems to attempt a reconciliation of the Saṁkhya dualism with Upanishadic monism, something which we will have occasion to assess later in this chapter.

But it is time now to turn our attention to how this discussion of the unmanifest relates to *bhakti yoga*, the key discussion of which is in Book 12. Leading up to this discussion in Book 11, we see Krishna revealing himself as the manifest universe to Arjuna (*BG* 11.15–16). This extraordinary vision encapsulates not just the physical universe, but the pantheon of Gods, demons, semi-divine beings, and humans in all their glory, the description of which takes up much of the Book. Arjuna is shaken to the core, but insightfully asks Krishna whether the yoga of worshipping the manifest (*bhakti yoga*) or that of pursuing the unmanifest (*sannyāsa* or *dhyāna yoga*) leads to the fullest knowledge (*BG* 12.1)? It is important to see that Arjuna's question arises for him despite his vision precisely because the tradition has always prioritized the pursuit of the unmanifest (and likely because the vision is not the same as the sage's insight since he sees it separate from himself). Moreover, while the *Gītā*'s general message seems to be that all paths lead to knowledge and freedom, it does not prevent the text from emphasizing one path at the expense of another in particular instances as it does the path of action (broadly construed) here (*BG* 12.12). But even as it does so, it does not deny the claims of the path that is concerned with the unmanifest (i.e., *sannyāsa* or *dhyāna yoga*), and has this to say in *BG* 12.5:

> The trouble of those whose minds
> Are fixed on the unmanifest are greater,
> For the goal of the unmanifest is attained
> With difficulty by embodied beings.

It is hard indeed for embodied beings (that therefore have what the *Upaniṣads* call "name and form") to know that which is unmanifest (and therefore without name and form). Much easier for many more of the embodied to pursue the Divine as manifest than as unmanifest, especially since Arjuna's vision clearly suggests that insights into key aspects of the Divine as unmanifest are plausible. Thus, Arjuna sees that the Divine is infinite in form (*BG* 12.16) and therefore more than the world that rests within It (*BG* 12.18); and describes the Divine as imperishable and beyond being, in language usually reserved for the unmanifest (*BG* 12.37).[4] Herein, then, lies the core of the *Gītā*'s rationale for the push to *Bhakti* especially in the face of Buddhist populism. If, as we saw in our earlier discussions of the *Gītā*, the life of action requires an embodied standard of right action like the good king Janaka who personifies the abstract principle of world-welfare, the personification of the Divine first principle in the *Gītā* of course is Krishna. Considered together, *karma* and *bhakti yoga* along with *jñāna yoga* truly make access to knowledge and hence freedom universal.

8.3 The Grounds for the Equalization of *Saṁkhya* and *Yoga*

Yet, and this is crucial, the *Gītā* is not simply saying that its version of universal access via multiple paths/*yoga*s is true; to do so, as we will now examine, it explicitly turns early Buddhism's views on the nature of action on its head.

Towards the end of Book 2 of the *Gītā* and following on the important presentation of how Arjuna should undertake *karma yoga* with detachment, Krishna describes the stable sage at Arjuna's behest (*BG* 2.54–72). This description involves, among other things, a discussion of the sage's self-control, intelligence, and focus, in ways that suggest Krishna is speaking of the life of renunciation rather than that of action (*BG* 2.66–67). This confuses Arjuna so that at the beginning of Book 3 he asks Krishna to clarify whether in fact he is speaking of the path of action or of renunciation. Krishna's response begins with a reminder of the distinction between the theoretical/Saṁkhya approach (which as we saw is renunciatory) and the one of Practical/Yoga (which is the life of action broadly construed to include *karma* and *bhakti yoga*). Yet his considered response in Book 3 to Arjuna's question seems to be that the distinction is ultimately provisional, and his central argument for this position can be found in 3.4–5:

> Not from abstaining from actions
> Does a man attain the state beyond karma,
> And not by renunciation (*saṁnyāsa)* alone
> Does he obtain perfection.
>
> Indeed, no one, even in the twinkling of an eye,
> Ever exists without performing action;

Everyone is forced to perform action,
even action which is against his will,
By the strands (*guṇas*) which originate in material nature

We have seen this line of argument in the specific context of *karma yoga* in chapter 5, but here we can see that the application is much broader. The *Gītā* seems to re-conceive the Buddha's views on incessant change in terms of the *guṇas* and asks us to think about the implications for the life of renunciation. While it is true that renunciation implies walking away from one's obligations in the world to work, family and society, the *Gītā* points out that this does not mean that such a life is without any action, especially if the world and all its constituents are constantly in flux. Thus, even sense-control, breathing, eating, and meditating are all actions so that no living being can stop action completely (*BG* 3.6–8, 6.2). If so, the difference between the Saṁkhya and Yoga, or the life of renunciation and that of action, when it comes to knowledge and freedom really amounts to a difference in the kinds of actions undertaken; but then it would seem that the wholesale recommendation to renounce the world in early Buddhism is unnecessary.

Moreover, if action is the common denominator of all the paths, then it would seem each path has different prescribed actions that, according to the *Gītā*, need to be undertaken in a particular way if it is to lead to knowledge and freedom. In the case of *karma yoga*, we saw in chapters 4 and 5 that the path entails living up to one's *dharm*ic obligations with detachment, which is paralleled by *bhakti yoga*, as I suggested above. The path of knowledge or renunciation is similarly discussed in the text, even as we are told that it traverses the path of action first for most of us (*BG* 5.6). This is because, as we saw, the stage-and-station schema requires working through the various stages of life (which presupposes *dharm*ic activity of one sort or the other) before one can renounce the world and walk away from it. If undertaken properly, *dharm*ic activity provides the opportunity to develop sense-control and intellectual restraint that is crucial for meditative endeavors (*BG* 4.39, 5.28). The activity of meditation itself is discussed rather quickly since it is discussed fully elsewhere in more specialized texts. Here we are told that meditation involves withdrawing to isolated places, sitting motionless (presumably in a lotus posture), and focusing the mind on a single object while breathing in a regulated fashion in ways that ultimately culminate in knowledge and insight (*BG* 6.10–15).

Since our focus here is not on the details of the technique involved in the path to knowledge but on knowledge itself, the following needs to be kept in mind. Recall that we have seen the negative dimension of such knowledge in the context of chapter 5, which involves the key insight that there is no enduring self that acts. Rather, what we have is strands/*guṇa*s acting on *guṇa*s so that the sage acts in harmony with the *guṇa*-constituted world precisely because there is the recognition of deep continuities with it. This is not to deny that such negative knowledge is a function of an intellect/*buddhi* working in consort with a mind-will/*manas* and an ego-sense/*ahamkāra* that constitute the embodied doer/*kartā*. The positive dimension of such knowledge is knowledge of the Higher Self/*Ātman*, which we postponed in 5.2 since it requires an understanding of the relation of the Higher Self/*Ātman* to the Universal Self/*Brahman*, and to which we turn next. But before we do, it is important to see that the knowledge that the text repeatedly tells us that the Higher Self/*Ātman* has of itself (what I call "Self-Knowledge") is distinct from the knowledge (or self-knowledge) that the lower self/*deha* has of the Self (which is, of course, the *deha*'s Self). After all, not only is Self-Knowledge the unchanging, essential nature of the Higher Self/*Ātman*, whereas self-knowledge is arrived at by a lower self/*deha* at the end of the path that seeks such knowledge. This distinction will hopefully allow us to solve some crucial problems arising in chapter 8 section 5.

8.4 The Nature of Knowledge

The advantage of maintaining an ultimate separation between Higher Self/*Ātman* and the Universal Self/*Brahman* is that it allows for a real distinction between the enjoyer and the enjoyed (conceived as the Highest Good). This in turn is key for the path of devotion/*bhakti yoga* which conceives the devotee and their devotion separately from the object of devotion (i.e., God). Unfortunately, as we saw above in chapter 8 section 2, the *Gītā* seems intent on maintaining Upanishadic monism so that an ultimate (i.e., transcendental) distinction between *Ātman* and *Brahman* seems implausible even if we will have to see if a provisional separation is not. Nor is an ultimate separation plausible at the empirical level for the same reason, and especially since we have seen that the *Gītā* agrees with early Buddhism in holding that the lower self/*deha* and even the doer/*kartā* is provisional especially post-insight. We will therefore have cause to assess the implications of the *Gītā*'s metaphysics here to fully understand the implications for *bhakti* (in the next section). Yet the main problem here seems to be misconstruing lower self-knowledge for Higher Self-Knowledge since the latter (*qua Ātman*) is persistent whereas the former is not. So let us examine the textual basis for this distinction before we see how eliding it is the cause of much difficulty. Once we have established the above distinction, we can then speak to the relation of Higher Self/*Ātman* and the Universal Self/*Brahman*.

One would think that self-knowledge is had by the agent/*deha* at the broadest level, since it is the agent that acts in the world and pursues knowledge. But it is the intellect/*buddhi* specifically that undertakes the task of obtaining the truth, a truth that is beyond the reach of the senses yet presupposes sense-control (*BG* 6.21, 12.8). But the intellect is not a free-standing faculty since it works in relation with the mind/*manas* and I-sense/*ahamkāra*, and the agent on the other hand does not transmigrate, whereas we have seen that self-knowledge ends transmigration (*BG* 14.26).[5] Since transmigration applies to the doer/*kartā*, it is to the doer that we would want to contextualize such knowledge in relation to the relevant considerations of freedom/*mokṣa*. Still, while the text insists that such a doer persists until death (*BG* 7.29–30, 8.5), we should not take this to mean that self-knowledge is not immediately transformative; after all, we saw, for instance, that it involves knowing that action is a function of strands acting on strands. Thus, the language of "self-knowledge" should be understood in context for it clearly involves an awareness that the self or doer is not ultimate. At the same time, there is a deep recognition that strands acting on strands is universally pervasive, and that such activity is guided by cosmological laws that are continuous with *dharmic* law so that the ensuing knowledge of the world (which is a part of self-knowledge) is wide-ranging yet unified (*BG* 18.20).

A similar expansion of self-knowledge from the bodily to Nature more broadly construed is evident in Book 13, where the discussion speaks analogically of the body as the Field (*BG* 13.1) but quickly expands to include the material world (*BG* 13.19–20). Such self-knowledge specifically includes knowledge/*jñāna* of the Field-Knower or *Puruṣa*/*Ātman* (*BG* 13.2), which I take to be distinct from *Ātman*'s Self-Knowledge (and which I discuss more fully below). So it would seem that the self-knowledge of the doer/*kartā* involves knowledge of the Field (that is of itself and the world) and the Field-Knower (*Ātman*/*Puruṣa*) in ways that are empowered by the *Ātman* so that:

> … for those in whom this ignorance of the Self
> Is destroyed by knowledge,
> That knowledge of theirs
> Causes the Supreme [Self] to shine like the Sun
>
> (*BG* 5.16)

A more accurate translation of the last two lines reads: "Their knowledge like the sun illuminates that Highest," which is more elegant but also makes the implicit point more clearly: the self's knowledge is illuminating for the self precisely because it is of the Self which is auto-luminous (see also *BG* 10.11). It reveals not only that one is not (an ultimate) self, but simultaneously, that one is the Self, a recognition that allows the self to become transparent to itself. Such an insight is no easy thing even if it is available to every path; yet for all paths it is plausible only because in every instance, and in accordance with different methods, the *kartā* is stilled as much as is possible for something that is part of an ever-changing Nature so that it approximates the unchanging activity of *Ātman* that is internally available to all (*BG* 2.53, 6.27, 12.8, 14.19). This positive dimension of the stilling where the *Ātman* is an anchor and lodestar to the lower self therefore complements what is said in chapter 5 sections 8–9, which has to do with *guṇa* reconfiguration so that *sattva* is predominant. It is this stilling coupled with the inward contemplation of *Ātman*, then, that is responsible for the immediate if epistemological undermining of agency that eventually ends transmigration at death. Such an end is to be understood in terms of a permanent disentanglement of the strands that constitute the doer/*kartā* rather than their ultimate destruction, as one would expect given the *Gītā*'s views on Nature/*Prakrati*.[6] While such understanding is generally called "knowledge" (*jñāna*) by the text, it is more appropriately termed "discrimination" or "insight" (*vijñāna*) when the text wants to distinguish a theoretical understanding from a living realization (*BG* 6.8, 7.2ff, 9.1).[7]

From everything we have seen so far, it is clear that knowing is not restricted to the *Ātman*/*Puruṣa* as later views on this matter would have it.[8] This is unsurprising since it is the empirical person who acts, and it is the doer/*kartā* that knows and is freed by such knowledge through a process of dissolution by insight (not unlike what we see in early Buddhism). When the text therefore says that desire, feeling, and the entire theater of consciousness that involves the body and thinking constitutes modifications of the field (*BG* 13.6), I take it to mean such experience is also had *by* the field rather than by the Field-Knower. Such a view is consistent with the *Gītā*'s reference to the empirical person whose mind and intellect are affected by the emotions, and who attains tranquillity through self-control (*BG* 2.52–64, for instance). This in turn allows us to maintain the integrity of *Ātman*'s unchanging Self-Knowledge even if it raises another puzzle about how such knowledge of the field can be excluded from the First Principle's Self-Knowledge within the context of the *Gītā*'s monism (setting aside for the moment the exact nature of the *Ātman-Brahman* relation). In fact, the text says that the *Ātman*/*Puruṣa* that abides in nature with a body does have or causes experiences (*BG* 13.20–21); and it also tells us that this is a semblance (*ābhāsam*) of what "experience" normally means since Ātman is in essence free from the *guṇas* (*BG* 13.14). I take "semblance" here to mean not that it appears to experience, but that *Puruṣa* therefore experiences in a very different way that does not include the modality of time (which applies within the realm of the *guṇas*) that is essentially mysterious to us. This would, I think, also explain how Self-Knowledge constitutes the nature of the Higher Self/*Ātman* (*BG* 3.37–42,[9] 5.15–16) which would otherwise be problematic since we are also told that the Self is no doer (*BG* 2.22, 2.30, 13.29–31, 14.19, etc.). Since activity is usually understood to occur within space and time which do not apply here, *Ātman*'s Self-Knowledge cannot be understood in terms of regular activity. Such Self-Knowledge is also a semblance of self-knowledge in another way since the Self's luminosity that presumably makes such Self-Knowledge possible is mysteriously responsible for the conscious activity in self-knowledge. I will say more on the nature of this mysteriousness when we address the ontological dimension of this epistemological phenomenon below.

8.5 The *Ātman-Brahman* Relation

What we see emerging in the context of the *Gītā*'s attempt to maintain the Upanishadic substance monism is an aspect dualism so that *Brahman* is both matter and spirit, even if it is yet unclear how that dualism might work. What is clear is that we have multiplicity and agency, pleasure and pain, and experience and freedom in the material context in the main. But if the unity of *Puruṣa* and *Prakrati* is hard to understand, matters are further complicated if *Puruṣa* itself is divisible or multiplex, at least from the point of view of maintaining the kind of unity that the *Gītā* envisions.

One important suggestion in the tradition by Rāmānuja has been to conceive *Ātman* as a mode of *Brahman* based on what is called "coordinate predication," which ironically enough, is a concept original to Śaṇkara's commentary (cf. *BGB* 2.16). Rāmānuja points out that cognition of the world by the knowing Self (*jiva/Ātman*) occurs simultaneously with that of its body. That is, when I see a table, I perceive myself as a body that perceives the table. Yet because it is possible for me to perceive the body (for example, when I say I am skinny), he thinks that the knowing Self cannot be reduced to the body even if perception is predicated both of the body and of the Self. But such coordinate predication/*sāmānādhikaraṇya* suggests that a distinction between the Self and the body is plausible as is their eventual separating and provides a model for *Brahman*'s (or who Rāmānuja calls

Iśvara's) relation to the world. For *Iśvara* is the ultimate subject of such coordinate predication so that it is not unreasonable to say that what is predicated (or is a mode) of my or any other Self, or anything else for that matter, is simultaneously predicated of Him (*RGB* 13.0). The nature of this relationship between *Iśvara* and everything else is expressed in terms of the mind and body (*RGB* 3.27–29), or that which controls (*śeṣin*) and that which is controlled (*śeṣaṇa*) (*RGB* 7.7). The elegance of this solution has to do with how Rāmānuja manages to find unity while maintaining diversity by reducing everything to modes of a single, organic substance. The mind/body analogy is not exact since *Iśvara*'s relation to the world as his body is mediated by individual Selves/*jivas*/*Ātmans* which are distinguishable from Him and from the material world (*RGB* 5.14, 15.16–17). Thus, we have *Brahman* as a unity that is qualified by attributes so that it is not, as Rāmānuja's predecessor, Śaṇkara suggests, undifferentiated.

Several issues arise from even this short presentation of Rāmānuja's views on the *Ātman-Brahman* relation, but I will focus on just two. First, that he does not really show how the mind and body are related as a unity, as much as he assumes the unity to make the larger point about the relation of *Iśvara* to the world. In fact he acknowledges the lack of explanation when he says that the relationship is unique and has no parallel anywhere (*RGB* 9.5). This by itself is not a problem, since he simply follows the *Gītā* in saying so, as we will see. Nor is he the first to use uniqueness as the basis of the inexplicability of the relation between *Brahman* and the world, since Śaṇkara uses it as well, as we will also see. The bigger problem arises because Rāmānuja seems to want to have his cake and eat it too. It is important for Rāmānuja to maintain a distinction between *Ātman* and *Brahman* (or in his language, between *jiva* and *Iśvara*) since his emphasis is on the path of devotion/*bhakti yoga*. Devotion, after all, presupposes a devotee distinct from God who is the object of devotion. One would think it is hard to see how a distinction might work in the context of the *Gītā*'s monism, which is precisely what Rāmānuja thinks he has accomplished with coordinate predication. The problem is that it is hard to see how *Ātman* as an attribute or mode of *Brahman* is really distinct from Him in the appropriate fashion. While it is true that an attribute or mode is distinct from that of which it is an attribute, it does not seem distinct enough to allow for autonomous activity of a devotee towards her God. For example, my brownness is a mode or attribute of my substance, but it certainly cannot get sunburned on its own volition. Rāmānuja's response is that the omnipotent God allows his subjects the freedom to act (*RGB* 18.15); if so, it seems to undermine Rāmānuja's philosophical work to explain the *Ātman-Brahman* relationship in terms of the subject-predicate relation by taking recourse to God's infinite power to do whatever He wants.[10]

So, it would seem that on our view, the *Gītā*'s aspect dualism may not allow for the undermining of the *Ātman-Brahman* identity. Such a view may seem like Śaṇkara's interpretation of the text which maintains the *Ātman-Brahman* identity at its core (*BGB* 9.10, 13.2, 15.7), but is not, since he denies aspect dualism. That is, Śaṇkara thinks that the world is the product of appearance/*māyā* and not material Nature/*Prakrati* so that while they look the same, they are actually very different, ontologically speaking (*BGB* 7.11). Thus, many readers have equated *māyā* with illusion and some of things that Śaṇkara himself says encourages this view, even if it is not entirely accurate (*BGB* 13.2, pp. 323–34, 13.31). In fact, it might be closer to the truth to suggest that Śaṇkara's views resemble a form of absolute idealism (where everything is reducible to the mind and its ideas); for he also says that *māyā* is constituted by ignorance which is clearly a mental phenomenon and that *Brahman* is pure, undifferentiated consciousness (*BGB* 5.19, 13.27, 13.2 p. 321, pp. 331–32). Even so, Śaṇkara tells us elsewhere that the relation between *Brahman* and *māyā* (which constitutes the world) is unique since all relations in experience are within *māyā* and which therefore has no analogue (for a related suggestion, see *BGB* 13.2 pp. 332–34). This admission is important because it is hard for Śaṇkara to explain how *Brahman* can remain unchanging when *māyā* clearly does not; nor can he easily explain the locus of *māyā* as distinct from *Brahman* since nothing exists besides *Brahman* on his view. Thus, Śaṇkara too, like Rāmānuja after him, thinks the relation between Brahman and the world is mysterious—though for very different reasons. We cannot go into all the details of Śaṇkara's position here (nor of its various interpretations), but we can easily see that despite these issues it avoids one important problem of aspect dualism: namely, how exactly *Puruṣa* and *Prakrati* relate to each other, since on his view *Prakrati* is simply continuous in nature in some way with *Puruṣa* (*BGB* 14.3).

The problem is Śaṇkara's reading comes at a high price that we may not be willing to pay. We have already seen that the *Gītā*, in responding to the proto-Saṁkhya, seems to deny substance dualism even while accepting that Nature/*Prakrati* is the material aspect of *Brahman*. Even early Buddhism, while denying that anything persists in the world (including the *guṇa*s), seems committed to a causal understanding of material nature. While the *Upaniṣad*s are generally committed to monism, they do not seem to make a hard distinction between matter and spirit nor do they therefore seem to be committed to idealism, for these distinctions come much later (see Appendix 2 for details). Yet even though Śaṇkara thinks that the world is not ultimately real, he does not want to deny that all our social commitments stay in place so long as there is no self-realization, which is consistent with what the *Gītā* says. Even so, his view differs from mine in that Śaṇkara emphasizes renunciation of the world since for him the path of knowledge is the only way to freedom; for on his view *Ātman* (which is identical to *Brahman*) always has Self-Knowledge so that no action is involved in something that has always been the case (*BGB* 6.2–4). Such a view seems problematic because it moves from the empirical level (where there is ignorance) to the transcendent (where there is none) at the moment of insight while denying just this movement. Whereas on the view I espouse in the previous section, self-knowledge is an action since the world is constantly in flux, even if Self-Knowledge is not.

It is because Śaṇkara denies that knowledge involves action, that he breaks with the *Gītā* (or at least on my reading of it) which allows multiple paths to freedom precisely because they involve action. In the process of so doing, he makes clear that his commitments to the world parallels his understanding of its lack of ontological ultimacy. The implications are particularly paradoxical for the realized individual for whom there does not seem to be any place despite all of Śaṇkara's efforts to the contrary, since on his view there is no distinction between the eternally unchanging *Brahman* and *Ātman*, and ignorance/*māyā* is overcome at insight.[11]

On the view that I espouse here, there is a place for the material world in the *Gītā*'s aspect dualism precisely because *Puruṣa* and *Prakrati* are distinct aspects of *Brahman*. On this view, it is because the world and the individuals in it are an important aspect of *Brahman* that Krishna (*qua Puruṣa*) manifests as an *avatar* to fix the world's problems (I will say more on this issue below); and it is for the same reason that the principle of world-welfare/*loksamgraya* is the highest principle of all action in it, and the universal renunciation of the world—*contra* early Buddhism—is resisted. This aspect dualism is mysterious not because as in Cartesian dualism, we have two different kinds of substances (immaterial soul and material body) interacting in ways that are hard to understand, but because we have a single substance that has these two seemingly distinct aspects (and is therefore closer to Spinoza's version). The advantage of the *Gītā*'s position over Descartes' is that internal aspect interaction seems less incommensurable than trying to relate two very different substances. Even so, the text itself acknowledges that this internal relation between *Puruṣa* and *Prakrati* is mysterious (*BG* 9.2), though it does suggest some ways for us to think about it in the early part of Book 9. So, we should at best expect to understand why the internal relations of *Brahman* are mysterious to us even if that is not the same as understanding or resolving the mystery. In so doing, we are following the tradition established by Śaṇkara and Rāmānuja who think that the relation is mysterious even if they do not faithfully conceive the relation (at least in the *Gītā*) in terms of *Puruṣa* and *Prakrati* as I attempt to do below.[12]

Here then is what we see in the early part of Book 9 regarding the relation between the spiritual and material: (a) the unmanifest *Brahman* pervades the material universe (*BG* 9.4.1–2); (b) that all (material) beings abide in, and are supported by, *Brahman* but not vice versa (*BG* 9.4.3–4, 9.5.3); (c) and yet in some way all beings do not abide in Brahman (*BG* 9.5.1); (d) and that the relationship of Brahman to beings is that of space/aether/*ākaśa* to an all-penetrating wind (*BG* 9.6); (e) that the unmanifest is unchanging, indifferent, and oversees material nature (*BG* 9.9–10). The language of pervasion (*tatam*) and abiding (*matsthāni*) should not be taken to mean that the interaction is the same as that of space to wind; rather, that it is like that but not quite that since wind is in space in ways that the material beings are not in immaterial *Brahman*, as (c) suggests. The point of course is that *Brahman* as unmanifest is not in space, nor in time as we saw earlier and as (e) suggests, in contrast to the material world. Thus, it would seem that the mysteriousness of the interaction for us has to do with the fact that explicable interactions concern entities that are in space and time. If we think about this ontological relationship in epistemological terms, we see why from the point of view of self-knowledge, what we get is at best an approximation of Self-Knowledge. For Self-Knowledge is the immediate, unchanging, and complete grasp that *Brahman* as *Puruṣa* has of itself and of *Prakrati* that is beyond space and time (*BG* 4.13, 13.29). Whereas self-knowledge of one's own Higher Self/*Ātman* (which is not distinct from *Brahman*), and which is had by the doer/*kartā* is in space and time (*BG* 6.20–21).

It is difficult to say more about the experience of Self-Knowledge from the perspective of mere self-knowledge, though we could say more about its implications for the individual, based on what the *Gītā* itself says. The steadfastness of the sage of stable insight (*sthitprajñaya*) is presumably the result of a stable intellect that approximates the state of *Ātman*'s Self-Knowledge (*BG* 2.51–72). Such stability is rare since change is the norm in the *Gītā*'s *guṇa*-based understanding of the world and is clearly anchored by the deep connection established in meditation between the sage and their *Ātman*. It is the contrast between the abiding *Ātman* and the changeful world, then, that perhaps provides the break in futurity of that doer and hence to freedom as it comes to terms with its lack of a persistent self (*BG* 13.23–25). Moreover, the even-mindedness of the sage is itself conferred by insight that consolidates the extensive practice of sense and mind control that the *Gītā* emphasizes. Thus, it would seem that it is in finding internal stability (distinct from finding an abiding self) that one comes to see the deep instability in all things that in turn leads to the eventual, permanent undermining of the doer. After all, the world otherwise provides no unchanging, stable context within which it is possible to see the incessant change within ourselves—and seems to be a possible way to think of what the *Gītā* takes to be a critical flaw in early Buddhism's theory of universal flux. In this sense, then, such self-knowledge (of the world and of the Self) is deeply impersonal since it involves insight into the workings of the I-sense/*ahamkāra* in relation to the intellect/*buddhi* and the mind/*manas*—and exemplifies one sense of what it means for knowledge to be objective.

This internal re-ordering imposed by the various *yoga*s that leads to self-knowledge runs parallel to Krishna's manifestation as an *avatar* to prevent the world from descending into chaos and gives us additional insight into the *Gītā*'s views on the *Puruṣa-Prakrati* relation. Krishna says that he is *Brahman* manifest in the world when *dharma*/law languishes in it (*BG* 4.7–8). The breakdown of the moral law (which I suggested is continuous with the cosmological one for the tradition) perhaps represents the crux of the relationship between the immaterial and material aspects of *Brahman*. Presumably, the process of the evolution of the world at the pinnace of its development represents a state of complete differentiation and cosmological (and *dharm*ic) order from which there is a gradual but inevitable decline. Such a decline (described in more detail in the later *Saṁkhya Karika*) leads to a state of devolution where the *guṇa*s exist in separation from each other (*BG* 2.28, 8.18). Interestingly enough, the *Mahābhārata* (in which, it should be remembered, the *Gītā* is ensconced), following tradition, speaks of the state of the world (and not just in terms of the Saṁkhya world view), and the stage of perfection (both *dharm*ic and cosmological) in particular as the Age of Excellence/*Krita Yuga*. In contrast, the age of *Kāli* is the last of four stages before the world is destroyed and returns to a state of disorder (or the unmanifest *prakriti*, on the *Gītā*'s view)[13] from which it re-emerges after a period in what the tradition says is an eternal, repetitive process. Each stage of the decline is not just cosmological but moral, political, and social as well. The dramatic date of the *Gītā* (and the *Mahābhārata*) puts it at the cusp of the third (*Dvapara*) and fourth (*Kāli*) age,[14] and therefore presents Krishna's remarks about preventing chaos in an interesting light. It suggests that while universal cosmological and moral perfection is no longer an option as in the *Krita Yuga*, staving off chaos presents an interesting opportunity: to either live up to *dharma* or not in ways that the different *yoga*s allow, so that internal harmony is the result of concerted individual choice and action. In fact, individual effort mirrors Krishna's own work in the face of the inevitable cosmic entropy, on which I say more in the conclusion below.[15]

8.6 Concluding Considerations

It could be objected that on this view the *Ātman*/*Brahman* identity undermines the plausibility of *bhakti yoga* which in turn weakens the overall reading, given the importance of devotion/*bhakti* in the text. After all, if the *Ātman* is not separable from *Brahman*, and the latter is the essence of every doer/*kartā*, then a viable distinction between God and devotee is hard to maintain. Such an objection is consistent with what was said in chapter 7, where following Śaṇkara, on my reading *bhakti yoga* does not have the same status as *jñāna* and *karma yoga*. I will attempt to nuance my view here to better explain why *bhakti yoga* has the standing it does in the text and suggest what it may be responding to in the ongoing discussions.

To be fair, there is a separation between Higher Self/*Ātman* and doer/*kartā* on my reading, even if there is not between *Ātman* and *Brahman*. This is a real separation insofar as the Self and the doer represent two different aspects of *Brahman* so that a plausible distinction between God and devotee can in fact be maintained. The problem is that the devotee *qua* doer does not persist post-freedom/*mokṣa* as she does on Rāmānuja's reading (even if his view has problems defending the doer's autonomy, as we saw above in section 5). The lack of persistence post-freedom approximates early Buddhism's understanding of *nirvana* as the annihilation of the self, and therefore does not allow for such freedom to be understood as existence on a super-mundane level as in traditional theism. But it is unclear if this consideration is persuasive, given that such persistence seems to have gained prominence in the context of much later developments in the tradition of *bhakti* that are closer in time to Rāmānuja many centuries later than they are to the *Gītā*. After all, if the *Gītā* is responding to early Buddhism (which is atheistic) and the early Upaniṣadic tradition (which is not obviously theistic in the main), then we need to say a little more about how even this nascent devotional theism arises in the text.

The responsible party is often thought to be the *Svetāśvtāra Upaniṣad (SV)* which is likely written prior to but in the same time period as the *Gītā*. Like the earlier *Upaniṣads* there is substantial evidence here of a spiritual monism, of the identity of *Brahman* and *Ātman* (*SV* 5.3, 6.12) as well as of their separation (*SV* 1.8), of striving via meditation to obtain freedom (*SV* 2.8–10), of *Brahman* being hidden and devoid of qualities, etc. (*SV* 6.11). We also see old Vedic themes of adoration of the Gods for wish fulfillment (*SV* 4.11), and what Max Muller has called henotheism (of temporarily raising one God above all others) (*SV* 1.4, 3.4). In addition, we see it speak of the world in terms of the *guṇas* and use the term "*Saṁkhya*" as theoretical understanding as in the *Gītā* (*SV* 5.5, 5.7,

6.13), as well as a likely reference to the founder of the Saṁkhya school Kapilla (*SV* 5.2)—all of these Saṁkhyan elements have led scholars to believe that it is a later *Upaniṣad*. But we also see a persistent and overriding theism where *Brahman* is spoken of as the Supreme God of Gods, creator, and protector (*SV* 4.13, 6.16–17); and interestingly enough, a hint of *bhakti* when the text tells us that only those who have the deepest love of God can see Him (*SV* 6.23). As suggested above, adoration of divinities in exchange for worldly favors is as old as the *Vedas*, but the love of God with the sole intention of seeing Him is new, even if it is not developed in the *Svetāśvatāra Upaniṣhad* as it is in the *Gītā*.

Bhakti in the *Gītā* involves a personal relation with *Brahman*, made possible by Krishna as *avatar* so that this *yoga* personalizes detachment. The devotee acts for the sake of the Lord and is driven by intense love and devotion to him (*BG* 12.9, 18.62, 65–66). Book 11, as we saw, presents us with the awe-inspiring vision of Krishna as the cosmos and beyond so that the discussion of devotion that follows is not merely abstract. If the *Gītā* seems to suggest that the principle of world-welfare is too abstract so that we need someone like King Janaka as the exemplar of *karma yoga*, then Krishna is the personification of divinity that becomes the focal point of love and devotion in *bhakti yoga*. Both therefore fall under the practical (as opposed to theoretical) approach to freedom by offering a way of acting without concern for personal fruit, as we saw in chapter 7 section 6, and therefore with detachment.

Yet there are important differences between *bhakti* and *karma yoga* as well, the key one being the place of emotion (and especially love) in these paths. This is very clear in the later tradition, where the devotee's relationship with Krishna is not cerebral; that is, it is not the result of a rational decision to love God. Rather, love is an upwelling of emotion often inspired by stories of the lives of the *avatars* (as found in the *Bhagavad Purana*, for instance) that are handed down from generation to generation in a lived tradition. In *karma yoga*, on the other hand, we saw a concerted effort in chapters 4 and 5 to downplay emotion by reducing desire through self-control so that the detached sage/*karma yogin* is eventually without desire and emotion.[16] Thus by emphasizing the direct, emotional relationship with God in *bhakti yoga* the *Gītā* seems intent on diminishing the role of the priestly middleman (parallel to what happens in later western Christian Protestantism), and thereby makes an important point. That is, if *karma yoga* opens access to ultimate freedom/*mokṣa* in ways that *jñāna yoga* does not, it is still too cerebral and austere to appeal to everyone. Whereas if the Buddhist threat is to be met so that the orthodox tradition can also offer genuinely universal access to freedom, the *Gītā* thinks that the emotions should not be eliminated but transformed by love in the way that *bhakti yoga* makes possible. Part of the appeal here is not just that there is a place for the emotions in this path, but that the devotee-Divine relationship accentuates their distinctness and the Divine's otherness in ways that are ultimately made irrelevant by insight into the truth that freedom/*mokṣa* brings. For in freedom there is recognition that the Self is not ultimately Other as it is the Self of all existence and is in fact the only Persistent, even as this recognition itself is not.[17]

The fullest flower of *bhakti* in the *Gītā* does not bear fruit until much later in the tradition, as mentioned earlier, when it is developed in a variety of ways.[18] But a more immediate impact might have been felt in Buddhism, where *bhakti* may have been partly responsible for the transformation of the ideal Buddhist sage/*arhat* to the adored and worshipped *bodhisattva*. For the *arhat*'s central characteristic is dispassion (which parallels how the *jñāna yogin* is characterized in the orthodox tradition) but makes way for a new ideal of the compassionate *bodhisattva* who acts to mitigate the suffering of all sentient beings—and does so out of love.

Notes

1 Thus *BG* 6.7 distinguishes Higher *Ātman* from *Ātman* so that the latter usage is traditionally taken to either mean the mind (in Rāmānuja) or the equivalent of the doer/*kartā* (in Śaṇkara).

2 Hence the suggestion that to emphasize one over—and hence explain away—the other is to undertake eisegesis as opposed to exegesis, according to Keith E. Yandell, "On Interpreting the 'Bhagavadgītā,'" *Philosophy East and West* 32, no. 1 (1982): 37–46. In my reading, I therefore try to walk a line between Śaṇkara and Rāmānuja so as to attempt a reconciliation.

3 See Daya Krishna, "Is Īśvara Kṛṣṇa's Sāṁkhya Kārikā Really Sāṁkhyan?," in *Indian Philosophy: A Counter Perspective*, by Daya Krishna (Oxford: Oxford University Press, 1991), 147, 153.

4 But note that the description offered up here is by the narrator Sanjaya, as the text very deliberately indicates, and therefore from an external point of view, rather than that, say, of a sage. This would explain why the vision does not constitute Arjuna's liberation even if it describes what Arjuna (and Sanjaya) see.

5 Perhaps this is why when Śaṇkara acknowledges that self-knowledge is had by someone other than the Self/*Ātman*, which he explicitly does in his commentary to *BG* 2.21, where he is speaking of the Self as seen by the mind/*manas* which I take to be representative of the doer/*kartā*. See *BGB* 46.

6 Thus Clooney is right to point out that Hegel is corrected by Madhusūdhana Saraswatī when he says that Self-Knowledge is not empty but is of consciousness. But on my reading at least, the inward stilling that is self-knowledge also has more content besides *Ātman* since it includes what I am calling "disentanglement" as opposed to mere emptiness that persists even with the outward turn. See Francis X. Clooney, "Much Ado About Nothing?," *The Owl of Minerva* 52, no. 1 (2021): 51–71.

7 I follow Śaṇkara in making this distinction between knowledge and discrimination (see *BGB* 188 and 240), though not everyone agrees with it, notably Aurobindo. I say more about issues arising from this denial below in section 5.

8 Thus, for the *Saṁkhya Karika*, the human being conceived in terms of *prakrati* only appears to know, whereas for Śaṇkara, the world itself is an appearance along with any knowledge in it and of it.

9 Following Radhakrihsnan in taking "*tenedam*" in 3.38.4 to refer to the *dehin*/Self in 3.40.4, rather than referring to the Universe (Edgerton) or the intellect (Sargent).

10 See Matthew D. MacKenzie, "The Five Factors of Action and the Decentring of Agency in the Bhagavad Gītā," *Asian Philosophy* 11, no. 3 (November 1, 2001): 145, who agrees that Rāmānuja is inconsistent in suggesting that God grants his subjects permission to act since determinism is the natural outcome of his view. Even so, it is unclear to me that this kind of theistic view that ultimately resolves into some version of grace is not anachronistic, since theism of the sort that is coupled with a fervent *bhakti* is many centuries in the future, as I have already suggested.

11 I have attempted to sympathetically motivate Śaṇkara's views in my "Śaṇkara on Action and Liberation," *Asian Philosophy* 17, no. 3 (November 1, 2007): 231–49. Such a view, as I say above, requires accepting that the world lacks ontological ultimacy in ways that do not seem to sit well with what I take to be the *Gītā*'s views on the matter.

12 I think therefore that Franklin Edgerton, *The Bhagavad Gita* (Cambridge, MA: Harvard University Press, 1997), 42–43, is right to suggest that Śaṇkara's extreme idealistic monism is not present in the *Gītā* though his dualistic reading differs from my substance monism and aspect dualism.

13 The unmanifest/*avyaktam* is used to refer to *Brahman*'s unchanging higher self (see *BG* 2.25, 7.24, 9.4, 12.1, 12.5 and esp. 8.20–21) as well as to its devolved lower state to which the world reduces and then evolves from again (see *BG* 2.8 and esp. 8.18).

14 See the *Adi Parva* Section 2, Vyāsa, Kisari Mohan Ganguli, *The Mahābhārata of Krishna-Dwaipayana Vyasa*, vol. 1 (New Delhi: Munshiram Manoharlal, 1990).

15 See Sandeep Sreekumar, "An Analysis of Consequentialism and Deontology in the Normative Ethics of the Bhagavadgita," *Journal of Indian Philosophy* 40, no. 3 (2012): 304, who thinks it is the *Ātman* that obtains liberation. But since the Higher Self is unchanging and free, it is hard to see how it is the subject of *mokṣa*, as I have shown.

16 Even though there is much else to admire in his work, I cannot therefore agree with Paul Deb, "A Chariot Between Two Armies: A Perfectionist Reading of the Bhagavadgītā," *Philosophy East and West* 71, no. 4 (October 2021): 864, who says that " … *bhakti* represents *karmayoga*'s further specification; that disinterested activity finds, as it were, its apotheosis in loving devotion to God."

17 But see Ithamar Theodor, *Exploring the Bhagavad Gita: Philosophy, Structure and Meaning* (London; New York: Routledge, 2016), 19, 99–100, Matthew D. MacKenzie, "The Five Factors of Action and the Decentring of Agency in the Bhagavad Gītā," *Asian Philosophy* 11, no. 3 (November 1, 2001): 149, and Richard De Smet, "A Copernican Reversal: The Gitakara's Reformulation of Karma," *Philosophy East and West* 27, no. 1 (1977): 53–63, who follow Rāmānuja in suggesting the priority of *bhakti* over the other paths so much so that the highest stage for them is one of separation from the Divine and one that is characterized by devotion to God. Such readings tend to emphasize the texts that separate the devotee from the object of devotion. But it is unclear to me that they do as much justice to the texts that suggest that the relation is ultimately one of non-duality. On the other hand, Aurobindo's integral yoga combines the *yoga*s of action, devotion, and knowledge and therefore unifies the volitional, emotional, and intellectual aspects of our being (see Ayon Maharaj, "Toward a New Hermeneutics of the Bhagavad Gītā: Sri Ramakrishna, Sri Aurobindo, and the Secret of Vijñāna," *Philosophy East and West* 65, no. 4 (2015): 1209–27). But then integral yoga is only available to the very few and seems inconsistent with the *Gītā*'s emphasis on accessibility of freedom to those in different walks of life.

18 Bilimoria rightly acknowledges the origin of *bhakti* in the popular prayer/*puja* practices that originate in the *Vedas* and is championed by the Mīmāṁsa school but places the text closer to the *bhakti* movement than I do, which diminishes its revolutionary impact. See Purushottama Bilimoria, "Metadialectics of the Bhagavadgitā," in *Ethics and the Contemporary Milieu* (University of Saskatchewan, Canadian Asian Studies Association, 1988). See also Richard H. Davis, *The Bhagavad Gita: A Biography* (Princeton, NJ: Princeton University Press, 2014), 43–44, who plausibly explains how Krishna's childhood provides a compelling basis of later *bhakti*.

9

Active and Contemplative Lives in the *Nicomachean Ethics*

9.0 Introduction

If freedom/*mokṣa* is the pre-eminent human goal in the *Gītā*, then the equivalent in the *Ethics* is happiness. We have already seen Aristotle say in chapter 6 that happiness is realized when a human being is functioning well, understood in terms of the excellent activities of reason. Here, we will examine these activities of reason in terms of the activities of practical and theoretical virtue insofar as they constitute happiness, especially since questions arise about whether the latter ultimately leads us away from our humanity in ways that are reminiscent of the *Gītā*. While the answer in the *Nicomachean Ethics* affirms our humanity by showing how theoretical virtue can be affected by fortune, it comes at the cost of restricting access to the highest human happiness to a select few.

It seems odd to leave to the end a discussion of happiness in Aristotle, especially since he begins the *Ethics* with it. But since his final word on the matter is left to the end of his text (in Book 10), it may not be inappropriate as it initially seems. "Happiness" translates "*eudiamonia*" and is not a perfect translation since we often take it to mean a feeling or something like contentment; whereas in Aristotle's context "*eudaimonia*" usually means "living and faring well," for which reason "flourishing" has often thought to be a better translation of the Greek. But since we can mean just as many things by "happiness" as we can by "living and faring well," and for other reasons as we will soon see, the consensus has been to stay with happiness (though I have used "flourishing" from time to time to remind us of *eudaemonia*'s relation to living and faring well). This openness of meaning in turn causes a key problem, since it allows us to question what Aristotle himself means by "happiness"—especially on the grounds of what is said in Book 10 which threatens to undermine the unity and consistency of his overall position. This problem is especially troubling since "happiness" is an enveloping term that shapes the content of all the discussions in the *Ethics*.

The problem is not that we do not know what happiness is, since we have seen, broadly speaking, that it is constituted by the excellent or virtuous activities of reason; what remains unclear is the relation between the kinds of excellent rational activity as well as of their relation to the life well-lived as a whole. It might therefore be useful to briefly reprise the considerations that lead Aristotle to equate happiness with excellent rational activity. But in order to fully understand this equation, we will need to consider why other candidates are set aside because of their inability to fulfill what Aristotle often implicitly takes to be the conditions of happiness. We will then consider how the excellent practical and theoretical activities of reason fulfill these conditions in differing ways before attempting to fit them together in the notion of happiness and in that of the good life.

9.1 Happiness: Candidates and Conditions

Happiness or what is the good for humans is essentially constituted by excellent rational activities for Aristotle. This, as we saw in chapter 6 section 2, is explained on the practical front in terms of functioning or doing the job of being human excellently or well, which involves both physiological and psychological considerations. After all, there is more to being a human than just a body and especially since these psychological features essentially involve reason. Thus, rationality here is deeply integrated with the emotional and appetitive drives in human nature, even as it takes the lead in organizing practical activities of human life that are consistent and remorse-free. Such activity, as it turns out, is not just what is good for a human being (that is, what makes for happiness), but what the good person does (that is, what is ethical). But the activities of reason in human well-functioning have more than just a practical sense; for rationality is manifest in exercising thought in the theoretical domain which, as we will see, is a key aspect of happiness (*NE* 1.7 1098a4–5).

Such a drift towards the theoretical in the notion of happiness is not entirely new, and its origins can be traced back to what many take to be the Socratic position in the *Apology* in terms of the examined life as the happy life (29d–29e; 36d–36e), which is then developed further—in more Platonic fashion—in the first six books of the *Republic*. In fact, many of the standard contenders for happiness/*eudaimonia* that Socrates battles in the dialogues are also discussed in the *Ethics* along with the Platonic candidate and set aside for reasons that are uniquely Aristotle's. In the process, Aristotle's reasons for why he conceives happiness the way he does become more obvious.

Money-making is a candidate that seems plausible because so many equate it with happiness; but Aristotle thinks that while we can make its pursuit our highest ambition, we should not since wealth is essentially a means rather than an end (*NE* 1.5 1096a5–9). We use wealth to come by other things (security, housing, sustenance, power, etc.), whereas happiness is an end and never a means to anything else so that it is not just an end, it is the most final end (*NE* 1.7 1197a34–35).[1] Now wealth can be a final end and perhaps even a most final end for those so pathologically inclined, but that is not what it essentially is, which is why Aristotle includes it as an instrumental external good (*NE* 1.8 1099a35–1099b1). Hence—and here the most important condition of happiness is articulated—it needs to be a most final end so that it cannot (rather than merely should not) be a means to any further end; after all, while everything can be pursued for the sake of happiness, happiness is never pursued for the sake of anything else (*NE* 1.7 1197a36–1097b7).

The pursuit of bodily pleasure is eventually rejected as the highest good for a similar reason, though the path there is not as straight-forward. Many people do equate pleasure with happiness, and it is not as obvious that they should not, especially since it is more plausibly a most final end than money-making. Hence we are not surprised if people say that having fun is their main goal in life, or when people who do substantial and interesting work seem to live for the sybaritic pleasures of the weekend. This is not helped, Aristotle thinks, by the fact that people in high places (tyrants and perhaps certain types of celebrity) set such a low standard. Low because, as the function argument will show in what follows in the text, there is nothing distinctively human in such a life that we share with animals. Hence to live in such a way is beastly and slavish, and perhaps, as the reference to tyrants implies, capable of addictive excess that even animals are not (*NE* 1.5 1095b19–22). This is not to say there is no place for bodily pleasure, as Aristotle's discussion of moderation shows. Bodily pleasures are desired by the virtuous in a moderate fashion so long as they make for the good condition of the body, and are not contrary to nobility or beyond the good person's means (*NE* 3.11 1119a11–20).

More interestingly, Aristotle explains the place of such moderately pursued bodily pleasure in happiness in Book 10, and thereby completes his case for why we should not make this our highest good even though we can. There, he says that the pursuit of bodily pleasure is an indulgence that allows us to relax since we cannot work continuously, and so that we are refreshed and capable of returning to serious work involved in the life of virtue (*NE* 10.6 1176b32–1177a10). Such work seems to be a reference to the arduous theoretical pursuits and their completion in the activity of contemplation in the discussion that quickly follows in *NE* 10.7.[2] But just in case we get the wrong impression that such pursuits are all intellectual drudgery, Aristotle tells us that the pleasures of the theoretical virtue are the pleasantest of human activities (*NE* 10.7 1177a23–27). We will soon have opportunity (in section 8 of this chapter) to see why he thinks this of the theoretical pursuits; but for the moment it is important to see the bigger picture in which the theoretical pleasures of virtue are seen together with their practical counterparts. After all, we saw that practical virtue centrally involves pleasure in the discussion of the relation of love and virtue in chapter 2. Not only does it become obvious that rational pleasures in the activities of reason permeate life extensively in ways that are distinctively human, but that they even subsume the way in which the bodily pleasures are pursued (i.e., in moderation) as an aspect of, as it turns out, the happy life.

What the discussion of pleasure implicitly assumes, and which is repeatedly articulated by Aristotle (*NE* 1.8 1098b30–1099a6; 1.13 1102a5; 9.9 1169b29, for instance), is that happiness therefore is not a product (like a painting), but an activity, since it is activities that are pleasurable actualizations of potential. This means, as has been pointed out, that virtuous activities can be a means to happiness while constituting it (as walking is a means to and constitutive of relaxing) in ways that would not have been possible if happiness were to be conceived as a product distinct from the means that produces it (as when saddles are distinct from saddle-making).[3] More on this in a moment.

Next, let us look at Aristotle's discussion of what he takes to be Plato's conception of the Good as the candidate for happiness. Aristotle's discussion of the Good understood as a universal is both revealing and more constructive than is often assumed, though I will focus on just two relevant aspects of it. Aristotle thinks that "good" is either the property of a subject (for example, a good horse) or of its attribute (because it has a good gait, for instance) or is relational (that its gait is better than that of a mule). Priority, therefore, as one would expect from his substance-driven world view, falls on the subject since the relational and predicative aspects of goodness would not exist without it. Whereas he thinks that for Plato, the Form of the Good is not a substance as much as it is a universal that substances, etc. somehow share in to be good; but such sharing, Aristotle therefore implies, wrongly reverses the priority of their existence (*NE* 1.6 1096a19–29), and by implication, of that which has value. The second concern for Aristotle is that even if there is such a thing as the Good, it seems far removed from human concerns and is hardly something that is achievable by humans. Whereas the human good is specifically human and something that should be so achievable since it is ideally in our power to obtain (*NE* 1.6 1096b32–35). Both these concerns are addressed, as we will see, in his discussion of contemplation wherein Aristotle finds a way of reconciling important dimensions of Plato's thinking discussed here with his own.

What emerges here, then, is not necessarily a new condition of happiness that must be satisfied, as much as a slightly different emphasis on one we have already seen: that the human good or happiness is an activity that the *agent* undertakes. Happiness therefore cannot be something that is merely given to the agent, as is possible in the case of wealth or honor, which means it is that much more difficult for it to be taken from the agent. Also implicit in the emphasis on happiness as something that we do, is the fact that it is not enough to simply be capable of, or have the potentiality to do; rather, it is constituted by the actual doing, as we saw above. This emphasis on doing is consistent with Aristotle's entire philosophy of actualization of potential (see Appendix 1); and the added implication that an activity is a means to happiness by being constitutive of it will soon have important consequences for his views on the place of fortune in human life.

This leaves us with the two remaining successful candidates: the political activities and the contemplative/theoretical ones, both of which manifest rationality in distinctively human ways as the function argument makes clear. Aristotle speaks of practical virtue not only because the citizen partakes in legislative life of the city as we saw in chapter 6, but because the ethical relations between the citizens that constitute justice broadly construed in the *polis* are an essential part of what makes us political animals. Practical virtue, we saw in chapter 2, involves not just the excellence of practical reason, but that of the non-rational parts of the soul (the appetitive and the emotional) in ways that centrally involve love. Love in turn points to the key way in which intentionality is central in practical virtue by being undertaken as good—that is, for its own sake and therefore as an end in itself—in ways that satisfy the finality requirements of happiness. After all, one of the key requirements of virtuous action is that it be chosen and chosen for its own sake (that is, for its *telos*), which I suggested is an alternate way of speaking of virtuous actions as loved. Grounded in virtuous dispositions, such choices cannot be undertaken for any other reason than virtue; that is, they cannot rather than merely should not be means to other ends. Thus, when a similar choice is undertaken as a means to a further end, it can only be by those who are not or not yet virtuous. However, this does not mean that the actions associated with the choice do not have outcomes, such as victory in battle. This is why Aristotle will eventually deny practical virtue the status of most final end. Since actions in accordance with practical virtue are up to us, these satisfy the requirement that happiness is something that we do; as well as the requirement that it is the activity rather than the capacity to so act that constitutes happiness.

But there are two additional requirements for happiness—completeness and self-sufficiency—that Aristotle now says also need to be fulfilled. That these are only discussed now in the context of rational activity's candidacy should not come as a surprise since the other candidates do not get as far in satisfying the already listed requirements. Unfortunately, their inclusion complicates matters even while making Aristotle's position more interesting, as I show below.

9.2 *Teleia* as Final and Complete

Aristotle tells us at the end of the function argument that:

> … [the] human good turns out to be activity of the soul exhibiting virtue, and if there are more than one virtue, in accordance with the best and most final (*teleiataton*). But we must add "in a complete (*teleia*) life." For one swallow does not make a summer, nor does one day; and so too one day, or a short time, does not make a man blessed or happy.
>
> (*NE* 1.7 1098a17–19)

The language of "most final" (*teleiataton*) here is consistent with Aristotle's rejection of money-making as the human good, since its nature is essentially that of a means rather than that of an end itself. Here, Aristotle is indicating how the hierarchy of virtues works by separating the final from the most final virtues (and thereby implicitly distinguishing the practical and theoretical virtues as I will show).[4] The problem is that he is also using "*teleia*" to speak of the complete sum of human life. Here "complete" is an appropriate translation, first, given what he says above about how the presence of a single swallow does not constitute summer (or a warm day in spring for that matter), it is possible that a short life in which the virtues are actualized would conceivably be incomplete. Second, because Aristotle specifically defines one meaning of "*teleia*" as that which is not missing any of its parts, as opposed to when it is used to mean "final" when it has reached its end (*Metaphysics* V.16 1021b12–25). Clearly then the translation of "*teleiataton*" as "most final" and "*teleia*" as "complete" is plausible here.

It should be evident now that I think Aristotle has been speaking of the *activities* of happiness (as final and most final) up to this point and now we have to consider the shape of the *life* of happiness (as complete) that these activities constitute. The problem is that the life/activity distinction is not straightforwardly acceptable since Aristotle also speaks here in the just preceding function argument of the life of reason and the life of perception and nutrition, wherein he clearly means the activities of reason, perception, and nutrition (*NE* 1.7 1097b35–1098a1). So perhaps more work needs to be done at the conceptual level to distinguish the activities that constitute a life from the life itself, happy or otherwise.[5] Fortunately, Aristotle provides the wherewithal to do so in his related discussion of the external goods of fortune. The connection between a complete life and the role of fortune is made obvious by his suggestion here in the function argument that a life can be cut short (and is therefore incomplete), presumably by fortune.

9.3 Fortune and the Ruptured Life of Happiness

Aristotle speaks of the effects of fortune on human life in terms of the kind of good it represents in two distinct but related ways. But first he separates goods of the agent's soul (virtue) from that of the body (health, beauty, fertility) and those that are external to the body (wealth, good birth, power, good children, etc.). Goods that are external to the soul (that is, goods of the body and goods that are external to the body) are further spoken of as necessary or instrumental for happiness (*NE* 1.9 1099b26–28), in ways that clearly suggest that the good of the soul (i.e., virtue, as the constituent of happiness) is not. Thus, the point seems to be that goods external to the soul are external conditions of happiness and therefore subject to fortune whereas the goods internal to the soul are not because these are up to us (because virtuous activity is something we do) and constitute happiness. This is troubling because the distinction seems too neat and I will say more about this soon, hopefully without derailing our discussion. For the moment, it is important to see Aristotle's point on why goods that are external to the soul (what I will simply refer to as "external goods") are subject to fortune and how they in turn affect happiness. Certain kinds of goods of the body (health) and external to the body (basic financial well-being so that one can afford food and shelter) are necessary conditions of happiness because these are necessary conditions of human life (*NE* 10.8 1178b35–1179a1, etc.). This therefore means that by themselves they are sufficient for living, even if Aristotle does suggest that it is possible to be happy with very little more than these, as we will soon see. Other external goods (such as wealth, position, power, good looks, etc.) are instrumental insofar as their presence can enhance virtuous activity (*NE*

1.8 1099a31–1099b5). Thus, we can be more generous if we have more money, do more for the deserving if we have the power and connections to help them, etc. Here too, the point seems to be that money and power are not internal or essential goods; only that they are useful for those that are so (i.e., the virtues).[6]

Aristotle's focus above seems therefore to be on the necessary and instrumental conditions of the activities of happiness *once the latter have been established*; and not on what it takes to establish them in the first place.[7] This is perhaps why he distinguishes the virtues as up to us even though it is his view that the development of virtue is dependent on familial, educational, and cultural infrastructure that we have already discussed extensively. While it may be of great concern to us to work out how much virtue really is a function of privilege, Aristotle is more concerned here on what can threaten the activities of happiness in ways that lead to an incomplete life. But if the established activities of happiness can be threatened, then it is not difficult to see how their very possibility might be affected by fortune, as I will attempt to show in the next and final chapter.

Now the lack of necessary external goods can cut short life and affect considerations of its completeness, happy or otherwise. Poor health can lead to an early death, as can accidents and adverse circumstances (such as by drowning in a storm at sea, or by starvation on being washed up on a desert island). In many such cases, it is easy to make the tragic assessment that a happy life is cut short as in the case of someone who has just completed their moral education and begun to undertake the activities of virtue independently; in others, shortness does not hamper the play of virtue, as in the case of an Achilles in his prime whose life was completed by his courageous brilliance on the battlefields of Troy. In yet others, it may be more difficult to say. Thus, would we say that our assessment of the completeness of the Platonic Socrates' life, for instance, be different if he died of natural causes twenty years earlier? Or thirty years earlier? The point of course is not that it is always easy to make the assessment of how much virtuous activity is enough for a complete, happy life, just as it is often hard to know when summer finally overcomes spring. The important thing to see is that a plausible distinction between the life and activities of happiness emerges here.

Even so, the assessment of their relationship is further complicated by the fact that shortness of life is not the only basis for its incompleteness, as Aristotle shows in his discussion of the life of Priam. Priam is the king of Troy and father of Hector and of Paris (paramour of Helen) in the *Illiad*. Priam is a wise and just king, with many children and a prosperous kingdom that is eventually laid to waste in the sack of Troy. In the course of the war between the Greeks and

Trojans set off by Paris's abduction of Helen, Priam loses everything: his children, notably his heir Hector, his wives, his kingdom and his wealth. Not only does Hector die at the hands of Achilles but oral accounts in the tradition suggest the eighty-year-old Priam himself is ignominiously killed by Achilles' son, Neoptolemus (and as is immortalized much later in Virgil's *Aeneid*). Aristotle trenchantly assesses Priam's life in the following way:

> For there is required, as we said, not only complete virtue/*teleías áretēs* but also a complete life/*teleíou bíou*, since many changes occur in life, and all manner of chances, and the most prosperous may fall into great misfortunes in old age, as is told of Priam in the Trojan Cycle; and one who has experienced such chances and has ended wretchedly no one calls happy.
>
> (*NE* 1.9 1100a4–9)

Priam's "*teleías áretēs*" here in its non-comparative usage is universally translated as "complete virtue" presumably to refer to "complete practical virtue." The point seems to be that while Priam has lived ethically, his life as a whole is incomplete despite its length because of the misfortunes that have befallen him.[8] The problem is that if we look at Priam's life from the point of the activities of virtue (and hence happiness) it is not as if he stops being virtuous in adversity, so that it is unclear then in what sense he can no longer be called happy. In fact, it is often the case that adversity offers greater opportunity for virtue, as is clear in the case of the life of Achilles; thus, as Aristotle acknowledges is the case with Priam, we might still call him happy in the sense that he would not act viciously (*NE* 1.10 1100b33–1101a6). Aristotle's response that ill-fortune can crush and maim happiness because it hinders activity may therefore seem disconcerting (*NE* 1.10 1100b24–32). Yet, if we see that fortune enhanced Achilles' courageous activities on the battlefield, whereas it progressively undermined Priam's as father, king, and husband, we might see Aristotle's point.[9] But I suggest that the assessment of this disruption is best made from the point of view of Priam's life as a whole rather than from the perspective of the activities themselves. From such a perspective, some disruptions are natural (when he might have handed over the reins of the kingdom to Hector and stopped being king), as opposed to not (when he is ignominiously killed). If Priam's retirement as a result of age had come to fruition, or if he had been able to recover his kingdom, etc., then in fact it may not have been inappropriate to say that it (among other things) enhanced the chances of completing his life (*NE* 1.11 1101a10–13). Not that death by itself is reason enough to deny him such completeness, as we may see in the case of Achilles.

Expanding on our discussion of self-skilling in the context of autonomy in chapter 3 section 5, we can see how our understanding of the life/activity distinction can be enriched if we remember the ways in which a life is a constructed artifact in the hands of the agent. There we saw that choice is an activity/*energeia* and therefore complete at that instant because it is undertaken for its own sake (or for its *telos*). Whereas the processes/*kinesis* such choice unleashes—understood in terms of the procurement of victory in battle (which is its aim/*skopos*), or in the maintenance of the dispositions that produce choice—takes time. Disruption (as in the case of Priam) or enhancement (as in the case of Achilles) as a result of fortune, then, makes the most sense at the level of the life of happiness because it affects the processes that constitute such a life—including, as we will see, the leisure to pursue theoretical ends—and thereby impacts its completeness since Aristotle explicitly says completeness requires both (*NE* 10.8 1178a35–1178b1). Completeness in turn allows us to see that such a life is a product of one's work and is therefore an artifact that can be aesthetically assessed in particularly human terms: tragic, mundane, or glorious.[10] This view of the role of fortune in happiness in the *Nicomachean Ethics* seems to represent a significant shift in Aristotle's position from the earlier *Eudemian* version and has profound implications for his views on happiness, as I will attempt to indicate later.[11] Thus "*teleia*" turns out to be two-dimensional in this context so far: "final" seems to fit better when applied to activities that are ends in themselves (such as activities undertaken for their own sake, or virtuous activities); even if such choices are essentially connected to processes that bring about external aims such as leisure that ultimately convince Aristotle that practical activities are therefore not most final. "Complete" seems more appropriate in the context of the totality of one's life, especially when we are assessing whether any of its parts are missing. Having undertaken an initial assessment of "*teleia*," it is time now to consider the remaining condition of happiness: self-sufficiency.

9.4 *Autarkia* as Self-Sufficiency: Activity and Life

Before we discuss *autarkia* here in the context of *NE* 1.7 as self-sufficiency, it is important to remind ourselves of the discussion of self-governance in chapter 3. There we saw that the virtuous individual comes to be self-governing because of the way in which the non-rational is harmonized with the commitments of the rational. Such harmony (as opposed to hegemony) is wrought by love, as discussed in chapter 2, in ways that allow for the transformation from a cultivated but essentially dependent human being into a self-governing and virtuous person. I suggested there that this understanding of a virtuous person as self-governing is crucial to seeing what Aristotle means by self-sufficiency here in the context of the conditions of happiness, which I now develop.

Aristotle speaks of both the self-sufficient activity and life that are more closely in parallel than is the case for *teleia* activity and life.[12] A self-sufficient activity is one that is undertaken independently even if it is dependent on external goods. Hence generosity presupposes resources in ways that may not be as necessary in acts of battlefield courage, even if both require others for their manifestation (*NE* 10.7 1176a35–1176b5). This more or less dependence on external goods does not take away from the fact that these acts of virtue are independent actions precisely because they are actions of a self-governing individual. Similar actions that are coerced or under the direction of a tutor are obviously not self-sufficient even if they are not involuntary. But, by implication, neither are the actions of children or the weak-willed primarily because of their capricious nature; nor that of the compulsively appetitive because of their excessive dependence on the external objects of desire which may therefore be exacerbated by the impact of ill-fortune.

Since human flourishing, as we have seen, is brought about in a familial, social, and political context, it would seem that the self-sufficient life like self-sufficient activity is also dependent. Not just on external goods and other ethical agents, but family, friends, and fellow citizens since for Aristotle we are social animals whose existence is embedded in a rich social fabric (*NE* 1.7 1097b7–12). Even so, such a life is not excessively dependent on others in the way in which a child's might be initially, since the self-sufficient activities of virtue that constitute happiness are undertaken by independent, self-governing individuals. The lack of self-sufficiency is closely intertwined with its incompleteness (*NE* 1.7 1097b15–21); for a life can have all the appearances of completeness but may not be so because of a lack of self-sufficiency—say, for instance, when an agent is excessively constrained by the family patriarch throughout their life. So it would seem that circumstances and hence fortune can affect self-sufficiency as much as it can completeness.

9.5 Happiness Yet Again

It might be useful now to see how the above-discussed considerations that we have developed mainly in the context of the practically virtuous life and its activities might apply to the theoretical ones. In the process, we will not only get a fuller sense of what Aristotle means in this context but also the opportunity to consider the implications it has for the good or happy life as a whole.

As it turns out, Aristotle thinks that theoretically virtuous activity of a certain sort (i.e., *theoria*/contemplation) is most self-sufficient and final and therefore more so than practical activity, and there are key reasons why he thinks it is the primary activity of happiness. Theoretical activity is more self-sufficient than practical activity because it needs very little beyond the necessities of life and is therefore less dependent on fortune (*NE* 10.8 1179a4–16). This may seem puzzling especially since we might think that such a life needs more resources in the form of a more than basic education, infrastructure, and social networks, which Aristotle acknowledges (*NE* 10.8 1178b1–7). But to focus on these is to focus on the development of our potential to become knowers; whereas what Aristotle has in mind here is the fullest actualization of this potential in the activity of knowing (and therefore on what it means to be a knower), which after all, is consistent with his repeated claims that happiness is an activity. We may think of this in terms of using, say, grammatical knowledge in the activity of writing rather than when it is in development in the process of education (*NE* 10.7 1177a22–24). Not only are such activities more pleasurable than the processes involved in their acquisition, but they are also less dependent than practical ones on external accoutrements for their actualization and thereby more self-sufficient (*NE* 10.7 1077a32–1177b1; 10.8 1178b2–3).

The focus on the use of knowledge in activity can be misleading since Aristotle thinks such usage has implications for finality. After all, if something is useful then it is not final even if we see that Aristotle's focus is on the contemplation/*theoria* of grammatical knowledge rather than its use. The point of course is that such knowledge can be used, which parallels the considerations in practically virtuous activity construed as final because virtuous choice is undertaken for its own sake, but not most final precisely because it engenders useful processes that reach goals. Thus, a well-written letter that helps confirm the commitment of a key ally, and an appositely brave choice, can both be useful in war. The most final activity of contemplation, by implication, then, must be of an object that cannot be useful in any other way than for its own sake, which for Aristotle is the contemplation of God (*NE* 6.7 1145b5–8; *Met.* 12.7 1072b14–15; 1072b24–25).

The key to understanding Aristotle's view is to see that not only is the intellect/*nous* which does the contemplating conceived as divine or more plausibly divine-like (*NE* 10.7 1177a16), but that the activity of human contemplation itself is modeled on divine contemplation (*NE* 1179a24–26). The discussion on the nature of divine contemplation is mainly negative in the *Ethics* and is focused on denying divinity any sort of practical activity, and therefore exemplifies the acme of uselessness (*NE* 10.8 1178b11–23). What seems implicit though is an affirmation of a commonality with human contemplation: that both assume a knowing that is only fully actualized in the act of contemplation. But while human contemplation is of God precisely because God grounds philosophical wisdom/*sophia (NE* 6.7 1141a20), nothing positive is said here about the nature of divine contemplation. This is perhaps because divine contemplation is discussed in the *Metaphysics* where Aristotle tells us that the divine's contemplation is of itself. There he says that human contemplation is *like* divine contemplation not because it is a contemplation of its own nature but because it is of divine nature,[13] which I will suggest, represents a significant shift in Aristotle's position (*Met.* 10.7 1172bb14–15). To understand why, we need to consider Aristotle's views in the *Metaphysics* and the *De Anima* on divine nature and human thinking.

9.6 Divine Thinking as Contemplation

The basis for denying useful activities to God in *Metaphysics* 12 is implicitly based on his perfection. Interestingly enough, "perfection" is the third meaning of "*teleia*" as discussed in *Metaphysics* 5, in addition to "final" and "complete." There we are told something is perfect when it cannot be excelled in terms of the goodness associated with its kind. Thus an excellent doctor is one who is not only good at her job, but is one who cannot be bettered in all her activities of healing (*Met.* 5.16 1021b14–15). The challenge is that healing is a qualitative exercise and is not as easy to measure as quantitative ones like speed. Aristotle seems to acknowledge this insofar as he accepts that human pleasures (as we will see below) can be more or less perfect. But in the case of God, there is less of a problem since God, one would think, by definition is perfect.[14] This is implicit in Aristotle's suggestion that God as first substance is not just good in the category of substances but good per se because for him, as we have seen already, substances are primary existents and everything else depends on substances for their existence (*Met.* 12.7 1072a26–11). So here then we see the beginnings of Aristotle's response to the first of his own concerns regarding Plato on the Good (discussed in section 2 of this chapter above); that the Good does not exist independently, but rather as an attribute of First Substance.[15] But it is unclear why God is good (and therefore perfect) without seeing how God's activities are most final and complete. This is especially so since Aristotle thinks God's being (or substance) is not distinct from his activity, and this activity in turn is not distinct from its object which is God.

It might be easiest to start with God's activity, which Aristotle thinks is one of undiminished knowing. One way to see this is in terms of a straight-forward extrapolation to perfection from what he famously claims is the essential desire of humans to know (*Met.* 1.1 980a22). But more importantly, it is a way in which he connects the divine's activities to human ones. But if God's being or substance is not distinct from his activity of thinking, then you would expect Aristotle to say that God is a pure immaterial actuality without any potentiality that would undermine God's unity or eternality, which he does (*Met.* 12.6 1171b11–22). Matter's absence in God has not only to do with matter's non-eternality for Aristotle, but also because on his view, thinking is not material for reasons we will see below. This view on the nature of God as a simple eternal and immaterial actuality is even more striking in relation to human thinking for Aristotle, since our grasp of ourselves as thinkers is usually reflexive and occurs when thinking is going on so that self-knowledge is dualistic (*DA* 3.4 429b5–10).[16] This is because there is more to human substance than the ability to think, as we have seen in chapter 3 section 2.2, and because human thinking involves material processes, as we will see. Whereas there is no such dualism in God's self-knowledge since there is no distinction between knower and the activities of knowing, and no potentiality involved in its activity.

Divine and human thinking are more isomorphic when it comes to the identity relation between thinking and thought object. For Aristotle insightfully points out that thinking about the shape of a snub nose is to abstract its snubness from its material aspect and consider it in mind, wherein that which is considered (the snubness) is not distinct from the considering (the thinking about the snubness) (*Met.* 12.9 1075a1–3). This insight is at least in part why Aristotle thinks that human thinking and therefore the mind which thinks is immaterial, despite his hylomorphism, even as the mind's immaterialism maintains the parallel with the Divine's immaterial nature.[17] Things get more complicated because Aristotle tells us that the object of God's thinking is himself. Aristotle thinks God's excellence entails that he cannot think of anything else but himself as it would otherwise undermine his excellence; for he is the best of all substances so that there is none better to think about or depend on (*Met.* 12.9 1074b17–23). The point therefore seems to be that divine perfection is self-sufficient in the extreme so that we can see how it sets the standard for self-sufficiency at the human level, both where thinking and living are concerned.

Yet when we consider all of this together, we get: an immaterial Thinker that is not distinct from its Thinking, Thinking that is not distinct from its Thought Object, and a Thought Object that is not distinct from the Thinker. Aristotle's view here seems to be deeply recursive, for you end up where you start, no matter where you start. Thus, if you ask what the Thinker is, then you see that it is no different from the Thinking which in turn is not distinct from the Thought Object which in turn is the Thinker itself. If you ask what is Thinking then you see it is no different from what is thought about or the Thought Object, which in turn is not distinct from the Thinker which is reducible to Thinking. If you ask what the Thought Object is, then it is no different from the Thinker which is not distinct from the Thinking and which is reducible to the Thought object. Interestingly enough, Aristotle chooses to emphasize neither the subject or the object in his description of divinity in this context. Instead, he focuses on the activity that is the bridge between them to which they can be reduced: a Thinking, Thinking about Thinking, which emphasizes the pure actuality that is divine being.

The recursive nature of Thinking makes God's activity more rather than less mysterious, and so it is time now to see how his perfection understood in terms of the other two meanings of "*teleia*" (i.e., "finality" and "completeness") might help us here. First, it should be noted that there is no life/activity distinction that applies to God since his singular activity is not distinct from his life or from his being/substance. Thus, *teleia* as perfection is at once about activity and life, unlike in the human instance, so that all of its meanings would apply, if at all, to Thinking (*Met*. 12.9 1074a33–34).

Divine perfection we saw is based on divine excellence or goodness so that divine thinking is of itself since there is none better. Now it becomes obvious that since there is no subject/predicate separation in God that God's goodness is not distinct from God and that God and Good are therefore interchangeable, so that the Good is a living substance and not an abstract Form as Plato would have it. Such activity is final not only because it continuously achieves its end in activity (as an *energeia*), but because there clearly can be no other end beyond it, which now fully explains why Aristotle says in the *Ethics* that practical activity cannot be associated with divinity (*NE* 10.8 1178b8–23). Divine activity is not only the highest good and therefore the most "endy" activity, but also the most useless for any other purpose since there is no purpose beyond its activity.

Teleia as completeness applies to divinity not because as in the human instance where it means not lacking in parts, but because Thinking is partless. The fact that Aristotle chooses to focus on God's thinking rather than his being is significant not simply because it emphasizes activity, but because it emphasizes its objectless nature. For if God's being is in fact distinct from his thinking about his being, then his thinking about his being would not have the highest possible level of completeness from moment to moment, as is the case since the Divine is in fact a unified, objectless activity (*Met.* 12.9 1075a5–10). What significance does this objectless Thinking have to make it the activity of the Good, we might ask, since it seems empty?

Recall that human self-awareness for Aristotle is incidental to thinking and perception, both of which involve awareness. Thus while thinking is going on the object of thought and thinking are identical; one is aware that one thinks incidentally to thinking even if thinking itself essentially involves awareness. That is, Aristotle's view seems to be that the thinking comes first and the awareness that we are thinkers follows as a kind of spillover effect. Whereas there is no such distinction in divine Thinking, as we have seen, so that all there is to Thinking is an objectless awareness that is, interestingly enough for Aristotle, deeply pleasurable and which human awareness approximates. Aristotle hints at this relation when he says that divine activity is pleasure (not a pleasure) and it is through (*dià*) this that presumably human perception, memory, and thought are pleasant (*Met.* 12.7 11072b15–17). Given divine nature's simplicity, it cannot be that the experience of pleasure is distinct from the awareness of it and is likely what Aristotle means when he says that divine activity is pleasure; pleasure that is therefore a non-composite unity of joyful awareness.[18]

Now why would such awareness be the acme of all possible activity? Perhaps because Aristotle is trying to show us that God as the first principle of knowing represents what is basic in all knowing: an awareness without which all conscious activity—desiring, thinking, imagining, perceiving, and remembering—would be impossible. Thus, not only would it be impossible to satisfy our most basic desire to know, but without awareness it would be impossible to know that we have a desire to know.

9.7 Human Thinking and Contemplation

It would seem, then, that there is a deep connection between the nature of certain kinds of human and Divine activity, which has interesting implications for the highest human activity of contemplation. We just saw that awareness is involved in perception, memory, and thinking of all kinds (discursive, intuitive, imaginative, etc.). But it remains unclear how such human awareness is related to pleasure in ways that approximate Divine activity. In his second and most discussed position on pleasure in the *Ethics*, Aristotle tells us that pleasure completes (*teleioī*) an activity/*energeia* (*NE* 10.4 1174b23). Such a view implies that there is no such thing as an experience of pleasure per se since it always accompanies activities such as thinking and perceiving (including those involved in bodily pleasures). The problem is that earlier he tells us that pleasure, like seeing, *is* an activity and therefore already complete/*teleia* from moment to moment (*NE* 10.4 1174a15–16). So how can pleasure and seeing both be complete activities and it be the case that pleasure completes seeing? One way to reconcile this seeming inconsistency is to deny that pleasure (which involves awareness of the pleasure) is different from the activity that it is said to complete (such as seeing). For seeing is only an activity when the pleasure/awareness is involved, as opposed to when we speak of its purely physical processes (such as when the sense organ is imprinted by the sensible form of a physical object, etc.) (*DA* 424a17–28). Thus, to say that seeing is an activity is to do so because pleasure/awareness is integral to what it means to be the activity of seeing; and to say that pleasure/awareness is an activity is to say that it is not found separate from what it completes (i.e., the processes involved in seeing). It would then follow that in humans we can, more or less, only theoretically separate this awareness/pleasure from the activity it completes, as much as we can separate such awareness/pleasure from the reflexive self-awareness/pleasure that it grounds.

The implications for our understanding of human pleasure, then, are profound. First, it means that it is possible for an activity to be more or less complete because it is more or less pleasurable, which Aristotle seems to allow. The rationale, if my view on the inextricable connection between pleasure and awareness is right, would have to do with more or less attention paid in the activity. This is precisely what Aristotle tells us when he says that the same activity of perception is more delightful at first because "we look hard at a thing," i.e., pay it more attention or are more aware of it. When such attention flags, so does the pleasure (*NE* 10.4 1175a3–10).

Aristotle goes further and suggests that different activities are more or less pleasurable depending on the completeness of the subjects and the objects they relate (*NE* 10.4 1174b14–19). This makes sense since there would plausibly be qualitative differences between divine and human pleasure because of the differences in substances involved. But Aristotle extends the point to speak of differences within human activities as well because of the different organs and objects involved. Thus, perception is pleasant if the eye is healthy and is perceiving, say, a beautiful animal, but thinking about the animal, Aristotle suggests, is more pleasant because such activity is better and thereby more complete. Here "better" which is the comparative of "good" is not the only basis of calling such activity "more complete" and thereby more pleasurable; for thinking (as he only suggests here and develops more fully in the *De Anima*) has only indirectly to do with material objects for Aristotle than perception (*DA* 3.4 429a29–429b18), and is more of the nature of awareness and therefore more pleasurable than perception.[19] It is plausible, then, that the activities of human thinking will not only be most pleasurable for those whose intellects are in the best condition (i.e., virtuous or well-educated) and are thinking about the best possible objects, and thereby as complete as humanly possible (*NE* 10.41174b20–23).[20] As we have seen Aristotle say that God is the best and most complete of substances (because he is without parts), it is not inappropriate to suggest that such contemplation's completion is derivative of God's. Considering the other meanings of "*teleia*" in the context of human contemplation is also illuminating, and appropriately enough, maintains a parallel with God's contemplation.

In the *Ethics* we are told that human contemplation presumes philosophical knowledge, explicitly in the specific discussions of contemplation in Book 10 (*NE* 10.7 1177a24–26), and implicitly in Book 6 where he discusses the relation between practical (*phronesis*) and philosophical wisdom (*sophia*) (*NE* 6.13 1145a7–11). His point seems to be that to contemplate is to already know, and not be in the process of coming to know; just as much as the use of grammatical knowledge already presupposes such knowledge. Thus, contemplating God represents the head/*kephalèn* of all knowledge, as *NE* 6.7 (1141a18–19) suggests, because such knowledge is most final as it is knowledge of the first principle (*Met.* 12.7 1072b11); after all, to come to see God's nature as awareness is to understand how basic it is to thinking, imagining, perception, and memory (*Met.* 12.7 1072b16–17). Aristotle tells us that unlike practically virtuous activity, contemplation is loved for its own sake since nothing arises from such activity (*NE* 10.7 1177b1–2). But Aristotle's point is even stronger, because nothing *can* arise from the contemplation of God (i.e., that such activity has no *skopos*) except knowing understood as an end in itself, which therefore makes such contemplation the most final of human activities. After all, understanding that God is the first principle that grounds all knowledge and so is not a means to any further end, even as it transforms and completes all the knowledge that it grounds. Thus Aristotle tells us that there is a difference between arguments and hence knowledge going from and so grounded in first principles as opposed to arguments that go to (and by implication seek to go beyond) first principles (*NE* 1.4 1095a31–1095b1).[21] Whereas practical virtue presupposes choice as an end in itself and is therefore a final but not a most final end, since it engenders goals such as victory in battle or a viable political state and the possibility of a theoretical life (*NE* 10.7 1177b4–15).[22] The language of love is unsurprising since as a lover of (theoretical) virtue, must love virtuous activity for its own sake, as we saw in chapter 2 section 1. Not surprising also is Aristotle's claim, therefore, that such activity, on first approximation, is deeply joyful (*NE* 10.7 1177a24–25), since in the above discussion in chapter 2 we saw him say that we enjoy doing what we love.

But is not just the activity of contemplation that is loved, since for Aristotle God is the object of love (*Met.* 12.7 1072b1–14). This makes sense for at least two reasons: first, because God as the Good—and therefore as living perfection—is the highest possible object of love. Aristotle is very clear in this context that love as a desire is consequent to the nature of God as the first, thinking being understood as the real good and therefore the true object of wish (*Met.* 12.7 1072a27–29); a position that complements a similar discussion in the practical context of the real good, wish, and love, as we saw in chapter 2. But if this is true, then God as good may be intuited in the way in which the real good is apprehended in practical activity by wish. This perhaps explains why Aristotle never speaks of choosing to contemplate. But it may be that the difference between seeing the practical and theoretical good is that the latter is only briefly seen in ways that are not up to us. If they were, then Aristotle would not say that we enjoy divine life and do so for a short time (*Met.* 12.7 1072b14–15); for if we could choose it, then it is unclear why such activity is only briefly available to us.[23]

The second reason why loving contemplation is not distinct from loving God has to do with having seen Aristotle say that the thinking and object of thought are not distinct. In thinking about a nose, the thinking is identical only with the theoretical or immaterial aspects of the nose (for example, its snubness). Whereas thinking about God makes the thinking identical with God in some sense since he is purely immaterial. One way to get at this identity might be to consider how our thinking of Thinking is an awareness of Awareness where the latter is not merely an intellectual apprehension of form. After all, human contemplation is to approximate the Divine's, and the Divine's contemplation of itself brooks no separation between subject, object, and activity. Thus, human contemplation is an activity in which, by approximating the Divine's partless activity, we lose ourselves for a while; for the reflective awareness that we are thinking is often attenuated when we are in contemplation of much lesser objects. Hence to lose oneself in thinking presumably means to lose the reflexive sense of self in everyday thinking as we approach the unity of Divine Thinking in contemplation; and it is the blissful nature of the unity of divine activity, then, that completes the explanation of why human contemplation at its acme is deeply pleasurable.[24]

However we may read this—especially since Aristotle doesn't give us much phenomenological detail about contemplation—it is quite clear that such activity is human and not divine. Hence, he insists in the *NE* that human activity is akin to divine activity (*NE* 10.8 1178b25–27; 1179a23–26), but sometimes seems to be in two minds on whether it is the activity of the divine or just the most divine element in us (*NE* 10.7 11777a16). But when pushed by a possible objection to his view that such a life would be too high for humans (a) if we are composites of human (i.e., of reason and passion which is perfected in the life of practical virtue) and divine, (b) why bother with the human when we can live the divine, immortal one (*NE* 10.7 1177b26–1178a1), he says (c):

> But (*d*) this [i.e., the intellect] seems to be each man himself, since it is the authoritative and better part of him. It would be strange, then, if he were to choose not the life of himself but that of something else … for man, therefore, the life according to intellect is best and pleasantest, since intellect more than anything else *is* man.
>
> (*NE* 10.7 1178a1–8)[25]

We have already seen in 3.3.3 that when Aristotle says reason is the person in the practical context that he does not mean that reason is all there is to the person understood as "personality" rather than "self." It seems eminently plausible to think that such a reading is the case here in the context of theoretical reason, especially since on my reading practical and theoretical reason are only distinct in application (cf. 3.3.2). That is, Aristotle clearly seems to be saying that the intellect *is* human so that to choose the life of theoretical virtue is to choose the human life as much as is the life of practical virtue.[26] So it remains now to consider how the practical and theoretical activities fit together in the happy life.

9.8 Happiness Reconsidered

We have discussed the relation between the activities of practical and theoretical virtues in terms of practical wisdom's/*phronesis* stewardship of philosophical wisdom/*sophia*, so we have some basic sense of the relationship. In closing, it might be useful to think of the different senses of "*teleia*" as they apply to such a life wherein we flesh out some more of the details of the relationship between the practical and theoretical activities of virtue.

Such a life is happy because it is complete since it involves the fullest actualization of rationality that is in turn a profound and joyful expression of love in both its practical and theoretical aspects. A life that has only one or the other is therefore substantially incomplete but not without merit. Many will pursue just the activities of practical virtue which will therefore constitute a life that Aristotle says is secondarily happy (*NE* 10.8 1178a9–23),[27] since it involves complete if not the most complete virtue, as might have been the case for a less unfortunate Priam. Aristotle is acknowledging here that the philosophical life is not for everyone in the way in which the life of practical virtue is essential in the pursuit of interpersonal relations that are continuous with political ones, as we have seen. It is no wonder then that he spends as much time as he does in the *Ethics* speaking to its practical ingredients and as little to the theoretical ones, in what he tells us is an outline of the human good (*NE* 1.3 1094a25–1094b7). For the language of "outline" in the context of the theoretical virtues applies more to their place and function in the good life, especially since their content is discussed elsewhere (for example, in the *Physics*, *Metaphysics*, etc.).

A different kind of incompleteness is the case for those who pursue theoretical wisdom without regard for the practical, as Aristotle says is the case of someone like the first Greek naturalist philosopher Thales. Such a life is not happy because it is not the human good of happiness that is sought (*NE* 6.7 1141b4–8); that is, the pursuit of philosophy is not contextualized as a good in a total human life since it is not shepherded by practical wisdom. Thus not only is it possible that such a life be a brilliant disarray, but that it can potentially be characterized by a lack of practical virtue as in the case of the unscrupulously brilliant. What seems unclear here is that perhaps the fullest actualization of theoretical wisdom/*sophia* in contemplation/*theoria* is not really possible without practical wisdom/*phronesis*, as I have suggested, and elaborate below.

A life of practical wisdom that culminates in *theoria* is a life that has reached its most final *telos*/end as opposed to one that only instantiates the final ends of practical virtue. This is because the former involves the actualization of all aspects of the rational human function and not just one or the other. Here, while it is more obvious that the actualization of final virtue is possible without that of the most final virtue, it is less so that the latter is possible without the former; after all, that which is most final than that which is final is higher in the hierarchy and therefore presupposes it, but not vice versa. Even so, Aristotle does not do more than suggest in places why this might be; for instance, that the kind of attention that culminates in contemplation presupposes an internal quietude that only practical virtue provides (*NE* 7.14 1154b22–31),[28] as discussed in chapter 3. For there we saw that practical virtue is understood in terms of an internal harmony and unity that makes not only the challenges of a sustained life of practical virtue possible, but even more so, the life of theoretical virtue. Put a different way, the practical intuition of the good and its theoretical counterpart are related in Aristotle; after all both are spoken of as fine/*kalon* even if God as the object of contemplation is its highest and most basic form (*Met.* 12.7 1072b10–11).

The happy life is humanly perfect/*teleia* when it achieves both the practical and theoretical good, because such a (human) good life cannot be exceeded.[29] Not by lives of practical or theoretical wisdom by themselves, and not by any other kind of life (of money-making, bodily pleasure, etc.) for reasons we have already seen. We saw in chapter 6 that practical wisdom is concerned with what is conducive to the good life in general. This follows from the fact that practical wisdom is the culmination of the moral and intellectual aspects of practical virtue, which *qua* individual virtues are concerned with the good in their respective spheres. Thus courage is concerned with the good in battle, temperance with the good when it comes to food and sex, and so on. Practical wisdom, then, is acting well in all practical endeavors and thereby securing the practical good. But what is conducive to the good life in general, as we saw, also involves bringing about as steward the possibility of contemplation/*theoria*. Such a possibility not only involves an extensive education, but the possibility to pursue such knowledge at leisure that practical wisdom brings about (*NE* 10.7 1177b3–15). Even if philosophy is not for everyone, practical wisdom *qua* political wisdom (since is the same state as political wisdom) sets its realization for the citizenry as the high-water mark for the state as we saw in chapter 6 (see also *NE* 1.2 1094a29–1094b11). But the fullest perfection entails the realization of both the practical and theoretical good in a life; and the latter as we saw in the previous section presupposes obtaining the highest human good of *theoria* because of its deep intertwining with the Good understood as divine.

It might be appropriate to end the discussion here by thinking about the impact of fortune on the life of happiness. While the philosophical life is practically virtuous even if private, it will not need extensive resources for its activities because the focus here is not on ruling land and sea (*NE* 10.8 1178b32–1179a16). This does not of course mean that the life of secondary happiness cannot be private but rather that its fullest and most lustrous expression is in the political domain, and to this extent, makes it more dependent on the external goods. Thus, paradoxically enough, the life of complete happiness needs less by way of external goods than the life of practical virtue, which is all the more reason to see the latter as a secondary form of happiness.

But it is important to be reminded of the fact that both the purely practical and the philosophical-cum-practical lives can be disrupted by fortune, for even if the latter needs less than the former, it can be undermined by war, pestilence, or just sheer economic misfortune. Such disruption can seriously affect the theoretical life so that it may not be possible to obtain its natural completion in *theoria*. Interestingly enough, Aristotle emphasizes its resilience once the knowledge has been obtained but does not speak to its extreme delicacy in process. In fact one could argue that the philosophical life is more easily disrupted by fortune whereas such disruptions are often grist for the purely political life's mill, though Priam's life is an important reminder of how to think about the nature of such disruptions. Thus, while the perfect life of happiness cannot be disrupted presumably once it has obtained completion in *theoria*, this may not always be so before-hand due to the delicate nature of the intellectual life in progress. Such a view is still consistent with Aristotle's earlier discussions in the *Ethics* where fortune is a necessary (at most) but not sufficient condition for happiness but represents a significant shift in Aristotle's thinking from the *Eudemian Ethics* where he suggests that fortune can be sufficient for happiness, as we will soon see. Aristotle's views on human happiness therefore are not only more restrictive in terms of access but also more prone to be affected by fortune, in ways that will make for an interesting dialogue with the *Gītā*.

Notes

1 I use W. D. Ross's original translation here of "*teleia*" as "final" rather than "complete" as is found in the updated one in the Revised Oxford Translation. For I think it has been rightly pointed out that when Aristotle uses "*teleia*" in a comparative context to speak of, say, the pursuit of honor as more final than the pursuit of wealth, for instance, it does not mean that the pursuit of honor necessarily includes within it (as comprehensive or complete) the pursuit of wealth. See Robert Heinaman, "Eudaimonia and Self-Sufficiency in the Nicomachean Ethics," *Phronesis* 33, no. 1 (January 1, 1988): 38; and Daniel Devereux, "Aristotle on the Essence of Happiness," in *Studies in Aristotle*, ed. Dominic J. O'Meara (Washington, DC: Catholic University of America Press, 2018), 247–60.

2 Of course non-bodily pleasures are broader than those involved in rational virtue, both practical and theoretical. For these can involve pleasures of the arts, sport, etc. See the distinction between bodily pleasures and those that are not as location

specific in W. F. R. Hardie, *Aristotle's Ethical Theory* (Oxford: Clarendon Press, 1968), 297–302.

3 The most influential of such readings have been J. L. Ackrill, "Aristotle on Eudaimonia," in *Essays on Aristotle's Ethics*, by Amélie Rorty, Major Thinkers Series 2 (Berkeley: University of California Press, 1980), 15–34; and John M. Cooper, *Reason and Human Good in Aristotle* (Cambridge, MA: Harvard University Press, 1975).

4 See the previous note on use of "final" to translate "*teleia*" in its comparative use. As we have seen in the discussion of how virtuous activity is completed by pleasure, it is possible for activities to be more or less complete as well, which complicates matters.

5 An influential problematizing of this distinction between the life and activities of happiness can be found in Cooper, *Reason and Human Good*, 159–160; important defences of the viability of the distinction can be found in David Keyt, "Intellectualism in Aristotle," *The Society for Ancient Greek Philosophy Newsletter*, December 1, 1978, https://orb.binghamton.edu/sagp/87; and Heinaman, "Eudaimonia and Self-Sufficiency," 33. My approach to the distinction, as I show below, is based on the discussion of fortune in the *Ethics*.

6 There is broad agreement that there is a distinction between necessary and instrumental conditions of happiness, even if there is disagreement on the details. See, for instance, John M. Cooper, "Aristotle on the Goods of Fortune," *The Philosophical Review* 94, no. 2 (May 1, 1985): 180; Heinaman, "Eudaimonia and Self-Sufficiency," 35; and Martha C. Nussbaum, *The Fragility of Goodness: Luck and Ethics in Greek Tragedy and Philosophy* (Cambridge: Cambridge University Press, 2001), 327–29.

7 See Marc Gasser-Wingate, "Aristotle on Self-Sufficiency, External Goods, and Contemplation," *Archiv für Geschichte der Philosophie* 102, no. 1 (March 1, 2020): 22, who makes this point in the specific context of all that is necessary to become a contemplator, which I will discuss more fully below.

8 The discussion here is of complete practical virtue and not of *theoria*/contemplation which for Aristotle constitutes the most complete virtue. This is why such a life is complete but not fully complete and therefore happy in a secondary sense, as we will soon see.

9 See Nussbaum, *The Fragility of Goodness*, 322–27; Cooper, "Aristotle on the Goods of Fortune," 180–81.

10 Hence I think Hirji's point about the distinction between the conditional exercise of virtue (that avoids bad things) and complete exercise of virtue (that produces good things) is best made in the context of a life of virtue. See Sukaina Hirji, "External Goods and the Complete Exercise of Virtue in Aristotle's Nicomachean Ethics," *Archiv für Geschichte der Philosophie* 103, no. 1 (March 1, 2021): 29–53. Jay Elliott's suggestion that it is difficult to see how happiness is up to us because virtue

constitutes happiness and is up to us, given that external goods can directly impact virtuous activity, may also be similarly addressed. For fortune only directly affects the processes and hence the life of virtue, but not the ability to choose virtuous action which is entirely in the control of the virtuous agent. See Jay R. Elliott, "Aristotle on Virtue, Happiness and External Goods," *Ancient Philosophy* 37, no. 2 (October 1, 2017): 347–59.

11 For the moment though, it may be enough to say that both texts seem to agree that external goods (which are a function of fortune) are either necessary or instrumental for the activities of happiness, even if the *EE*'s position is based in the common discussion of pleasure (in 7.13). But the *EE* also seems to think that fortune is sufficient for well-doing (*EE* 8.2) and therefore approximates the intrinsic good of virtue which normally produces good actions, for reasons we will consider in the Conclusion.

12 See Anthony Kenny, "The Nicomachean Conception of Happiness," *Oxford Studies in Ancient Philosophy* (1991): 73–74; Gasser-Wingate, "Aristotle on Self-Sufficiency," 6–7; and Eric Brown, "Aristotle on the Choice of Lives: Two Concepts of Self-Sufficiency," in *Theoria: Studies on the Status and Meaning of Contemplation in Aristotle's Ethics*, ed. Pierre Destrée and Marco Zingano (Leuven: Peeters Publishing, 2014), 111–33. In what follows I will consider the possibility of disruption in the development and in the maintenance of both kinds of self-sufficiency in a variety of scenarios.

13 See Richard Kraut, *Aristotle on the Human Good* (Princeton, NJ: Princeton University Press, 1989), 73–6.

14 See Plato's *Republic*, 381a10–381c for the possible basis of this view.

15 See Stephen Menn, "Aristotle and Plato on God as Nous and as the Good," *The Review of Metaphysics* 45, no. 3 (1992): 546–47, who thinks that Aristotle collapses Plato's notion of the Good and the Divine Craftsman of the *Timeus*. See also White who explains why Aristotle does this in terms of synthesizing his naturalism with Platonism (Nicholas P. White, "Goodness and Human Aims in Aristotle's Ethics," in *Studies in Aristotle*, ed. Dominic J. O'Meara (Washington, DC: Catholic University of America Press, 2018)).

16 That Aristotle is speaking here of self-knowledge rather than autonomous thinking is accepted by many. See W. D. Ross, *Aristotle* (London: Methuen, 1923), 144–45; Joseph Owens, "The Self in Aristotle," *The Review of Metaphysics* 41, no. 4 (1988): 707–22; Charles H. Kahn, "Aristotle on Thinking," in *Essays on Aristotle's De Anima*, ed. Martha C. Nussbaum and Amelie Oksenberg Rorty (Oxford: Clarendon Press, 1992), 359–80. But I do not think, as Kahn does, that such reflexive self-awareness is ultimately different from that involved in contemplation, as I show below.

17 Additional reasons for the mind's immateriality are presented in *DA* 3.4 429a13ff, of which the argument from intensity seems the most interesting. Here, Aristotle suggests that thinking is essentially different from sensation because intense

perceptions simultaneously undermine perceptual ability in ways in which just the opposite is the case for intense or powerful insights. Presumably since much of the disruption caused by the intensity of perception has to do with its material apparatus, the suggestion seems to be that thinking does not have one since it is not similarly disrupted by powerful insights. For more on why Aristotle thinks human mind/*nous* and Divine mind/*nous* are immaterial, see my "The Relation of Divine Thinking to Human Thought in Aristotle," *American Catholic Philosophical Quarterly* 73, no. 3 (August 1, 1999): 377–406.

18 I have argued for a variation of this reading in my "Relation of Divine Thinking to Human Thought," *American Catholic Philosophical Quarterly* 73, no. 3 (August 1, 1999): 377–406. Others who hold a similar view include Aryeh Kosman, "What Does the Maker Mind Make?," in *Essays on Aristotle's De Anima*, ed. Martha Nussbaum and Amelie Rorty (Oxford: Oxford University Press, 1992), 343–58, and Charles H. Kahn, "Aristotle on Thinking," in *Essays on Aristotle's De Anima*, ed. Martha C. Nussbaum and Amelie Oksenberg Rorty (Oxford: Clarendon Press, 1992), 373–75. But there is a long tradition of scholars who think that God's thinking is of the forms of the world including Richard Norman, "Aristotle's Philosopher God," in *Articles on Aristotle. 4, Psychology and Aesthetics*, ed. Jonathan Barnes, Malcolm Schoefield, and Richard Sorabji, vol. 4 (London: Duckworth, 1969); Joseph P. Lawrence, "The Hidden Aporia in Aristotle's Self-Thinking Thought," *The Journal of Speculative Philosophy* 2, no. 3 (1988): 155–74; Jonathan Lear, *Aristotle: The Desire to Understand* (Cambridge: Cambridge University Press, 1988), 295–96; Rolf George, "An Argument for Divine Omniscience in Aristotle," *Apeiron* 22, no. 1 (March 1, 1989): 61–74; etc. The main problem with such "nomological" readings is that it may undermine God's simplicity since God's knowledge of himself (even if he is the highest instantiation of all the forms) would be incidental to such knowledge. But see Thomas DeKoninck, "Aristotle on God as Thought Thinking Itself," *The Review of Metaphysics* 47, no. 3 (August 1, 1994): 488–89, who thinks that because self-knowledge is always incidental to what is known, God must have nomological knowledge if he is to have self-knowledge at all.

19 For a good discussion of the psychological aspects of thinking and its continuities with perception, see D. K. Modrak, "Chapter Seven: Aristotle on Thinking," *Proceedings of the Boston Area Colloquium in Ancient Philosophy* 2, no. 1 (1986): 209–36.

20 See Keyt, "Intellectualism in Aristotle," 179 and Francisco J. Gonzalez, "Aristotle on Pleasure and Perfection," *Phronesis* 36, no. 2 (1991): 141–59, even if the latter may not agree with my view on the nature of pleasure itself.

21 Thus it is important to emphasize that such knowledge is not useless in terms of what it grounds since it completes knowledge by making it possible, as suggested at the end of the last section. What Aristotle denies is that there is anything beyond

God as first principle as we move towards him. See Matthew D. Walker, *Aristotle on the Uses of Contemplation* (New York: Cambridge University Press, 2018), 151–53. Walker makes a similar point by taking recourse to the *Protrepticus* and by conceiving contemplation quite differently than I do, as I show below.

22 This text is the culmination of the *telos/skopos* distinction in the *Ethics*, though a denial of this distinction seems to be an important basis of Frede's view that *NE* 10.7–8 are inconsistent (because earlier) than the rest of the text. See Dorothea Frede, "New Perspectives on an Old Controversy: The Theoretical and the Practical Life in Aristotle," *Zeitschrift für Philosophische Forschung* 73, no. 4 (2019): 481–510.

23 How might we reconcile this suggestion of brevity in the *Metaphysics* with Aristotle's claim in the *Ethics* that we can contemplate the truth more continuously than we can do anything (*NE* 10.7 1177a22)? Perhaps because he means there that an activity can be continuous (or holds together, *sunexetatē*) and uninterrupted without necessarily being lengthy. I say more below about the continuity in terms of absorption which contemplation allows us to lose ourselves for a while.

24 But Walker, *Aristotle on the Uses of Contemplation*, 175–82, thinks that our self-awareness is like God's self-awareness in that it makes us aware of our upper limits as humans (in the contemplation of God) and lower ones (insofar as we are capable of higher activity than other animals). But then it is hard to see how such self-awareness is any different from awareness of any other sort of knowledge that we may possess. Whereas Aristotle seems to think that contemplation is the purest and most pleasurable of all our activities (*NE* 10.7 1177a24–25), and therefore by implication quite different from the rest.

25 Many recent discussions affirm that contemplation is a human activity. See, for instance, Walker, *Aristotle on the Uses of Contemplation*, and Mor Segev, "Aristotle on the Proper Attitude Toward True Divinity," *American Catholic Philosophical Quarterly* 94, no. 2 (April 3, 2020): 187–209. But see Ackrill, "Aristotle on Eudaimonia," 33. Ackrill's influential position takes Aristotle to be explaining why we should live the life of our divine element here (along with what is said in *De Anima* 3.4 regarding the Active Intellect), even if it means to set aside the practical life since the divine element is what is essentially human. But this results in thinking of Aristotle's position as "broken-backed" since it means accepting that this life is too high for humans unless we are not human but in fact divine, and requires reading the objection as ending at (a) and Aristotle's response beginning at (b). Whereas I take the objection to be stated in (a) and (b) with Aristotle's response coming in (c) which avoids the problem of breaking the back of Aristotle's position. See also Caleb Cohoe, "Living Without a Soul: Why God and the Heavenly Movers Fall Outside of Aristotle's Psychology," *Phronesis* 65, no. 3 (2020): 281–323, for a different approach. Cohoe argues that human and divine *nous* are distinct because human *nous* is an aspect of a human soul, where soul for Aristotle is always

associated with matter of which the soul is a principle (*qua* form); whereas God is a different kind of *nous* since he is life without matter so that the language of soul cannot be applied to him.

26 Hence in the next chapter when Aristotle uses the language of "composite" to refer to the activities of practical virtue and separates these from the excellence of theoretical reason, he still insists that the latter is human though it needs only the bare necessities of life (*NE* 10.8 1178a19–26). This is true regardless of the fact that Aristotle says (to the consternation of many) that mind is immaterial (*DA* 3.4 429a20–25) for the mind that thinks is human mind which does not persist at death (*DA* 3.5 430a24–25).

27 I acknowledge that I have changed my mind on several related matters here on which I have published before. First, I no longer think that the life of practical virtue leads to contemplation and hence to the life of complete happiness without philosophy, though I still continue to believe this is true of Aristotle's earlier *Eudemian Ethics* (*EE*). This shift is essentially the result of coming to see that unlike in the *EE*, the *NE* holds that we are not divine nor do we have internal access to the divine in ways that obviate the need for philosophy (and as outlined above in the previous section). I realize that the *EE*'s position is closer to the *Gītā*'s but not only in the *NE*'s position later, it is also much more consistent with Aristotle's substance-driven philosophy in general, and is how his ethics is read in particular by the tradition. For a full discussion of my earlier position, please see my "On the Eudemian and Nicomachean Conceptions of Eudaimonia," *American Catholic Philosophical Quarterly* 79, no. 3 (August 1, 2005): 365–88.

28 See Howard J. Curzer, "The Supremely Happy Life in Aristotle's Nicomachean Ethics," *Apeiron* 24, no. 1 (March 1, 1991): 47–70, esp. 61–2.

29 This view of how the best life involves both practical and theoretical activity is now well accepted. See, for instance, Curzer, "The Supremely Happy Life in Aristotle's Nicomachean Ethics," 801–34; Sarah Broadie, *Ethics with Aristotle* (New York; Toronto: Oxford University Press, 1991), 413–14; John M. Cooper, "Contemplation and Happiness: A Reconsideration," *Synthese* 72, no. 2 (1987): 187–216; etc.

10

Conclusion

10.0 Introduction

We are finally in a position to bring the developing themes of this exercise to fruition. With the completion of our discussion of contemplation as the highest happiness in the *Ethics*, we can fully consider the relation of the means (*dharma*, virtue) to the ends (freedom, happiness) in both. What we will see is that in different ways, the highest good is out of direct focus of action so that the ethical always has priority, even if what constitutes the ethical and shapes the practical outcomes is a function of their respective commitments to the social or to the individual. These commitments also fashion the nature of the highest good in both despite deep similarities in the ways in which divinity is conceived and contributes to the good. While rationality is more important for the *Ethics* and the emotions even less for the *Gītā*, their focus on the stability of personality means that both find ways of working with desire in all its manifestations, even if one is interested in satisfying desire and the other in eliminating it. Yet the focus on the individual's happiness by way of philosophy does not seem to lead to the possibility of every citizen's happiness in the *Nicomachean Ethics*—something that will be confirmed by a short excursion into the earlier *Eudemian Ethics*; whereas the *Gītā*, perhaps in response to early Buddhism, does just that by making freedom accessible to all via multiple paths/*yoga*s. Finally, reflecting on the role of fortune in human life will give us insight into our texts' overarching commitments to the individual and to the whole.

10.1 Means and Ends

We have previously considered and reflected on the relation of *dharma*/duty-bound action and its relation to *mokṣa*/freedom, but it may be useful to review these considerations in preparation for our discussion of the relation of practical virtue to theoretical contemplation in the *Ethics*. There seem to be three important dimensions to fully *dharmic* action. First, that the action be undertaken without consideration of personal fruit. This is the intention with which the action is to be undertaken, and it is not inappropriate to articulate the intention positively as "acting because it is one's *dharma* to do so." Second, the specific content of such action is determined by one's stage and station based in an evolving tradition and grounded ideally in the origin texts/*Vedas* of the tradition. Third, that the outcomes of such action are directed at world-welfare understood as the staging for the possibility of freedom/*mokṣa* for all. These considerations in turn have two important implications. First, that *dharma* is, ideally, always the agent's highest priority even if it is not of the highest value (as is *mokṣa*) so that there are no shortcuts to their own freedom; for the agent to make their own freedom (understood as freedom from the self) their highest priority enhances rather than undermines the self. Second, that *dharma* encompasses all human activity (social, political, familial, economic, etc.) since it consists of rules for how human activity is undertaken. Taken together, *dharma* always has overriding priority in every sphere of human activity so that it directly promotes the welfare of all and the agent's freedom only indirectly.

Turning to the *Ethics*, the familiar *telos*/*skopos* distinction will initiate our parallel discussion of the dimensions of virtuous action. The "why" or *telos* of virtuous action, we have seen, is virtue itself for Aristotle, who also speaks of the end in terms of "the noble." What he seems to mean by this is that the action needs to be chosen because it is what virtue requires, and which therefore is very much about the intention with which the action is chosen. The "what" of virtue is more complicated and involves deliberative choice as it instantiates the wish to act virtuously. Such deliberation is guided by the requirements of the particular virtue in question (such as courage) that is consonant with the law which is itself ideally a construct of the virtuous citizenry *qua* legislators. This legislative activity in turn is informed by the ultimate goal of creating a society in which the highest human activity of philosophical contemplation (and therefore by implication much of the activity of culture) is possible. For along with the activities of practical virtue, the highest actualization of theoretical virtue in contemplation together constitutes human flourishing. Thus, the outcome/*skopos* of practical virtue is driven by essentially social considerations of promoting every citizen's flourishing, as opposed to just the agent's own highest happiness. For contemplation for the individual is not possible without the ethical, even if it is not chosen, and is in fact the intuited completion of a philosophical investigation into the nature of form that culminates in the knowledge of God. Such knowledge is an end in itself and has no outcome even as it grounds all other knowledge and thereby completes wisdom/*Sophia*.

Both texts, we saw, make the ethical the highest priority and think that it is an internal, psychological prerequisite for obtaining the highest good without reducing the ethical to a mere means to such an end. In the *Gītā* the process is much more explicit and seems to be based on a transformation of practical activity to meditative practice via detachment (see chapter 5 section 8). Whereas the process seems implicit in the *Ethics* in the discussions of stability and internal harmony that the ethical life brings about which thereby enables the sustained pursuit of knowledge and its completion in contemplation. The big differences arise because of how the highest good is conceived and relates to agency.

10.2 Happiness and Freedom

Complete happiness in Aristotle, as we have seen, is very much about the agent even if it is impossible without the context of the city-state/*polis*. Completeness here is clearly inclusive so that both the practical and theoretical virtues are necessary for the fullest human flourishing. So, this position allows for the possibility of a life of practical virtue to be happy but only in a secondary sense even if it involves theoretical pursuits that are not philosophical, which to many seems too limited an either/or (and on which more below).

The key is to see the way in which the satisfaction of desire relates agency to the completeness of happiness, since we are rational animals and therefore have rational and non-rational desires. But desire cannot simply be satisfied in any and every way, which is why virtue is the transformation of the dispositions that desire. The non-rational desires of appetite (for food and sex) and those based on emotion (such as the desire to confront the enemy based on fearlessness and confidence) are cultivated and satisfied in the practical life in terms of the practical virtues (such as moderation and courage). Aristotle thinks the rational desires are only partly satisfied in the practical life insofar as they guide its activities by harmonizing with the non-rational desires; a harmony that we saw centrally involves love. The completion of the satisfaction of rational desire also involves love whose fulfillment requires the pursuit of philosophy (i.e., the love of wisdom) and its culmination of human understanding in the Divine first principle.

Aristotle's inclusive notion of complete happiness therefore, ironically enough, ends up being too exclusive. Only a select few of the select few who are philosophically minded and live practically virtuous lives may obtain it, with the vast majority of us approximating this happiness to a greater but more likely lesser extent. It is no wonder that various efforts have been made to either downgrade contemplation's place in Aristotle's conception of happiness, eliminate it, or change its scope. But I think these attempts speak more to our own democratic leanings and anti-theological commitments than to what is given to us in the text.

It may be that Aristotle is right that the highest human good is difficult for most of us to obtain, something that the *Gītā* agrees with; still, consistent with its holism, the *Gītā* thinks that access to the good should not be restricted by one's path in life even if its preceding tradition does just this in ways that seem more consistent with Aristotle's position. The wider access to the highest good in the *Gītā* is possible because the internal stability that makes a sustained form of internal reflection possible is crucially available to all ways of life within the orthodox fold. The path of action/*karma yoga* procures such stability by correlating mindful (in terms of right intention) duty-bound action on the back of a sustained cultivation of sense-control. The path of knowledge/*jñāna* and devotion/*bhakti* presuppose much of this *dharm*ic training since all partake in society to some extent. *Jñāna yoga* adds an explicit meditative dimension in retirement whereas *bhakti* transforms *karma yoga*'s impersonal mindfulness into a single-minded focus on the Godhead.

In the *Gītā*, it helps that access to the highest truth—i.e., to the Higher Self/*Ātman* which is not distinct from access to the Universal Self/*Brahman*—is internal to us. This critically ensures that regardless of path, freedom/*mokṣa* is in fact universally available, in ways that may not apply to Aristotle's wise person even if philosophy were not the only approach to complete happiness.[1] The eternal unchangingness of the Self we saw is crucial for the insight that liberates the self from its bondage perhaps because of the stark contrast It provides to all that changes. Thus, this contrast provides the basis of the internal breakage of the self that constitutes freedom, even if, ironically enough, this is only possible if the self (and specifically the doer/*kartā*) is in a relatively stable (i.e., *sattv*ic) configuration in the first place.

The negative nature of this insight into the Self—in terms of what the self is not—is worth considering further. It is as if someone born on board a ship at sea comes upon land for the first time in their middle age. Their recognition of the difference in permanence between land and vessel is visceral, as they struggle to reconsider the meaning of safe harbor. Similarly, to see that there is no self but the Self is a visceral insight that reveals the impermanence of the self that must involve rationality, even if the positive nature of the insight may not. Thus, the culmination of rationality's negative role in human endeavor according to the *Gītā* is consistent with its view on the elimination of desire, rational and non-rational. This consistency is so even if the negative dimension is mediated by the satisfaction of desire in the service of world-welfare, and by the needs of stage-and-station rather than of the individual per se.

It may be easier to accept the limiting of rational rather than non-rational desire, given how central feeling is to human nature. The *Gītā* is mindful of traditional Brahmanism's austere approach to sentiment that is clearly in evidence in the paths of knowledge and action. Hence it finds a way to begin the transformation of devotion away from trading favors to one that allows for the emotions to find their fulfillment in the love of God. Even so, the *dharm*ic life does not involve the fulfillment of the non-rational—as it does in Aristotle where it is, like the fulfillment of reason, very much about what it means to live the good human life, ideally conceived—since *dharma* is shaped to ultimately take us away from our humanity.

To end this section, it may be appropriate to discuss the deep similarities between contemplation/*theoria* and freedom/*mokṣa*, even if our texts say little about them. Aristotle's hylomorphism of form/soul and body attempts to maintain the unity of the individual even if the discussion of *nous* as immaterial, and by implication not being the form of any part of the body, complicates the picture. Essentially the same mystery haunts the *Gītā* at the global level in relating Spirit/*Puruṣa* and matter/nature/*Prakrati* in its aspect dualism and ontological monism. Both texts emphasize the deeply pleasurable experience of what amounts to the essence of knowing (i.e., awareness or consciousness), though both are fairly reticent on the details. Even the *Gītā* which repeatedly speaks of freedom says quickly of it as the experience of light, bliss, and peace without saying much more (*BG* 5.24, 6.27, 6.28), and which reminds of the ecstatic elements in Aristotle's discussion of contemplation. As we would expect, the *Ethics* emphasizes the transitory nature of the experience which marks a return from the divine to the human in ways that complete human happiness; whereas the *Gītā* thinks that perfectly detached action ensues from insight so that a return to our humanity (and to some form of attachment) is not what should be normally expected.

10.3 Individualism and Holism

Aristotle's commitment to individual happiness as the highest social value is enormously influential in the western tradition, even if the conception of flourishing has broadened, morphed, and even transformed. It may therefore be useful to consider the value of holism as a way of potentially reflecting on these commitments.

Aristotle, we saw, thinks leisure is essential for philosophy and therefore for the highest good of contemplation/*theoria*. This seems plausible since so many of the activities of culture—from religion, literature, theatre, poetry, art, and especially philosophy—depend on society progressing beyond mere subsistence. It also means that since the distribution of leisure in traditional societies is usually unequal (and historically persistent), the excessively restrictive nature of the form of highest happiness as contemplative philosophy in Aristotle also has an economic dimension. One kind of response has been to broaden the notion of contemplation to include art, friendship, theoretical pursuits of all sorts, and in general, all the kinds of activities that humans find themselves reflecting on in their lives.[2] But to do so is to go against Aristotle's own considerations in the *Ethics* as to the essential connection of philosophy to contemplation (based on considerations of finality), and its association with divinity in that text as well as in the related discussions in the *Metaphysics*.

Moreover, his view in the *Nicomachean Ethics* reflects a reduction in but not an elimination of his theological commitments that are more in line with the *Metaphysics,* when compared to the older *Eudemian Ethics* (*EE*), and therefore more likely to be his considered position. Let me explain without getting bogged down in the details. A different conception of divinity seems to be in place in Aristotle's discussion in the *EE* of contemplation as the criterion (or mark) of the goals of a society (spoken here in terms of the pursuit of the natural goods such as wealth, etc.). Not only is Aristotle more explicit here that contemplation is of God, but that the criterion is "the service and contemplation of God"[3] (*EE* 8.3 1249b15–20). Whatever "service of God" might mean here including possibly just ethical activity, it certainly suggests a different divinity from the remote, austere one we see in the *Metaphysics* which seems more consistent with the one implicit in the *Nicomachean* version; for this language in the *EE* suggests that at the very least there is some kind of divine expectation of human activity.

Another aspect of the different theological commitments in the *EE* is the suggestion that the Divine can be the origin of well-doing in us that is consistent but not rational and therefore lucky.[4] "Well-doing" here clearly refers to what "living well and doing well" do in the Nicomachean version, and therefore to happiness. Thus we have the startling view that divinely inspired, irrational luck can be the cause of happiness, whereas on the Nicomachean view, good fortune (which is a form of luck) is at best a necessary or instrumental condition of happiness.[5] More importantly, the Nicomachean version insists that it is the rationality of well-doing that is essential to it counting as happiness, whereas this does not seem to be so in the *Eudemian Ethics* perhaps in light of its seemingly more substantial theological commitments.

Returning to the *Ethics*, we saw that the brief albeit enthralling nature of contemplation as the highest most final form of happiness leaves an enduring mark on the contemplator because of the purity of its pleasure (*NE* 10.7 1177a24–26). Yet it is, as we have seen, the delicate fruit of a complete life of intellectual labor that presupposes an intensive education and practical cultivation which in turn is supported by an extensive infrastructure that is familial, social, and cultural. It would therefore be plausible to say that such a complete life is more easily disrupted in process than a life like Priam's that is practical in the main; for while obstacles can be grist for the practical life's mill, the theoretical aspects of a complete life can more easily be undermined in progression by war, family disruption, financial difficulties, etc. This means that complete happiness is more exclusive and elusive even as it remains the ideal for the strivings of the city-state.

The *Gītā* on the other hand initiates universal access to the highest good of freedom, likely in response to early Buddhism. Such a move is revolutionary in a tradition that is renowned for its emphasis on elitism and secrecy, as it attempts to maintain a world order that it takes to be divinely sanctioned and continuous with the cosmological one. Its approach to universal access is based on bringing a certain kind of intentionality and mindfulness to duty/*dharma* regardless of one's walk of life. Since duty is pervasive across class and station and permeates all aspects of life (and even when it does not), the *Gītā* seems to bring meaning and value to all human activity. To accommodate different human proclivities, the path/*yoga* of devotion offers a less austere, more personal, and richly emotional approach to freedom than that of action, whereas the path of knowledge is more austere and cerebral than either.

It may be useful to consider how the problem of misfortune affects the *Gītā*'s position on accessing the highest good. For it would seem that we can easily imagine Arjuna ending up like Priam: defeated, bereft, and broken, which could clearly affect his pursuit of freedom. The *Gītā*'s response I think might be to emphasize that the problem of misfortune is a problem from the point of view of the individual and their flourishing, whereas from the *Gītā*'s perspective, misfortune always provides opportunity for insight. After all, misfortune is, in essence, that which goes against the individual and is consistent with, and even conducive to, seeing through individuality. It is true that adversity often encourages the reverse, since anger, hatred, self-pity, etc.—which are often a response to misfortune—can end up strengthening the hold of the self rather than undermining it. But this is exactly why the *Gītā* extensively addresses just these kinds of response with discipline/*yoga* of more than one sort.

It may be objected that this kind of response is conducive to maintaining the social (and usually corrupt) status quo since it encourages members of society to accept their lot; for the worse one's lot the better the opportunity for freedom from it. But such an objection, it is important to note, assumes the primacy and irreducibility of the individual which the *Gītā* denies, even as it attempts to combat the stench of corruption in the social order. Not only is the text more accessible to the masses as part of the *Mahābhārata*, but it is critical of the priestly class and its attempt to exploit its monopoly on ritual. The *Gītā*'s solution—predating similar moves in Protestant Christianity—is to shift control of the religious life away from the priestly class, even if it does so by transforming religious (and it must be insisted, everyday) existence into something more spiritual and contemplative. But the issue of a decaying social order is worth pursuing further especially in light of the *Gītā*'s monistic commitments.

If the world is an aspect of the Divine understood as perfect, we need to consider in what sense it can be corrupt. In the western tradition, the influential and considered view that "divinity" means perfection originates in Plato, who then argues that perfection must be unchanging since any change must entail a move away from perfection.[6] Plato's views on divine perfection seem to powerfully impact the way in which he conceives of knowledge in terms of unchanging Forms that have kinship with the divine. The world on the other hand is separated from the divine and can only approximate perfection insofar as it varyingly and imperfectly participates in form.

We see this view emerge in Aristotle with a distinctively Aristotelian twist, since the Divine is conceived as unchanging perfection by distinguishing Its activity/*energeia* from change/*kinesis*. Substance and hence form is found in the world for Aristotle (rather than separated from it as in Plato)—as we saw in the case of the human soul as form of the body. But form in the world therefore tries to approximate the Divine's unchanging activity by maintaining the persistence of form (if not the mortal individual) in the world through reproduction. In the very special case of humans, a very small subset gets to participate in the Divine's perfection additionally if fleetingly through contemplation, so that our relation to immortality is not just through species-form.

A view that is in some ways similar can be found in the *Gītā* in its discussion of the unmanifest, unchanging perfection of *Brahman* who is beyond space and time and therefore beyond change. But the *Gītā*'s combination of substance monism and aspect dualism means that a separating of divine perfection from the world's imperfections is not available to it. One kind of response (as found in Spinoza) is to insist that the world understood as inseparable from God is a living perfection, especially if seen from the point of view of eternity (that is, as being beyond time).[7] But such a move may not be available to the *Gītā* because of its insistence that the relation between the unmanifest, unchanging and manifest, changeful aspects of *Brahman* is mysterious precisely because the latter is in space and time and the former is not. Such a view is repeatedly articulated in the text so that it seems to be its considered view. Hence the *Gītā* speaks of Krishna's unchanging perfection even while he works in the world (*BG* 4.13); of the Divine's unchanging, higher manifestation in relation to Its lower changing one as *māyā* (*BG* 7.24–25); and of the moving and unmoving universe unified in the divine body of Krishna (*BG* 11.7), for instance. Moreover, it is unclear that the *Gītā* would find Spinoza's suggestion attractive since it thinks that the world's development is cyclical and therefore subject to disorder as much as it is to order.

We are therefore at a point in the discussion where we need to revisit the role of Krishna's intervention in the world. He tells us that his manifestations in the world (as an *avatar*) occur regularly to protect the good and re-establish righteousness, and thereby encourage their progression to freedom on the various paths (*BG* 4.6–11). Such a need for re-establishing the *dharm*ic order, I suggested, seems consistent with the *Mahābhārata*'s view (in which the *Gītā* is ensconced) that the world is in a state of decline. Part of the decline is clearly to be explained in terms of the deterioration of *dharma* as the social world's accelerating decline is consistent with the waning of the cosmological order (or what we call "heat-death"). The shoring up of *dharma* by Krishna's intervention seems therefore to be a stopgap measure to maintain the passage to freedom that *dharma* represents.

The question then arises as to why such an intervention is necessary if the world (and by implication all of its living and non-living constructs) is in the process of devolving into its constituent strands? In other words, it may seem that *dharma* does not need fortifying since its job is to help its adherents see through the individual self, which the process of dissolution of the world might naturally engender on its own. But I think the problem of selfing is particularly acute at our (late) stage of cosmological decline (i.e., the *kaliyuga*) though why this may be so needs to be motivated.

Presumably, at the most and least developed state of the world, the problem of what I'm calling "selfing" is not a problem. Selfing is not a hurdle in the former because the world is most fully differentiated and individuated and yet works as a unified organism because of the predominance of *sattva*; selfing is not an obstacle in the latter because the *guṇa*s exist only in separation, from where the cosmological cycle begins anew. At some stage in the decline a less problematic version of selfing that is still able to keep the larger perspective likely arises as a coping mechanism as the breakdown proceeds apace. Perhaps selves become increasingly blinkered as the decline extends so that the myopia (which is itself a function of the decline of *sattva*'s predominance) and the ensuing self-centeredness is a symptom of a late stage of the decline and is therefore a cause as much as it is a symptom of the destructive nature of the *kaliyuga*. Such resistance, on the *Gītā*'s view, may be the result of inertia as selves cling more and more desperately to the echo of a misremembered unity.

It is in this context then that Krishna's intervention with the notion of detachment should be understood. Clearly his embodied incarnation/*avatar* can be seen from the human perspective as an extraordinary intrusion to alleviate evil but is more likely just routine maintenance to keep the world's eventual dissolution on track. Hence detachment's central focus on living up to the letter and spirit of *dharma* that not only keeps the world from reducing to a premature and jumbled chaos but smoothens the passage to full dissolution by removing/freeing the kinks and folds that have naturally developed within it.

A different view of perfection, if one wants to call it that, emerges here. While there is a place for Plato and Aristotle's partiality to unchanging perfection, it would seem that ordered cyclical change is very much a part of it as well. Rather than thinking that such change approximates perfection, the *Gītā* seems to imply that organized change is simply a different aspect of it. Perhaps it thinks that the world's perfection arises from the sheer monotony of change—its organized cyclical and hence unchangingly changing Hereclitean nature—that balances the unchanging perfection of its spiritual counterpart.

10.4 Final Considerations

I have attempted to show how our two texts' commitments to the individual and to holism shape their response to common problems on the practical front including access to the highest good. It is because of Aristotle's substantialism that we see the highest good conceived in terms of a completion of individual nature with all the ethical and political infrastructure directed to this end, even if it means that such access is restricted to a few. The broader access to the highest good in the *Gītā* seems consistent with its holism, which is reflected in its practical and social commitments.

The impact of their influence on their respective cultures is extensive, as briefly discussed in chapter 1, and perhaps a little more here is in order before we close. Even if the decline of virtue's influence in the western tradition in early modernity is only revived in the mid-twentieth century, the influence of Aristotle's substantialism is more persistent. Despite the deep continuities between Plato and Aristotle on ethical matters, Aristotle's character-based ethics represents a huge shift from Plato's soul-body dualism to hylomorphism; for now, virtue becomes very much about flourishing in this world so that it transforms the nature and role of society that reverberates well into the future. This influence can be seen in early modern thinkers continuing to use the language of substance, but also in the way in which renaissance humanism and eventually liberal democracy make the individual the primary unit of consideration. While it is true that the primacy of the individual in liberal democracy broadly speaking is much more egalitarian than in Aristotle, the *Gītā*'s views should make us wonder how much of the pervasive problems of inequality are ultimately foundational in such individualism.

The *Gītā*'s views, on the other hand, impact especially the ethics of most of the orthodox and even the later Buddhist schools and is perhaps even instrumental in orthodoxy's resurgence in the culture at the expense of Buddhism. The much later decline in the state of discussion amongst the orthodox schools seems to be related to the rise of colonialism with the already powerful Vedanta schools gaining ascendency. This ascendency is manifest in the persistent influence of the *Gītā* (which is a central text for these schools) both in terms of the traditionally educated Indians, and western-educated ones, some of whom encounter the text first in English translation.[8] This is not to deny that many of the founding fathers of the Indian Constitution are powerfully influenced by their education in western liberal democracies. It is to suggest that the egalitarian considerations at the heart of the constitution (in a deeply inegalitarian context, made worse by colonialism) are inspired by the *Gītā*'s emphasis on freedom for all, even if the text might think such a focus on individualism is in the final analysis misconstrued.

Notes

1 See Roopen Majithia, "The Relation of Divine Thinking to Human Thought in Aristotle," *American Catholic Philosophical Quarterly* 73, no. 3 (August 1, 1999): 377–406. Here I have argued that Aristotle thinks we do have such internal access

to the Divine if in fact we see that the Prime Mover is not distinct from the Active Intellect which is crucial for human thinking, even if this view is controversial. In our context here in the *Nicomachean Ethics*, the issue is moot since philosophy seems to be the only approach to happiness as will become more obvious in our discussion of the *Eudemian Ethics* below.

2 See, for instance, Amélie Rorty, "The Place of Contemplation in Aristotle's Nicomachean Ethics," in *Essays on Aristotle's Ethics*, Major Thinkers Series 2 (Berkeley: University of California Press, 1980), 377–94; and Matthew D. Walker, *Aristotle on the Uses of Contemplation* (New York: Cambridge University Press, 2018).

3 I follow Kenny here in keeping the original text of the manuscript to say "*ton theon theapueuein*" as opposed to the amended version in the Oxford Classical Texts, *Ethica Nicomachea* ed. Ingram Bewater, 1920 Clarendon Press which reads "*to en hemin theion therapuein*." See Aristotle, trans. with an Introduction and Notes by Anthony Kenny, *The Eudemian Ethics*, Oxford World's Classics (Oxford; New York: Oxford University Press, 2011).

4 See my "On the Eudemian and Nicomachean Conceptions of Eudaimonia," *American Catholic Philosophical Quarterly* 79, no. 3 (August 1, 2005): 365–88. Here I have argued that Aristotle in fact is suggesting that all human thinking originates in the Divine, which might explain why he seems to think in the *EE* that human thinking is divine (*EE* 8.2 1248a22–28) rather than like the divine's thinking as I have argued (in 9.5) he does in the *NE*.

5 There is a discussion of good fortune in *EE* 6.13 1153b15–25 that makes a similar distinction between the necessary and instrumental role of external goods, but this, it should be remembered, is a book that is in common with the *Nicomachean Ethics* (where it is Book 7). Moreover, it is quite possible that Aristotle thought he could hold both positions consistently in the *EE* since one can have terrible luck with external goods as necessary or instrumental for well-doing, but still be lucky when it comes to acting well.

6 See Plato, *Republic*, 381a10–381c.

7 See Spinoza's *Ethics* Proposition 29, Scholium, for instance.

8 I agree with and follow much of what is said on these matters in Sanjay Palshikar, *Evil and the Philosophy of Retribution: Modern Commentaries on the Bhagavad-Gita* (New Delhi: Routledge India, 2014), 1–24. But while Palshikar is right in suggesting that many of the great proponents of *bhakti* in the middle ages make no reference to the *Gītā*, I am not sure that is enough to deny the *Gītā*'s persistent influence. For it is plausibly the case that *bhakti*'s philosophical basis is found in the *Gītā*, as I have suggested in 8.6, and is maintained through the ongoing influence of the various Vedanta schools.

Appendix 1

Aristotle on Potentiality and Actuality, and on Activity and Process

The distinction between actuality/*energeia* and potentiality/*dunamis* is key in Aristotle and is best understood with examples. Seeing and building are standard examples for actualities even if, as we will see, they are different because the former is an activity whereas the latter is a process. But as actualities, seeing and building are actualizations of capacities to see and build where the former is natural, and the latter learnt. But this means that with building at least we have a prior or first potentiality that is developed into the capacity to build which in turn is therefore a second potentiality or a first actuality. Whereas we are born with the capacity to see, or with the second potentiality/first actuality for sight that is then fully actualized as second actualities in seeing just as the capacity to build is fully actualized in building (*Phy.* 9.6 1048a30–1048b8).

Seeing is further distinguished from building because seeing is an activity/ (*energeia* in a narrower sense than "actuality") and building is a process/*kinesis*. Essentially seeing is complete in form from moment to moment; whereas building is only complete when its product, the building, is finished so that the form of the parts of the process are different from the form of the process as a whole (*NE* 10.4 1174a14–24). It is important for our purposes to see that the fully actualized second actuality of virtue is an activity and not a process.

Personal Identity in the Tradition

When philosophers investigate the self of personal identity, what they are pursuing is the nature of the person. Rocks and snails cannot be persons, because we usually think that persons have a mental life of some sort; they have memories, beliefs, preferences, and aspirations which make them who they are (all or most of which essentially involve rationality in some way). But, more importantly, to ask this question about personal identity is to really ask if and how it is possible for the person to remain the same (i.e., to be identical with oneself) over time (i.e., through the past, present, and future). Clearly, this investigation pursues what seems obvious to any person, that they are in fact the same person now as in the past. Yet it is notoriously difficult to pin down the basis for what seems so obvious to us. We pursue the matter here because the issue is relevant to ethics in general, and therefore to Aristotle's ethics in particular. After all, we hold present and future person X responsible for his past and present actions on the assumption that X is the same person in some way. If not, then it is hard to see how moral responsibility is possible over time.

Numerous attempts have been made in the history of the tradition to determine a viable candidate for personal identity, including psychological continuity, the body, and the soul. Briefly, memory is the central plank in psychological continuity's candidacy for being the basis of personal identity. Tom knows himself to be the same person as the child that grew up on Wellesley Street in Toronto because he has the memory of doing so. Even if Tom doesn't remember everything between the present and his childhood, it is reasonable to allow him that arc of identity, especially if there are a reasonable number of recallable memories on it. One of the key problems with this view is that it conflates evidence for personal identity with what constitutes it; for as it has been pointed out, memory of the past at best is a recognition of being the same person but not the basis of such personhood, which must therefore be different.

So, since the body is often the basis of the continuity we experience over time, it has been proposed as a candidate for the basis of personal identity. After all, Tom's body now is continuous with (even if it is not the same as) his body as a child in ways that are not the case for any other body. The problem here is that the body in general is not usually essential to personhood as a part of it (i.e., the brain, which is where memory, belief, preference, etc. are thought to reside). Thus, if Tom's brain is transferred from his body to another one successfully, we would usually agree that the new body now houses Tom the person, which means that the old body cannot be the basis of personal identity.

Soul, the third candidate, is often dismissed since it is usually taken to be immaterial, and the existence of immaterial entities in general is thought to be implausible within the context of a scientific world view. Even beyond such a world view, the interaction between immaterial (soul) and material (body) entities has been difficult to explain in the history of the tradition. If humans are constituted by both and given that soul and body seem fundamentally different from each other, it is hard to imagine how they might causally interact in a way that is explicable. This is a real problem since causal interaction in science is understood in purely material terms (e.g., where a neuro-chemical process as opposed to the soul in a body causes the body to move). Aristotle's position on personal identity essentially involves the soul, but in ways that crucially avoid the obvious difficulties we have just outlined.

Aristotle on Personal Identity

Aristotle's view on personal identity is best understood in terms of his substantialism and hylomorphism. Substantialism may be understood as the view in which substances are the key building blocks of the universe because everything that exists is either a substance or dependent on it. A substance for Aristotle is a composite of matter and form (*Phy.* 191a7–12); for instance, when the craftsman imposes the form of chair on wooden matter so that it is wooden chair X (which is a particular "this" that we can point to) which is a substance.[1] Another way to make the point is to say that X is a chair because being a chair is essential to X so that if it loses the ability to be called a chair (because, for instance, it comes under a persistent axe), it is no longer an X but something else. Suppose we say that the chair is now reduced to pieces of wood. Then we see that the wood itself is a natural substance which has the form (woodiness) imposed on matter (say, cellulose), which in turn has a form and matter composition all the way down to what Aristotle calls "prime matter" which is completely denuded of form (*Phy.* 2.1).

Now Aristotle's point is that X can have many changing predicates that are not part of its essence (or form) that still allow us to say that it is X. For example, the chair X could be painted yellow or green, could lose a leg, could become weathered over time, could change hands, etc., and still be a chair. All of these attributes qualify the substance X, which is why they are thought to be its qualities rather than its essence and would not exist without the substance. (Substance in turn would not exist as that substance without its form or essence, i.e., chairness that is common to all chairs and is therefore not the basis of the chair's identity on its own as X.) Another kind of thing that can be said of X the chair is that it is furniture. But unlike "being yellow" which is in the chair, being furniture is not in the chair but is rather said of it. This is because, like chairness, "furniture" is a form (or universal) albeit of a secondary kind that classifies tables, chairs and sofas and would not exist without these substances whose essences are primary forms (*Categories* 3 1a10–24).

The upshot then is that everything that exists is a substance (such as cats, trees, earth, water, cars, etc.) or exists in a substance (all its predicates such as its size, shape, position, weight, color, etc.) or is said of it (its classifications such as species and genus). Put another way, substances are fundamental building blocks of the universe because they are subjects and everything else is a predicate. For substances are in and of themselves (since they are not in or said of anything else) whereas everything else is in or said of a substance (*Categories* 5 2a11–14). Now let us see what implications such a view has for personal identity.

Essence or form in living beings like humans is called "soul," since it is soul that organizes the matter and gives it the structure that allows us to identify it as human (*DA* 2.1 412a18–21). Such form is transmitted from parent to child and differs from an externally imposed form like chair in that it brings about changes in the matter from within (*Met.* 17.7 1072b35–1073a3). Thus, an embryo grows because it has a soul or form that is an internal principle of change whose purpose is the fullest actualization of that form in an adult human being (*Phy.* 2.1 193a35–193b9).

One could be forgiven in thinking that form is simply another way of talking about DNA, but in fact that is not so; for DNA is a material principle that organizes matter. DNA's material nature—i.e., the sequencing of its four chemical bases, adenine, guanine, cytosine, and thymine—is the blueprint, if you will, of how the body will grow, organize, and maintain itself. Whereas form or essence is a formal principle which is not reducible to the matter it organizes. Yet form is not something that has separate being (or is ontologically distinct) from the matter either, even if we can separate it intellectually when we grasp form in our minds. So, for Aristotle, a naturalist grasps the form of toad in her mind after extensive observation of many toads in their habitat and over their life cycle. Such an essence no doubt involves an intellectual definition (for starters, that it is a tailless amphibian, etc.) that separates it from other, similar creatures (frogs, for instance) and classifies them into its appropriate sub-species and genus.

But an intellectual definition of a human (or any living) being is only the cognitional aspect of form for Aristotle, which is why he calls its lived manifestation "soul." This is because he does not think that soul/form can be reduced simply to the organization of its matter. If it could have been, then, the dead yet organized body of Socrates post-hemlock would still be ensouled, which Aristotle obviously would deny. But the possession of soul/form means that the body is not just organized but can persist in its organization precisely because it can potentially sustain itself through activity. This makes sense, given that we get at the cognitional aspect of soul/form only by observing the activities of the organized body in the world, which in turn allows us to say that the living being has a soul in the first place.

Aristotle's point is still more nuanced, for there is intermediacy between being dead and being active, what we might say is being alive or what he calls having the potentiality for activity. This is why, while happiness is defined as an activity, the happy person is one who has the potential to act in such fashion even if she is asleep (*DA* 2.1 412a21–29). Soul, then, is the potentiality to act of an appropriately organized body, something that the body of the post-hemlock Socrates clearly does not possess. The application of Aristotle's hylomorphism (from *hulē*, matter and *morphē*, form) to humans is interesting because it neither reduces the human being to matter, nor does it say that we are constituted by a material body and an immaterial soul. Rather, it seems to walk a fine (and attractive) line between the two, even if it is not without its problems.

For Aristotle, therefore, Socrates persists so long as this particular hylomorphic combination of matter and form persists. This does not mean, of course, that change cannot be associated with persistence so long as it is accidental (paleness, musicality, height, etc.) and not essential or substantial (i.e., where Socrates is no longer capable of undertaking the activities of Socrates).

Notes

1 The challenge is to try and understand Aristotle's seeming suggestions in the *Metaphysics* that it is form that is ultimately substance, and not the composite, for reasons we need not go into here (*Met.* 7.7 1032a33–1032b2; 7.8 1033b15–18; 7.11 1037a27–30; 8.3 1043b28–32). But there are good reasons to think that the composite is substance since forms of the same kind (e.g. of individual humans) are exactly the same whereas the composites are not, which therefore makes the latter the only plausible basis of personal identity. More importantly, the tradition that follows Aristotle seems to take the composite as substance for the most part and not the form.

Appendix 2

Philosophical Context of the *Gītā*

Since the *Gītā* presupposes many philosophical ideas from the tradition as it responds to criticisms from rival schools, a short précis of some of these positions will help contextualize our discussions.

The *Upaniṣads*

The *Upaniṣad*s are a part of the *Vedas* and hence considered *śruti*/heard, even if they seem to have been a later addition to them. As part of the *Brahmana*s they differ from the *Āranyaka*s that purportedly explain ritual, for they are often anti-ritualistic, speculative, and suggestive. In fact, many of the core ideas that engage the philosophical discussions both within and without the orthodox tradition that the *Vedas* initiate may be found here: rebirth that is determined in some sense by one's actions (*karma*), renunciation of the world and the practice of *yogic* disciplines such as meditation to obtain freedom/*mokṣa*, and, perhaps most importantly, discussions of the relations between Higher Self/*Ātman* and the universal cosmic principle/*Brahman*. The early *Upaniṣad*s are all thought to have been composed prior to the common era, with the essential divide being whether they are pre-Buddhistic (*Brahadaryaka*, *Chandogya*, *Taittariya*, *Aitariya*, and *Kausitaki*) or not (*Katha*, *Isa*, *Svetāśvatāra*, and *Mundaka*). It is generally agreed that what distinctively unites the early *Upaniṣad*s is their monism in terms of the variety of ways in which the *Ātman-Brahman* relation is expressed, even if there is often much more to the texts.[1] The texts do not therefore easily reduce to an anachronistic form of monistic idealism since the world's unity is often discussed in terms of being and non-being, body and mind, name and form, etc. Idealism itself seems a development in Vasabandhu's mind-only Yogācāra Buddhism which comes much later (fourth–fifth century CE).

Saṁkhya

"Saṁkhya" literally means "enumeration" which has led some to think that the earliest versions of such thinking represent the shift from *Upaniṣad*ic monism to the dualism of *Puruṣa*/Spirit and *Prakrati*/Nature.[2] In keeping with the non-theistic version of *Brahman* in the *Upaniṣads* it is likely that theism only develops in intermediate strains whereas the understanding of Nature in terms of strands/*guṇas* probably developed early. Thus, we begin with a dualism of the kinds of substance even if at first only individual instances of each are conceived. The strands of *sattva*, *rajas*, and *tamas* represent a radical re-conceiving of elementary entities which in *Upaniṣads* are spoken terms of the five elements (air, water, fire, earth, and space). These strands are ultimately reducible to some kind of ur-matter since they are the expressions of primordial Nature. Classical or later Saṁkhya as found in Kapilla's *Saṁkhya Karika* (probably fourth century CE) carefully consolidates much of the above and also develops on the early position. A sophisticated cyclical process now explains how the unmanifest Nature becomes a manifest multiplicity and then back again to a singularity, in relation to a multiplicity (as opposed to a singularity) of unchanging Spirits/*Puruṣas* that act like catalysts in the process. The *Gītā*'s views seem intermediate to the early and classical Saṁkhya where it seems first and foremost to be construed as a theoretical approach to freedom whose essential dualism of kinds of substance the text attempts to reconcile with *Upaniṣadic* monism.

Early Buddhism

Early Buddhism's outlook seems reactionary and reform-minded even while maintaining continuities with the Vedic tradition in many ways. While eschewing faith in texts like the *Vedas* and in ritual, perhaps because of the pervasive corruption of Brahmanism that even the *Gītā* acknowledges, the Buddha's views seem to rely on his own experience lensed through rational analysis. The use of rationality seems to be common to other heterodox (i.e., non-orthodox, non-Brahmanical) often renunciatory/*sramaṇa* traditions only some of whose legacies remain (as is the case for the Charvāka and the Jaina schools as opposed to, for example, early schools of Indian skepticism).

The core ideas of early Buddhism are encapsulated in the view of the world as a universal flux that is an extrapolation of a multidimensional, causal assessment of the individual. A person is an interdependent causal complex of five ever-changing aggregates/*skandas* of form/body/*rupa*, feeling/*vedanā*, perception/*saṃjañā*, predispositions/*saṃskāras*, and consciousness/*vijñāna*. But "person" or "Ram" are simply convenient designators that we use to carve off and address an aspect of the universal flux of which others include table, planet, and star.[3] The Buddha takes this understanding of the world and of the person to result in a deep contradiction: we act as if we persist in some essential sense as selves and relate to the world of things and people as if they do as well when in fact this is simply not the case. This contradiction is manifest in desire which is essentially an expression of hope for the persistence of either subject, object, or both. The Buddha's solution is to help find a way to overcome our essential ignorance in terms of an eight-fold path that involves, among other things, the life of monastic renunciation and mindfulness (or meditation) in addition to right action and right living (on charity). Hence *nirvana*, which literally means "blowing out," is not just a theoretical but lived insight into the nature of things that frees us from suffering, and which therefore ends with this life. For while the Buddha does not think there is a persistent self that transmigrates across lives, he does believe that that there is a persistence of the constantly shifting causal configuration or pattern that does, unless it is overcome by knowledge at insight. Thus, Buddhism does seem to have a great deal in common with the *Gītā* (such as on renunciation, desire, nature conceived in terms of change, etc.) and its preceding tradition, even if they differ on many of the details.

Ends, Stages, and Classes in the Tradition

The orthodox tradition develops a complex web of commitments in relation to one's stage and station in life that concern the ethical/*dharma*, material/*arthā*, pleasurable/*kāma*, and ultimate/*mokṣa* aims of human life.

"Duty" translates "*dharma*," a word that originates in the *Vedas* and which has a much-discussed wider meaning in the tradition that is useful to rehearse briefly. (The *Vedas* themselves are light on details, and the particulars of *dharma*, and its associated concepts discussed below, are discussed in the *dharmaśastras* (or *dharma* texts), of which the *Manusmṛiti* is preeminent.)

The Sanskrit root of "*dharma*" is *dhṛ*, which literally means to uphold, maintain, or support, usually in the context of society. But "*dharma*" means not only whatever is necessary to maintain the social order, but the cosmological one as well, a combination that is originally found in the Vedic term *ṛta*. Thus, depending on the context, "law" (both moral and natural) is an appropriate translation; "essential characteristic" or "function" is legitimate (i.e., an entity's *dharma* or essential characteristic gives us its role in nature or in society); as is "virtue," "duty," or "justice" in the human context (insofar as humans either do or do not live up to their *dharma*).[4] Clearly, in *BG* 2.7, quoted above, when Arjuna is bewildered about his *dharma*, the appropriate translation is "duty." Yet, as we can plausibly see, to do one's duty is to act justly and even virtuously, and this clearly involves intellectual deliberation.

But these deliberations are complicated by *dharma*'s relation to an individual's class/*varṇa*, stage in life/*āśrama*, or, taken together, his stage and station/*varṇāśramadharma*. As societies evolve, class stratification seems to be a natural concomitant, often driven by specialization of work. We might all start as hunter-gathers, but over multiple generations, move into farming, herding, construction, trading, fighting, teaching, and so on. Such stratification may originate in ability but often ossifies—in the name of social stability—into a class system, especially in traditionally static agrarian political economies. In India, four classes evolved into a hierarchy to fulfill four broad functions of society: the *Brahmin* or intellectual class that is responsible for sacred and educational work, the *kshatriya* or warrior class that is concerned with the administration and defence of the state, the *vaiśya* or economic class that undertakes agricultural, trades, and market-related work, and the *śudra* class for menial work in the service of the other three classes. Eventually, classes/*varṇa*—where mobility between classes was thought to have been possible, if difficult—hardened further into castes/*jati* and sub-castes, where membership was determined solely by birth. While class and caste mobility were prohibited within a lifetime, appropriately fulfilling one's class function within society was understood to lead to "upward" mobility over lifetimes. The underlying assumption here, which we will eventually examine, is that the maintenance of personal identity in some sense is possible over lifetimes.

The life stages/*āśrama* for members of every class are based on biological considerations so as to optimize the possibility of class function and hence overall social well-being. In the *brahmācārya* or student stage, the individual is given the appropriate education befitting his place in society.[5] After all, it not only makes sense to start early with mapping the imprint that will inform the rest of his life, but it is also when the individual is thought to process such an education most efficiently. In the *gṛhasthya* or householder stage, the individual takes on the responsibilities of family and work. This stage is considered to be the pillar of the entire system, for procreation keeps the wheel of life turning and economic activity and social commitments are its lubricants. The *vansprasthya* or semi-retirement stage is given to social service and contemplative activity, where the individual begins to withdraw from worldly life. The idea here seems to be to ease the transfer of occupation and assets to the next generation by having the experienced older generation on hand. Partial withdrawal from the world also helps the older generation to prepare for the final ascetic stage of *sannyāsa* or world-renunciation.

The class and stage interplay in determining duty is complex. A student member/*brahmācari* of the warrior class/*kshatriya* will have different duties from a more mature member/*gṛahastya* of the same class. (Broadly speaking we may say that the former's duty is to learn and the latter's is to apply what he has learnt.) Similarly, two householders of the warrior and priestly class will have different though interrelated duties from each other. Thus, individual life paths are carefully mapped and enmeshed in an optimal, social grid of trajectories, which in turn is part of the vast play of cosmic law/*dharma*.[6]

To complicate matters further, one's duty/*dharma* is not just determined by one's stage-and-station/*varṇāśramadharma*, but by its relation to the other ends of human life—*artha*, *kāma*, and *mokṣa*. Since duty/*dharma* is concerned with the moral dimension of human life, it is not inappropriate to say that it is a human end or goal. After all, morality is a priority as well as an aspiration that we work towards. But human life has other dimensions, which is precisely what *artha*, *kāma*, and *mokṣa* attempt to encapsulate for the tradition.

Artha is concerned with the material aspects of human life such as wealth and power, and therefore impacts everyone. So, while it has the most to do with the householder stage in life since this is where wealth is created in economic activity, it affects the stages as well, even if it concerns the world-renouncer the least. *Artha* has different material implications for the different classes so that, for instance, the working and warrior classes are generally more prosperous than the serving classes. Moreover, a certain level of overall economic well-being is necessary if the activities of leisure (including the broadly cultural activity of the *brahmin*/intellectual class) are even possible.

Kāma is concerned with pleasure, broadly construed so that it includes sensual and aesthetic pleasures. The inclusion of this end acknowledges the place of such pleasures in human life, especially in the householder stage and for the non-*brahmin* classes. The *Kama Sutra* tends to distort this broad emphasis not just because of its outsized notoriety, but also because of its focus on the lives of urbane men and courtesans. Better insight into the place of pleasure in the life of an orthodox Indian is provided indirectly by texts such as the *Manusmṛiti*, when it discusses appropriate and inappropriate kinds of sexual activity and food (*MS* 3 and 5). The *Nātya Śastra*, on the other hand, is a handbook for dancers and actors that articulates in sophisticated detail techniques to evoke the pleasures of aesthetic emotion in an audience. The *Nātya Śastra* initiates a nearly two-thousand-year-old tradition of commentary, disputation, and discussion that makes important advances in aesthetics while simultaneously reflecting developments in the arts and their place in the Indian culture.[7]

Finally, *mokśa* is concerned with freedom from the concerns of the other three ends of human life. Such freedom is variously conceived, for instance, as a life in Heaven according to *Vedas*, or the freedom of the Higher Self (*Ātman*) from the empirical self and hence from the possibility of future reincarnation according to the *Upaniṣads*. While freedom/*mokśa* is the focus of the last, renunciant stage of life, its presence is pervasive. For instance, the framework for what it means and how it is achieved is set in the studentship stage. Freedom, however it is conceived, is therefore the ultimate point of upward class mobility, and seems to be restricted to the highest priestly/intellectual class.

Of the worldly ends, *dharma* is primary (though not in relation to *mokṣa* (or freedom from the worldly ends) since it is concerned with the maintenance of social order and is involved at every stage of life). This means that the pursuit of wealth, power, and pleasure, for instance, are subordinate to *dharma*'s dictates in one's stage and station in life. The pursuit of sex, for example, is forbidden during the studentship stage, just as kingship is forbidden to the *śudra*. Moreover, when sex is permitted (as in the householder stage), it must be pursued as one's *dharma* ordains. *Dharma* itself is subordinate to *mokṣa* in that it is usually thought to be a means to *mokṣa* (though how this might work is controversial). What is implicit in this relation it would seem is that *dharma*'s goal of the maintenance of the social order has ultimately to do with the release *from* the social order. Later I will suggest how this might consistently work in the context of the *Gītā*.

We have here, then, a theoretical construct about the organization of society akin to what we see in Plato's *Republic*. Astonishingly though, this orthodox, Brahmanical worldview is not just a theoretical construct since its broadest features—with modifications, adaptions, developments, corruptions, and more—pervade the subcontinent's culture and society for over two millennia, regardless of political circumstances. One well-known problem that results from the class-stratification in the sub-continent needs to be highlighted in particular. Not only do the intellectual *Brahmin* class—whose status is determined by birth—benefit by being at the top of the hierarchy when it comes to other-worldly matters such as ultimate freedom/*mokśa*, they do so in worldly matters as well. So for instance, it is the *brahmin* who determines whether *dharm*ic law is being upheld appropriately by all who are within the orthodox fold; and it is he who conducts the rites and rituals of daily life for all the classes that are conducive to their spiritual progress and well-being, in exchange for material consideration. Unsurprisingly the ensuing abuse of power explains the rise of heterodox traditions like Buddhism that are grounded in a rejection of the orthodox Vedic texts and the priority of the priest/*brahmin*. We will soon see how the *Gītā* attempts to mount a defense of the tradition even as it moves it forward in important, even revolutionary ways.

Notes

1 See Patrick Olivelle, *The Early Upanishads: Annotated Text and Translation* (Oxford: Oxford University Press, 1998), 26–27. Olivelle emphasizes many important themes found in the *Upaniṣads* that are common with other texts and therefore are not what make them truly distinctive: power, fame, a good afterlife, children, etc.

2 See Gerald James Larson and Ram Shankar Bhattacharya, *The Encyclopedia of Indian Philosophies*, vol. 4, *Samkhya, A Dualist Tradition in Indian Philosophy* (Princeton, NJ: Princeton University Press, 2014), 3. See also Daya Krishna, *Indian Philosophy: A Counter Perspective* (Oxford: Oxford University Press, 1991), 147, 153. While such dualism may have been basic in early Saṁkhya, it is likely that there were several strands of this basic dualism that otherwise only bore a family resemblance. See Mikel Burley, *Classical Samkhya and Yoga: An Indian Metaphysics of Experience* (London: Routledge, 2006), 15.

3 See Henry Clarke Warren, *Buddhism in Translations*, Harvard Oriental Series, vol. 3 (Cambridge, MA: Harvard University, 1896), 165–68.

4 For more on the term "*dharma*," see Purusottama Bilimoria, Joseph Prabhu, and Renuka M. Sharma, *Indian Ethics* (Aldershot; Burlington, VT: Ashgate, 2007), chs. 1 and 2. A discussion of some of the issues in translating "*dharma*" can be found in Austin Creel, "'Dharma' as an Ethical Category Relating to Freedom and Responsibility," *Philosophy East and West* 22 (1972): 155–68. A good study of the continuities between the social and cosmological order can be found in John M. Koller, "Dharma: An Expression of Universal Order," *Philosophy East and West* 22, no. 2 (1972): 131–44.

5 I have restricted myself to the masculine here because the tradition does so when it comes to the distribution of social functions. This does not mean that women have no place in the scheme, even if their role is more uniform across classes and restricted to home and child care.

6 The category of obligatory action includes actions that must be performed daily or on special occasions (*nittya* and *naimittika karma*), and are part of a larger scheme of actions that include non-obligatory actions (that are desirable to the agent, *kāmaya karma*) and forbidden ones (*pratiṣiddha karma*). For more on these distinctions, see J. A. B. Van Buitenen, "Dharma and Moksa," *Philosophy East and*

West 7 (1957): 33–34, and Karl H. Potter, *Presuppositions of India's Philosophies* (New Delhi: Motilal Banarsidass Pub., 1991), 36–46.

7 For a sense of the trajectory of this discussion, see Sheldon Pollock, "A Rasa Reader: Classical Indian Aesthetics," in *A Rasa Reader* (New York: Columbia University Press, 2016).

Bibliography

Ackrill, J. L. "Aristotle on Eudaimonia." In *Essays on Aristotle's Ethics*, by Amélie Rorty, 15–34. Major Thinkers Series 2. Berkeley: University of California Press, 1980.

Allen, James. "Practical and Theoretical Knowledge in Aristotle." In *Bridging the Gap between Aristotle's Science and Ethics | Ancient Philosophy*, edited by Devin Henry and Margarethe Nielsen, 49–70. Cambridge: Cambridge University Press, 2015.

Anderson, Joshua. "Sen and the Bhagavad Gita: Lessons for a Theory of Justice." *Asian Philosophy* 22, no. 1 (February 1, 2012): 63–74.

Angier, Tom. *Techne in Aristotle's Ethics: Crafting the Moral Life*. London: Bloomsbury Publishing, 2010.

Annas, Julia. "Plato and Aristotle on Friendship and Altruism." *Mind* 86, no. 344 (1977): 532–54.

Annas, Julia. "Self-Love in Aristotle." *The Southern Journal of Philosophy* 27, no. 5 Supplement (February 1, 1989): 1–18.

Annas, Julia. *The Morality of Happiness*. New York: Oxford University Press, 1993.

Annas, Julia. "Virtue as a Skill." *International Journal of Philosophical Studies* 3, no. 2 (September 1, 1995): 227–43. Available online: https://doi.org/10.1080/09672559508570812.

Annas, Julia. ""Virtue Ethics and the Charge of Egoism." In *Morality and Self-Interest*, edited by Paul Bloomfield, 205–21. Oxford: Oxford University Press, 2007.

Anscombe, G. E. M. *Intention*. 2nd ed. Ithaca, NY; Oxford: Cornell University Press, Blackwell, 1963.

Appelbaum, David. "Tangible Action: Non-Attached Action in the Bhagavadgıta." *Sanskrit and Related Studies: Contemporary Researches and Reflections*, 99–111. Delhi: SRI Satguru Publications, 1990.

Aristotle. *De Anima Book II, III*. Translated by D. W. Hamlyn. Oxford: Oxford University Press, 1983.

Aristotle. "Eudemian Ethics." In *The Complete Works of Aristotle: The Revised Oxford Translation*, edited by Jonathan Barnes, translated by J. Solomon. Bollingen Series 71. Princeton, NJ: Princeton University Press, 1984.

Aristotle. *The Complete Works of Aristotle: The Revised Oxford Translation*. Edited by Jonathan Barnes. Bollingen Series 71. Princeton, NJ: Princeton University Press, 1984.

Aristotle. *The Eudemian Ethics*. Translated by Anthony Kenny. Oxford World's Classics. Oxford; New York: Oxford University Press, 2011.

Aristotle. *Nicomachean Ethics*, 3rd ed. Translated by Terence Irwin. Indianapolis, IN: Hackett Publishing Co., 2019.

Aristotle, W. D. Ross, and Lesley Brown. *The Nicomachean Ethics*. Oxford; New York: Oxford University Press, 2009.

Atkinson, David. "The Gita and Gandhi's Moral Vision." In *The Contemporary Essays on the Bhagavad Gita*, 1–14. New Delhi: Siddharth Publications, 1995.

Baker, Samuel H. "A Monistic Conclusion to Aristotle's Ergon Argument: The Human Good as the Best Achievement of a Human." *Archiv für Geschichte der Philosophie* 103, no. 3 (September 1, 2021): 373–403.

Barnes, Jonathan, ed. "Metaphysics." In *The Complete Works of Aristotle: The Revised Oxford Translation*, 2: 1552–728. Bollingen Series 71. Princeton, NJ: Princeton University Press, 1984.

Barnes, Jonathan, ed. "Nicomachean Ethics." In *The Complete Works of Aristotle: The Revised Oxford Translation*, 2: 1729–868. Bollingen Series 71. Princeton, NJ: Princeton University Press, 1984.

Barnes, Jonathan, ed. "On The Soul." In *The Complete Works of Aristotle: The Revised Oxford Translation*, 1: 641–92. Bollingen Series 71. Princeton, NJ: Princeton University Press, 1984.

Barnes, Jonathan, ed. "Politics." In *The Complete Works of Aristotle: The Revised Oxford Translation*, 2: 1986–2129. Bollingen Series 71. Princeton, NJ: Princeton University Press, 1984.

Barnes, Jonathan, ed. "Topics." In *The Complete Works of Aristotle: The Revised Oxford Translation*, 1: 166–277. Bollingen Series 71. Princeton, NJ: Princeton University Press, 1984.

Barnes, Jonathan, Malcolm Schoefield, and Richard Sorabji, eds. *Articles on Aristotle*, vol. 4, *Psychology and Aesthetics*. London: Duckworth, n.d.

Barney, Rachel. "Aristotle's Argument for a Human Function." *Oxford Studies in Ancient Philosophy* 35 (2008): 293–322.

Beever, Allan. "Aristotle on Equity, Law, and Justice." *Legal Theory* 10, no. 1 (March 2004): 33–50.

Berg, Richard. "An Ethical Analysis of the Bhagavad Gita." In *The Contemporary Essays on the Bhagavad Gītā*, 15–35. New Delhi: Siddharth Publications, 1995.

Bilimoria, Purushottama. "Varieties of Interpretation of the Bhagavadgītā." In *The Gītā in World Literature*, 1–15. Delhi: Sterling Publishers, 1990.

Bilimoria, Purushottama. "Metadialectics of the Bhagavadgitā." In *The Contemporary Essays on the Bhagavad Gita*, edited by Sinha, 52–68. New Delhi: Siddharth Publications, 1995.

Bilimoria, Purushottama. "Protestant Ethic and Hindu Dharma: With Reference to Kant and Gandhi." In *The Contemporary Essays on the Bhagavad Gita*, edited by Sinha, 69–101. New Delhi: Siddharth Publications, 1995.

Billimoria, Purshottama, and Raphael Lataster. "Panentheism(s): What It Is and Is Not." *Journal of World Philosophies* 3, no. 2 (2018): 49–64.

Bilimoria, Purushottama, Joseph Prabhu, and Renuka M. Sharma. *Indian Ethics*. Aldershot; Burlington, VT: Ashgate, 2007.

Bilimoria, Purushottama, Joseph Prabhu, and Renuka Sharma. *Indian Ethics: Classical Traditions and Contemporary Challenges*, vol. I. London; New York: Routledge, 2017.

Bloomfield, Paul. *Morality and Self-Interest*. Oxford: Oxford University Press, 2007.

Broadie, Sarah. *Ethics with Aristotle*. New York; Toronto: Oxford University Press, 1991.

Brodbeck, Simon. "Calling Krsna's Bluff: Non-Attached Action in the Bhagavadgītā." *Journal of Indian Philosophy* 32, no. 1 (February 1, 2004): 81–103. Available online: https://doi.org/10.1023/B:INDI.0000014005.76726.ea.

Brown, Eric. "Aristotle on the Choice of Lives: Two Concepts of Self-Sufficiency." In *Theoria: Studies on the Status and Meaning of Contemplation in Aristotle's Ethics*, edited by Pierre Destrée and Marco Zingano, 111–33. Leuven: Peeters Publishing, 2014.

Brown, Lesley. "What Is the Mean Relative to Us in Aristotle's Ethics." *Phronesis: A Journal of Ancient Philosophy* 42, no. 1 (1997): 77–93.

Buitenen, J. A. B. *The Bhagavadgītā in the Mahābhārata: Text and Translation*. Chicago: University of Chicago Press, 1981.

Burley, Mikel. *Classical Samkhya and Yoga: An Indian Metaphysics of Experience*. London: Routledge, 2006. Available online: https://doi.org/10.4324/9780203966747.

Burnyeat, Myles. "Aristotle on Learning to Be Good." In *Aristotle's Ethics: Critical Essays*, edited by Nancy Sherman, 205–30. Critical Essays on the Classics. Lanham, MD: Rowman & Littlefield, 1999.

Chakrabarti, Arindam. "The End of Life: A Nyāya-Kantian Approach to the 'Bhagavadgītā.'" *Journal of Indian Philosophy* 16, no. 4 (1988): 327–34.

Chatterjea, Tara. *Knowledge and Freedom in Indian Philosophy*. First paperback edn. Lanham, MD: Lexington Books, 2003.

Clooney, Francis X. "Much Ado About Nothing?" *The Owl of Minerva* 52, no. 1 (2021): 51–71. Available online: https://doi.org/10.5840/owl202153137.

Cohoe, Caleb. "Living Without a Soul: Why God and the Heavenly Movers Fall Outside of Aristotle's Psychology." *Phronesis* 65, no. 3 (2020): 281–323.

Coomaraswamy, Ananda Kentish. *The Dance of Śiva: Fourteen Indian Essays*. New York: Sunwise Turn, 1924.

Cooper, John M. *Reason and Human Good in Aristotle*. Cambridge, MA: Harvard University Press, 1975.

Cooper, John M. "Friendship and the Good in Aristotle." *The Philosophical Review* 86, no. 3 (July 1, 1977): 290. Available online: https://doi.org/10.2307/2183784.

Cooper, John M. "Aristotle on Friendship." In *Essays on Aristotle's Ethics*, edited by Amélie Oksenberg Rorty, 301–40. California: University of California Press, 1980.

Cooper, John M. "Aristotle on the Goods of Fortune." *The Philosophical Review* 94, no. 2 (May 1, 1985): 173–96.

Cooper, John M. "Contemplation and Happiness: A Reconsideration." *Synthese* 72, no. 2 (1987): 187–216.

Cooper, John M. “An Aristotelian Theory of the Emotions.” In *Reason and Emotion: Essays on Ancient Moral Psychology and Ethical Theory*, by John M. Cooper, 406–26. Princeton, NJ: Princeton University Press, 1999.

Cooper, John M. *Reason and Emotion: Essays on Ancient Moral Psychology and Ethical Theory*. Princeton, NJ: Princeton University Press, 1999.

Corcilius, Klaus. “Aristotle’s Definition of Non-Rational Pleasure and Pain and Desire.” In *Aristotle’s Nicomachean Ethics: A Critical Guide*, edited by Jon Miller, 117–43. Cambridge Critical Guides. Cambridge: Cambridge University Press, 2011. Available online: https://doi.org/10.1017/CBO9780511977626.007.

Creel, Austin. “‘Dharma’ as an Ethical Category Relating to Freedom and Responsibility.” *Philosophy East and West* 22 (1972): 155–68.

Cremaldi, Anna. “Aristotle on Benefaction and Self-Love.” *Epoche: A Journal for the History of Philosophy* 26, no. 2 (2022): 287–307.

Curzer, Howard J. “The Supremely Happy Life in Aristotle’s Nicomachean Ethics.” *Apeiron* 24, no. 1 (March 1, 1991): 47–70. Available online: https://doi.org/10.1515/APEIRON.1991.24.1.47.

Darwall, Stephen L. *Virtue Ethics*. Blackwell Readings in Philosophy 10. Malden, MA: Blackwell, 2003.

Davis, Richard H. *The Bhagavad Gita: A Biography*. Princeton, NJ: Princeton University Press, 2014.

De Smet, Richard. “A Copernican Reversal: The Gitakara’s Reformulation of Karma.” *Philosophy East and West* 27, no. 1 (1977): 53–63.

Deb, Paul. “A Chariot Between Two Armies: A Perfectionist Reading of the Bhagavadgītā.” *Philosophy East and West* 71, no. 4 (October 2021): 851–71.

DeKoninck, Thomas. “Aristotle on God as Thought Thinking Itself.” *The Review of Metaphysics* 47, no. 3 (August 1, 1994): 471–515.

Devereux, Daniel. “Aristotle on the Essence of Happiness.” In *Studies in Aristotle*, edited by Dominic J. O’Meara, 247–60. Washington, DC: Catholic University of America Press, 2018.

Dhand, Arti. “The Dharma of Ethics, the Ethics of Dharma: Quizzing the Ideals of Hinduism.” *Journal of Religious Ethics* 30, no. 3 (Fall 2002): 347–72.

Divanji, P. C. “‘Atman’ and the Terms Allied to It in the Bhagavad Gita.” Presented at the 32nd Session of the Indian Philosophical Congress, Srinagar, Kashmir, June 1957.

Dorter, Kenneth. “A Dialectical Reading of the Bhagavadgita.” *Asian Philosophy* 22, no. 4 (2012): 307–26.

Dowd, Joseph. “Maximizing Dharma: Krsna’s Consequentialism in the Mahābhārata.” *Praxis* 3, no. 1 (2011): 33–50.

Edgerton, Franklin. *The Bhagavad Gita*. Cambridge, MA: Harvard University Press, 1997.

Elliott, Jay R. “Aristotle on Virtue, Happiness and External Goods.” *Ancient Philosophy* 37, no. 2 (October 1, 2017): 347–59.

Flannery, Kevin L. "Moral Taxonomy and Moral Absolutes." In *Wisdom's Apprentice: Thomistic Essays in Honor of Lawrence Dewan, O.P.*, 237–59. Washington, DC: Catholic University of America Press, 2007.

Fortenbaugh, William W. *Aristotle on Emotion: A Contribution to Philosophical Psychology, Rhetoric, Poetics, Politics, and Ethics*. London: Duckworth, 1975.

Framarin, Christopher G. "The Desire You Are Required to Get Rid of: A Functionalist Analysis of Desire in the Bhagavadgita." *Philosophy East and West* 56, no. 4 (2006): 604–17.

Frede, Dorothea. "New Perspectives on an Old Controversy: The Theoretical and the Practical Life in Aristotle." *Zeitschrift für Philosophische Forschung* 73, no. 4 (2019): 481–510.

Ganeri, Jonardon. *The Collected Essays of Bimal Krishna Matilal: Ethics and Epics*. New Delhi: Oxford University Press, 2002.

Gasser-Wingate, Marc. "Aristotle on Self-Sufficiency, External Goods, and Contemplation." *Archiv für Geschichte der Philosophie* 102, no. 1 (March 1, 2020): 1–28.

Gomez-Lobo, Alfonso. "The Ergon Inference." *Phronesis* 34, no. 1–3 (1989): 170–84.

Gonzalez, Francisco J. "Aristotle on Pleasure and Perfection." *Phronesis* 36, no. 2 (1991): 141–59.

Gopalan, S. "The Concept of Duty in the Bhagavad Gita: An Analysis." In A. Sharma, *New Essays in the Bhagavadgita: Philosophical, Methodological and Cultural Approaches*, 1–13. New Delhi: Books & Books, 1987.

Green, Jerry. "Self-Love in the Aristotelian Ethics." *Newsletters for the Society for Ancient Greek Philosophy* 11, no. 2 (2010): 12–18.

Gupta, Bina. "Bhagavad Gita as Duty and Virtue Ethics: Some Reflections." *Journal of Religious Ethics* 34, no. 3 (2006): 373–95.

Gurtler, Gary M. "The Activity of Happiness in Aristotle's Ethics." *The Review of Metaphysics* 56, no. 4 (2003): 801–34.

Hacker, Paul and Donald Davis. "Dharma in Hinduism." *Journal of Indian Philosophy* 34, no. 5 (2006): 479–96.

Halbfass, Wilhelm. *India and Europe: An Essay in Understanding*. Albany, NY: State University of New York Press, 1988.

Halbfass, Wilhelm. *Tradition and Reflection: Explorations in Indian Thought*. Albany, NY: State University of New York Press, 1991.

Hardie, W. F. R. *Aristotle's Ethical Theory*. Oxford: Clarendon Press, 1968.

Harrington, Tiffany. "The Significance of a Bipartite/ Tripartite Division of the Psyche." *Equilibrium* 2, no. 1 (October 11, 2018). Available online: https://doi.org/10.5070/q22141229.

Heinaman, Robert. "Eudaimonia and Self-Sufficiency in the Nicomachean Ethics." *Phronesis* 33, no. 1 (January 1, 1988): 31–53. Available online: https://doi.org/10.1163/156852888X00027.

Henry, Devin, and Margarethe Nielesen, eds. *Bridging the Gap between Aristotle's Science and Ethics | Ancient Philosophy*. Cambridge: Cambridge University Press, 2015.

Herman, A. "Ethical Theory in the Bhagavad-Gītā: Teleological Attitude Liberationism and Its Implications." *Journal of Vaishnava Studies* 3, no. 2 (1995): 47–70.

Hewitt, Annie. "Universal Justice and Epieikeia in Aristotle." *Polis: The Journal of the Society for the Study of Greek Political Thought* 25, no. 1 (2008): 115–30.

Hirji, Sukaina. "Acting Virtuously as an End in Aristotle's Nicomachean Ethics." *British Journal for the History of Philosophy* 26, no. 6 (2018): 1006–26.

Hirji, Sukaina. "External Goods and the Complete Exercise of Virtue in Aristotle's Nicomachean Ethics." *Archiv für Geschichte der Philosophie* 103, no. 1 (March 1, 2021): 29–53. Available online: https://doi.org/10.1515/agph-2017-0107.

Hurka, Thomas. "Aristotle on Virtue: Wrong, Wrong, and Wrong." In *Aristotelian Ethics in Contemporary Perspective*, edited by Julia Peters, 9–26. Routledge Studies in Ethics and Moral Theory 21. New York: Routledge, 2013.

Hursthouse, Rosalind, and Glen Pettigrove. "Virtue Ethics." In *The Stanford Encyclopedia of Philosophy*, edited by Edward N. Zalta and Uri Nodelman Winter, 2022. Metaphysics Research Lab, Stanford University, 2022. Available online: https://plato.stanford.edu/archives/win2022/entries/ethics-virtue/.

Ingalls, Daniel. "Dharma and Moksa." *Philosophy East and West* 7 (1957): 41–48.

Irwin, T. H. "Beauty and Morality in Aristotle." In *Aristotle's Nicomachean Ethics: A Critical Guide*, edited by Jon Miller, 239–53. Cambridge: Cambridge University Press, 2011.

Irwin, T. H. W. *The Development of Ethics: A Historical and Critical Study*, vol. 1, *From Socrates to the Reformation*. Oxford: Oxford University Press, 2011.

Jacobsen, Knut A., Helene Basu, Angelika Malinar, and Vasudha Narayanan. *Brill's Encyclopedia of Hinduism*. Handbuch Der Orientalistik. Zweite Abteilung, Indien 22. Leiden; Boston: Brill, 2009.

Jean-Hyuk Kim, Bradford. "Aristotle on Friendship and the Lovable." *Journal of the History of Philosophy* 59, no. 2 (2021): 221–45. Available online: https://doi.org/10.1353/hph.2021.0025.

Jimenez, Marta. "Aristotle on Becoming Virtuous by Doing Virtuous Actions." *Phronesis* 61, no. 1 (December 10, 2016): 3–32. Available online: https://doi.org/10.1163/15685284-12341297.

Kahn, Charles H. "Sensation and Consciousness in Aristotle's Psychology." *Archiv für Geschichte der Philosophie* 48, no. 1–3 (January 1, 1966): 43–81.

Kahn, Charles H. "Aristotle and Altruism." *Mind* 90, no. 357 (1981): 20–40.

Kahn, Charles H. "Aristotle on Thinking." In *Essays on Aristotle's De Anima*, edited by Martha C. Nussbaum and Amelie Oksenberg Rorty, 359–80. Oxford: Clarendon Press, 1992.

Kant, Immanuel. *Grounding for the Metaphysics of Morals: With On a Supposed Right to Lie Because of Philanthropic Concerns*. Translated by James W. Ellington. 3rd ed. Indianapolis, IN: Hackett Publishing Co., 1993.

Kenny, Anthony. "The Nicomachean Conception of Happiness." *Oxford Studies in Ancient Philosophy* (1991): 67–80.

Keyt, David. "Intellectualism in Aristotle." *The Society for Ancient Greek Philosophy* Newsletter, December 1, 1978. Available online: https://orb.binghamton.edu/sagp/87.

Koller, John M. "Dharma: An Expression of Universal Order." *Philosophy East and West* 22, no. 2 (1972): 131–44. Available online: https://doi.org/10.2307/1398120.

Kosman, Aryeh. *Aristotle on the Human Good.* Princeton, NJ: Princeton University Press, 1989. Available online: https://doi.org/10.1515/9780691225128.

Kosman, Aryeh. "What Does the Maker Mind Make?" In *Essays on Aristotle's De Anima*, edited by Martha Nussbaum and Amelie Rorty, 343–58. Oxford: Oxford University Press, 1992.

Kosman, L. A. "Being Properly Affected: Virtues and Feelings in Aristotle's Ethics." In *Essays on Aristotle's Ethics*, edited by Amélie Rorty, 103–16. Major Thinkers Series 2. Berkeley: University of California Press, 1980.

Kraut, Richard. "The Peculiar Function of Human Beings." *Canadian Journal of Philosophy* 9 (1979): 467–78.

Krishna, Daya. *Indian Philosophy: A Counter Perspective.* Oxford: Oxford University Press, 1991.

Krishna, Daya. "Is Īśvara Kṛṣṇa's Sāṁkhya Kārikā Really Sāṁkhyan?" In *Indian Philosophy: A Counter Perspective*, 144–55. Oxford: Oxford University Press, 1991.

Kwasniewski, Peter A. *Wisdom's Apprentice: Thomistic Essays in Honor of Lawrence Dewan, O.P.* Washington, DC: Catholic University of America Press, 2007.

Lännström, Anna. *Loving the Fine: Virtue and Happiness in Aristotle's Ethics.* Notre Dame, IN: University of Notre Dame Press, 2006.

Larson, Gerald James, Ram Shankar Bhattacharya, and Karl H. Potter. *The Encyclopedia of Indian Philosophies*, vol. 4, *Samkhya, A Dualist Tradition in Indian Philosophy.* Princeton, NJ: Princeton University Press, 2014.

Lawrence, Joseph P. "The Hidden Aporia in Aristotle's Self-Thinking Thought." *The Journal of Speculative Philosophy* 2, no. 3 (1988): 155–74.

Lear, Jonathan. *Aristotle: The Desire to Understand.* Cambridge: Cambridge University Press, 1988.

Lee, Chang-Uh. "Friendship & Self-Love in Aristotle's Ethics, Focused on the Nicomachean Ethics, Book 8–9." *CHUL HAK SA SANG – Journal of Philosophical Ideas* 79, no. 79 (2021): 3–37. Available online: https://doi.org/10.15750/chss.79.202102.001.

Leighton, Stephen R. "Aristotle's Courageous Passions." *Phronesis* 33, no. 1–3 (January 1, 1988): 76–99. Available online: https://doi.org/10.1163/156852888X00045.

MacIntyre, Alasdair. *After Virtue*, 2nd ed. Notre Dame, IN: University of Notre Dame Press, 1984.

MacIntyre, Alasdair. *After Virtue: A Study in Moral Theory*, 3rd ed. Notre Dame, IN: University of Notre Dame Press, 2007.

MacKenzie, Matthew D. "The Five Factors of Action and the Decentring of Agency in the Bhagavad Gītā." *Asian Philosophy* 11, no. 3 (November 1, 2001): 141–50. Available online: https://doi.org/10.1080/09552360120116883.
Maharaj, Ayon. "Toward a New Hermeneutics of the Bhagavad Gītā: Sri Ramakrishna, Sri Aurobindo, and the Secret of Vijñāna." *Philosophy East and West* 65, no. 4 (2015): 1209–33. Available online: https://doi.org/10.1353/pew.2015.0107.
Majithia, Roopen. "The Relation of Divine Thinking to Human Thought in Aristotle." *American Catholic Philosophical Quarterly* 73, no. 3 (August 1, 1999): 377–406. Available online: https://doi.org/10.5840/acpq199973326.
Majithia, Roopen. "Self and Soul in Aristotle." *Transcendent Philosophy* 5 (2004): 181–206.
Majithia, Roopen. "On the Eudemian and Nicomachean Conceptions of Eudaimonia." *American Catholic Philosophical Quarterly* 79, no. 3 (August 1, 2005): 365–88.
Majithia, Roopen. "Function, Intuition and Ends in Aristotle's Ethics." *Ethical Theory and Moral Practice* 9, no. 2 (April 1, 2006): 187–200. Available online: https://doi.org/10.1007/s10677-006-9015-9.
Majithia, Roopen. "Śaṇkara on Action and Liberation." *Asian Philosophy* 17, no. 3 (November 1, 2007): 231–49. Available online: https://doi.org/10.1080/09552360701625429.
Majithia, Roopen. "Love and Virtue in Aristotle's Ethics." *Archive of the History of Philosophy & Social Thought/Archiwum Historii Filozofii i Mysli Spolecznej* 59 (2014): 25–35.
Majithia, Roopen. "The Bhagavad Gītā's Ethical Syncretism." *Comparative Philosophy: An International Journal of Constructive Engagement of Distinct Approaches toward World Philosophy* 6, no. 1 (January 9, 2015). Available online: https://doi.org/10.31979/2151-6014(2015).060108.
Manu. *The Laws of Manu*. Penguin Classics. London; New York: Penguin, 1991.
Matilal, Bimal Krishna. *Moral Dilemmas in the Mahābhārata*. Delhi; Varanasi: Motilal Banarasidass, 1992.
Matilal, Bimal Krishna. "Caste, Karma and the Gita." In *Philosophy, Culture, and Religion: The Collected Essays of Bimal Krishna Matilal. Volume 2: Ethics and Epics*, 136–44. Oxford; New York: Oxford University Press, 2001.
Matilal, Bimal Krishna. *Philosophy, Culture, and Religion: The Collected Essays of Bimal Krishna Matilal. Volume 2: Ethics and Epics*. Oxford; New York: Oxford University Press, 2001.
Matilal, Bimal Krishna. "Dharma and Rationality." In *Indian Ethics*, 89–112. London; New York: Routledge, 2007.
Menn, Stephen. "Aristotle and Plato on God as Nous and as the Good." *The Review of Metaphysics* 45, no. 3 (1992): 543–73.
Mill, John Stuart. *Utilitarianism*. Indianapolis, IN: Hackett Publishing Co., 2001.
Miller, Jon, ed. *Aristotle's Nicomachean Ethics: A Critical Guide*. Cambridge Critical Guides. Cambridge: Cambridge University Press, 2011. Available online: https://doi.org/10.1017/CBO9780511977626.

Mohanty, J. N. *Classical Indian Philosophy*. Lanham, MD: Rowman & Littlefield, 2000.

Mohanty, J. N. "Dharma, Imperatives, and Tradition: Toward an Indian Theory of Moral Action." In *Indian Ethics: Classical Traditions and Contemporary Challenges*, vol. I, edited by Purushottama Bilimoria, Joseph Prabhu, and Renuka Sharma, 57–78. London; New York: Routledge, 2017.

Moss, Jessica Dawn. *Aristotle on the Apparent Good: Perception, Phantasia, Thought, and Desire*. Oxford Aristotle Studies. Oxford: Oxford University Press, 2012.

Müller, Jozef. "What Aristotelian Decisions Cannot Be." *Ancient Philosophy* 36, no. 1 (2016): 173–95.

Müller, Jozef. "Practical and Productive Thinking in Aristotle." *Phronesis* 63, no. 2 (April 2, 2018): 148–75. Available online: https://doi.org/10.1163/15685284-12341345.

Nicolás, Antonio T. de. "The Problem of the Self-Body in the Bhagavadgītā: The Problem of Meaning." *Philosophy East and West* 29, no. 2 (1979): 159–75. Available online: https://doi.org/10.2307/1398554.

Nielsen, Karen Margrethe. "Deliberation as Inquiry: Aristotle's Alternative to the Presumption of Open Alternatives." *The Philosophical Review* 120, no. 3 (July 1, 2011): 383–421.

Nikam, N. A. "Detachment." *Philosophy East and West* 3, no. 2 (1953): 167–75.

Norman, Richard. "Aristotle's Philosopher God." In *Articles on Aristotle*, vol. 4, *Psychology and Aesthetics*, edited by Jonathan Barnes, Malcolm Schoefield, and Richard Sorabji. London: Duckworth, 1969.

Nussbaum, Martha. "The Discernment of Perception: An Aristotelian Conception of Private and Public Rationality." *Proceedings of the Boston Area Colloquium in Ancient Philosophy* 1 (1985): 151–201.

Nussbaum, Martha. *The Fragility of Goodness: Luck and Ethics in Greek Tragedy and Philosophy*. Cambridge: Cambridge University Press, 2001.

Olivelle, Patrick. *The Early Upanishads: Annotated Text and Translation*. Oxford: Oxford University Press, 1998.

Olivelle, Patrick. *Dharma: Studies in its Semantic, Cultural and Religious History*. Delhi: Motilal Banarsidass, 2009.

Olivelle, Patrick. "Dharmashastra." In *Brill's Encyclopedia of Hinduism*, by Knut A. Jacobsen et al. Handbuch Der Orientalistik. Zweite Abteilung, Indien 22. Leiden; Boston: Brill, 2009.

O'Meara, Dominic J., ed. *Studies in Aristotle*. Washington, DC: Catholic University of America Press, 2018.

Owens, Joseph. "The Self in Aristotle." *The Review of Metaphysics* 41, no. 4 (1988): 707–22.

Palshikar, Sanjay. *Evil and the Philosophy of Retribution: Modern Commentaries on the Bhagavad-Gita*. New Delhi: Routledge India, 2014.

Panagiotou, Spiro. *Justice, Law and Method in Plato and Aristotle*. Academic, 1987.

Pearson, Giles. "Non-Rational Desire and Aristotle's Moral Psychology." In *Aristotle's Nicomachean Ethics: A Critical Guide*, edited by Jon Miller, 144–69. Cambridge

Critical Guides. Cambridge: Cambridge University Press, 2011. Available online: https://doi.org/10.1017/CBO9780511977626.008.

Pearson, Giles. *Aristotle on Desire*. Cambridge Classical Studies. Cambridge: Cambridge University Press, 2012. Available online: https://doi.org/10.1017/CBO9781139161770.

Perrett, Roy. "Caste, Karma and the Gita." In *Indian Philosophy of Religion*, 47–56. Dordrecht; Boston: Kluwer Academic Publishers, 1989.

Perrett, Roy, ed. *Indian Philosophy of Religion*. Dordrecht; Boston: Kluwer Academic Publishers, 1989.

Perrett, Roy. *Hindu Ethics: A Philosophical Study*. Honolulu: University of Hawaii Press, 1998.

Peters, Julia. *Aristotelian Ethics in Contemporary Perspective*. Routledge Studies in Ethics and Moral Theory 21. New York: Routledge, 2013. Available online: https://doi.org/10.4324/9780203072769.

Pollock, Sheldon. "A Rasa Reader: Classical Indian Aesthetics." In *A Rasa Reader*. New York: Columbia University Press, 2016.

Potter, Karl. "Dharma and Moksa from a Conversational Point of View." *Philosophy East and West* 8 (1958): 49–64.

Potter, Karl. *Presuppositions of India's Philosophies*. Delhi: Motilal Banarsidass Pub., 1991.

Prasad, Rajendra. *Karma, Causation and Retributive Morality: Conceptual Essays in Ethics and Metaethics*. New Delhi: Indian Council of Philosophical Research in association with Munshiram Manoharlal Publ., 1989.

Price, A. W. "Choice and Action in Aristotle." *Phronesis: A Journal of Ancient Philosophy* 61, no. 4 (2016): 435–62.

Rāmānuja. Translation by Swami Adidevananda. *Sri Rāmānuja Gita Bhasya: With Text and English Translation*. Madras: Sri Ramakrishna Math, 2007.

Ram-Prasad, Chakravarthi. *Divine Self, Human Self: The Philosophy of Being in Two Gita Commentaries*. London: Continuum, 2013.

Rogers, Kelly. "Aristotle's Conception of Tò Καλόυ." *Ancient Philosophy* 13, no. 2 (October 1, 1993): 355–71. Available online: https://doi.org/10.5840/ancientphil19931327.

Rogers, Kelly. "Aristotle on Loving Another for His Own Sake." *Phronesis* 39, no. 3 (January 1, 1994): 291–302. Available online: https://doi.org/10.1163/156852894321052090.

Rolf, George. "An Argument for Divine Omniscience in Aristotle." *Apeiron* 22, no. 1 (March 1, 1989): 61–74.

Rorty, Amélie. *Essays on Aristotle's Ethics*. Major Thinkers Series 2. Berkeley: University of California Press, 1980.

Rorty, Amélie. "The Place of Contemplation in Aristotle's Nicomachean Ethics." In *Essays on Aristotle's Ethics*, 377–94. Major Thinkers Series 2. Berkeley: University of California Press, 1980.

Ross, W. D. *Aristotle*. London: Methuen, 1923.

Saenz, Victor. "Shame and Honor: Aristotle's Thumos as a Basic Desire." *Apeiron: A Journal for Ancient Philosophy and Science* 51, no. 1 (2018): 73–95.

Sargeant, Winthrop, trans. *The Bhagavad Gita: Twenty-Fifth–Anniversary Edition*. Albany: State University of New York Press, 2010.

Śastry, Alladi Mahadeva. *The Bhagavad Gita: With Commentary of Sri Sankaracharya*. India: Samata Books/Lotus Light Publications, 1992.

Schneewind, J. B. "The Misfortunes of Virtue." *Ethics: An International Journal of Social, Political, and Legal Philosophy* 101, no. 1 (1990): 42–63.

Segev, Mor. "Aristotle on the Proper Attitude Toward True Divinity." *American Catholic Philosophical Quarterly* 94, no. 2 (April 3, 2020): 187–209.

Sharma, Arvind. *New Essays in the Bhagavadgītā: Philosophical, Methodological, and Cultural Approaches*. New Delhi: Books & Books, 1987.

Sherman, Nancy. "The Fabric of Character: Aristotle's Theory of Virtue." *Classical World* 100, no. 4 (July 1, 1990): 894–5. Available online: https://doi.org/10.2307/4350927.

Sherman, Nancy, ed. *Aristotle's Ethics: Critical Essays*. Critical Essays on the Classics. Lanham, MD: Rowman & Littlefield, 1999.

Sherman, Nancy. "The Habituation of Character." In *Aristotle's Ethics: Critical Essays*, edited by Nancy Sherman, 231–60. Critical Essays on the Classics. Lanham, MD: Rowman & Littlefield, 1999.

Shetty, Manu. "The Bhagavad Gita in the Mahābhārata." *Journal of Indian Council of Philosophical Research* 10, no. 3 (1993): 89–107.

Shiner, Roger. "Ethical Perception in Aristotle." *Apeiron: A Journal for Ancient Philosophy and Science* 13 (1979): 79–85.

Sinha, Braj M. "The Bhagavad Gita: A Mimamsic Approach." In *The Contemporary Essays on the Bhagavad Gita*. New Delhi: Siddharth Publications, 1995.

Sinha, Braj M., ed. *The Contemporary Essays on the Bhagavad Gītā*, 1st ed. Siddharth Indian Studies Series. New Delhi: Siddharth Publications, 1995.

Skultety, Steven C. "Disputes of the Phronimoi: Can Aristotle's Best Citizens Disagree?" *Ancient Philosophy* 32, no. 1 (2012): 105–24.

Slote, Michael. "Law in Virtue Ethics." *Law and Philosophy: An International Journal for Jurisprudence and Legal Philosophy* 14, no. 1 (1995): 91–113.

Smart, J. J. C., and Bernard Williams. *Utilitarianism: For and Against*. Cambridge: Cambridge University Press, 1973.

Sorabji, Richard. "VII—Aristotle on the Rôle of Intellect in Virtue." *Proceedings of the Aristotelian Society* 74, no. 1 (June 1, 1974): 107–29. Available online: https://doi.org/10.1093/aristotelian/74.1.107.

Sreekumar, Sandeep. "An Analysis of Consequentialism and Deontology in the Normative Ethics of the Bhagavadgita." *Journal of Indian Philosophy* 40, no. 3 (2012): 277–315.

Stansell, Ellen Briggs. "The Guna Theory of the Bhagavad Gita." *Journal of Indian Council of Philosophical Research* 25, no. 4 (2008): 61–80.

Stark, Susan. "Virtue and Emotion." *Noûs* 35, no. 3 (2001): 440–55.

Suits, Bernard. "Aristotle on the Function of Man." *Canadian Journal of Philosophy* 4 (1974): 23–40.

Teschner, George. "Anxiety, Anger and the Concept of Agency and Action in the 'Bhagavad Gita.'" *Asian Philosophy* 2, no. 1 (1992): 61–77.

Theodor, Ithamar. *Exploring the Bhagavad Gita: Philosophy, Structure and Meaning.* London; New York: Routledge, 2016.

Tilak, Bal Gangadhar and S. B. Sukthankar. *Śrīmad Bhagavadgīta Rahasya, or, Karma-Yoga-Śāstra.* New Delhi: Asian Educational Services, 2007.

Upadhyaya, K. N. "The Impact of Early Buddhism on Hindu Thought: With Special Reference to the Bhagavadgita." *Philosophy East and West* 18 (1968): 163–73.

Urmson, J. O. *Aristotle's Ethics.* Oxford: Blackwell, 1988.

Vācaspati Misra. *The Samkhya-Tattva*-Kaumudi, 2nd ed. Translated by Ganganatha Jha. Poona: The Oriental Book Agency, 1934.

Van Buitenen, J. A. B. "Dharma and Moksa." *Philosophy East and West* 7 (1957): 33–41.

Vander Waerdt, P. A. "Kingship and Philosophy in Aristotle's Best Regime." *Phronesis: A Journal of Ancient Philosophy* 30 (1985): 249–73.

Vasiliou, Iakovos. "Aristotle, Agents, and Actions." In *Aristotle's Nicomachean Ethics: A Critical Guide*, edited by Jon Miller, 170–90. Cambridge Critical Guides. Cambridge: Cambridge University Press, 2011. Available online: https://doi.org/10.1017/CBO9780511977626.009.

Vyāsa, and Kisari Mohan Ganguli. *The Mahābhārata of Krishna-Dwaipayana Vyasa.* 12 vols. New Delhi: Munshiram Manoharlal, 1990.

Walker, Matthew D. *Aristotle on the Uses of Contemplation.* New York: Cambridge University Press, 2018.

Walker, Rebecca L. and P. J. Ivanhoe. *Working Virtue: Virtue Ethics and Contemporary Moral Problems.* Oxford; New York; Toronto: Clarendon Press; Oxford University Press, 2007.

Warren, Henry Clarke. *Buddhism in Translations.* Harvard Oriental Series, vol. 3. Cambridge, MA: Harvard University Press, 1896.

Weiss, Paul. "The Gita: East and West." *Philosophy East and West* 4 (1954): 253–58.

Wexler, Steve and Andrew Irvine. "Aristotle on the Rule of Law." *Polis: The Journal of the Society for the Study of Greek Political Thought* 23, no. 1 (2006): 116–38.

White, David. "The Bhagavadgītā's Conception of Human Freedom." *Philosophy East and West* 34, no. 3 (1984): 295–302.

White, Nicholas P. "Goodness and Human Aims in Aristotle's Ethics." In *Studies in Aristotle*, edited by Dominic J. O'Meara. Washington, DC: Catholic University of America Press, 2018.

Whiting, Jennifer. "Human Nature and Intellectualism in Aristotle," 68, no. 1 (January 1, 1986): 70–95. Available online: https://doi.org/10.1515/agph.1986.68.1.70.

Whiting, Jennifer. "Aristotle's Function Argument: A Defense." *Ancient Philosophy* 8 (1988): 33–48.

Wilkes, Kathleen V. "The Good Man and the Good for Man in Aristotle's Nicomachean Ethics." In *Essays on Aristotle's Ethics*, edited by Amélie Rorty, 341–58. Major Thinkers Series 2. Berkeley: University of California Press, 1980.

Yandell, Keith E. "On Interpreting the 'Bhagavadgītā.'" *Philosophy East and West* 32, no. 1 (1982): 37–46. Available online: https://doi.org/10.2307/1398750.

Index

activity 51–2, 219
actuality 219
ahamkāra. *See* I-sense/*ahamkāra*
Alcibiades 17, 115
anger 26, 93
apparent good 19
appetites 22–3, 48, 50
Aristotle. *See also Nicomachean Ethics*
  activity and process 219
  autarika as automony or self-governance 49–51
  autarkia as self-sufficiency 188–9
  bipartition and tripartition 41–3
  choice 16
  deliberation 16–18
  desire 14, 19, 87, 101–2, 209
  desire and character 22–4
  desire and intention 21–2
  development of character 27–30
  divine perfection 214
  divine thinking as contemplation 191–4
  equity and harmony in self-love 46–9
  fortune 185–8, 200–1
  friendship 36–8
  happiness/*eudiamonia* 179–84, 189–91, 198–201, 209–10
  human function 107–12
  human thinking and contemplation 194–8
  individualism and holism 211–12
  intention in virtuous action 15–16
  love and virtue 24–7
  the Mean 114–17, 118–20
  moral intentionality 100
  natural and legal justice 121–2
  personal identity 81–2, 221–3
  personhood and personality 40–1, 102–3
  potentiality and actuality 219
  practical and theoretical intellects 43–5
  rationality and latitude 148–9
  relation of the ethical and political 147–8
  right rule 118–19
  rule of law 120–2
  self 40–6
  self-love or self-friendship 39, 40
  substantialism 216–17, 221–2
  teleia as final and complete 184–8
  teleia as perfect 191–3
  tripartition 42–6
  virtue 15–6, 208
  virtue and rule of law 112–14
  virtue and skill 51–5
  virtuous action 106–7
  wish 18–21
Arjuna
  bhakti yoga 161–2
  dharma 65–6, 67, 132–3
  introduction to *Bhagavad Gītā* 7
  moral dilemma 60–2, 73–4 n.2
  Providence 80
  renunciation 162
  scriptural injunction 129–31
  svadharma 131–2
  transformation 89–92
artha 228
aspect dualism 167–70
Ātman 81–2, 95–6 n.1. *See also* higher self/*Ātman*; self/*Ātman;* individual self/*Ātman*
Ātman-Brahman relation 167–73
autarkia as autonomy or self-governance 49–51
autarkia as self-sufficiency 188–9

Bhagavad Gītā
  Arjuna's transformation 89–92
  Ātman-Brahman relation 167–73
  class membership 87–8
  classes, stages, and aims of life 64–6
  continuities with the tradition 129–31
  cross-cultural conversation 3–6

detachment 66–9, 71–3, 88–9
dharma 127–8, 138–42
dharma and supererogatory action 133–6
discontinuities with the tradition 131–3
emerging consequentialism 137–8
ends, stage, and classes in the tradition 226–30
equalization of *saṁkhya* and *yoga* 162–4
ethical action 2–3
freedom 210–11, 217
higher self/*Ātman* 78–9
individual self/*Ātman* 156–8
intellect, mind, and I-sense 61–4
introduction to 7
knowledge/*jñāna* 155–6, 164–7
lower self/*deha* 79–81
misfortune 213–14
mokṣa 138–42
moral intentionality 59–60
organized change 216
past lives 82
paths/*yogas* 158–62
personality traits 83–7, 87–8
personhood and personality 81–2, 102–3
philosophical context of 224–6
philosophical discussions between orthodox Brahmanism and various competing views 2
priority and circumscription of *dharma* and virtue 150–1
sage 92–5
saṁkhya/theory 158–62
self-knowledge 156–8
sense-control 69–71
similarities and differences with *Nicomachean Ethics* 1
śruti and *smṛiti* 128–9
status of the world 151–2
tripartition 100–2
universal self/*Brahman* 78–9, 156–8
Upaniṣads 160–1
bhakti yoga. *See* devotion/*bhakti yoga*
bipartition 41–3
bodily pleasure 181
Brahman. *See* universal self/*Brahman*
buddhi. *See* intellect/*buddhi*
Buddhism 2, 80, 128–33, 225–6

ceṣṭas. *See* predispositions/*ceṣṭas*
character 22–4, 27–30, 52
Charvāka 5
choice 14, 16, 31 n.10
class membership 87–8
comparative philosophy 3, 10 n.4
completeness/*teleia* 184–5
consequentialism 67, 137–8
contemplation/*theoria* 194–8, 199–201
courage 115, 116
cross-cultural conversation 3–6

daivaṁ. *See* Providence/*daivaṁ*
deha. *See* lower self/*deha*
deliberation 16–18, 31 n.11
deliberative desire 14
Descartes 5, 6
desire 14, 21–2, 22–4, 87, 108–9
detached sage 93–4
detachment 59–60, 66–9, 71–3, 74 n.10, 88–9, 90–2, 93–4
devotion/*bhakti yoga* 140–1, 161–2, 174–5, 177 n.17, 177 n.18
dharma
classes, stages, and aims of life in *Bhagavad Gītā* 64–5
detachment 68, 132–3
duty 226–7
ethical and political 148
mokṣa/freedom 138–42, 207–8
moral action in the *Bhagavad Gītā* 127–8
priority and circumscription 150–1
supererogatory action 133–6
dhyāna yoga. *See* meditation/*dhyāna yoga*
divine contemplation 190–1
divine perfection 214–15
divine thinking as contemplation 191–4

early Buddhism 225–6
emotions 22–9, 48, 64–70
equity 46–9, 55
ethical action 2–3, 13, 105
ethical intentionality 13–30
eudiamonia. *See* happiness/*eudiamonia*
examined life 6, 10 n.8

food 27–9
fortune 185–8
freedom 210–11, 217, 229
friendship 36–8, 46–8

Golden Rule 13, 105–6
Good 182
goodwill 36, 37
guṇas. *See* strands/*guṇas*

happiness/*eudiamonia* 179–84, 189–91, 198–201, 209–10
harmony 46–9, 55
higher self/*Ātman* 78–9
holism 9, 103, 149, 210, 211–16
honor 47
human contemplation 190–1
human function 107–12
human thinking 194–8
hylomorphism 223

I-sense/*ahamkāra* 61–4, 80, 92, 94
incommensurability 4–5
incontinence 15, 21, 23, 33 n.22, 39, 42
individual self/*Ātman* 156–8
individualism 211–12
intellect/*buddhi* 61–4
intention 21–2
Iśvara 168

jñāna. *See* knowledge/*jñāna*

kāma 228–9
Kama Sutra 228
karma yoga 162–3, 174
knowledge/*jñāna* 155–6, 164–7
Krishna
  bhakti yoga 161–2
  consequentialism 67
  detachment 88–9
  dharma 132–3
  introduction to *Bhagavad Gītā* 7
  renunciation 162
  scriptural injunction 129–31
  svadharma 131–2
  theoretical wisdom 65–6
Kurukṣetra 7, 11 n.12

latitude in ethical action 148–9
law and virtue 112–14
legal justice 121–2
love 24–7, 197
lower self/*deha* 79–81

manas. *See* mind/*manas*
Manusmṛiti 133–6
material aspects 228
the Mean 114–17, 118–20
meditation/*dhyāna yoga* 140
Mill, John Stuart 137–8
mind-as-sense 70–1
mind-as-will 63
mind/*manas* 61–4
misfortune 187, 213–14
mokṣa 138–42, 229
moral intentionality 59–60, 99–100
moral virtues 22, 23

natural justice 121–2
Nātya Śastra 228–9
Nicomachean Ethics. *See also* Aristotle
  cross-cultural conversation 3–6
  dharma 207–8
  ethical action 2–3
  ethnical intentionality 13–30
  influence by Plato and Socrates 1
  introduction to 6–7
  priority and circumscription of *dharma* and virtue 150–1
  similarities and differences with *Bhagavad Gītā* 1
non-rational desire 14, 15, 27–9, 101–2, 108–9

organized change 216

past lives 82
paths/*yogas* 158–62, 162–4
perfection/*teleia* 191–3
personal identity 219–23
personality 40–1, 81–2, 102–3
personality traits 83–7, 87–8
personhood 40–1, 81–2, 102–3
philia 36
Plato 214
pleasure 19, 181–2, 194–6, 228–9
Plotinus 5
potentiality 219
practical and theoretical intellects 43–5
practical knowledge 51

practical virtue 199–200
practical wisdom 118–19
predispositions/*ceṣṭas* 80
Priam 186–8
process 219
productive knowledge 51
prohairesis 18
proslaboûsa 18
Providence/*daivaṁ* 79–80
puruṣa 78, 96 n.1, 157–8

rajas 83–7, 88, 89–92
Rāmānuja 78–9, 167–9, 176 n.10
rational desire 14, 15, 27–9, 101–2, 109
rational love 25–6, 33 n.26
rationality 108–11, 148–9, 180–4, 199
relation of the ethical and political 147–8
remorse 109
renunciation, life of 162
right rule 118–19
rule of law 112–14, 120–2

sage 92–5
saṁkhya/theory 158–62, 162–4, 173–4, 224–5
Śaṇkara 78–9, 88, 168–70, 176 n.11, 176 n.12
sattva 84–7, 88, 89–92
self/*Ātman* 164
self-friendship 35, 36
self-governance 49–51
self-knowledge 156–8, 165–7, 170, 171, 176 n.6
self-love 35, 39, 40, 46–9
self-sufficiency 188–9
selfing 215–16
sense-control 69–71, 91
skill 51–5
skopos 16, 18, 21, 31 n.9
smṛiti 128–9
Socrates 17, 19, 40, 115, 116
soul/form 222–3
Spinoza 5, 6
śruti 128–9
stability 55
Stoics 5
strands/*guṇas* 83–7, 87–8
substantialism 216–17, 221, 223 n.1
supererogatory action 133–6
svadharma 131–2
Svetāśvtāra Upaniṣad (SV) 173–4

tamas 83–7, 88, 101
teleia as final and complete 184–5
teleia as perfect 191–3
telos 16, 18, 21, 31 n.9, 52
theoretical virtue 199–200
theoria. See contemplation/*theoria*
theory. *See saṁkhya*/theory
thinking 192–4, 203–4 n.17
thumos 42
tripartition 41–3, 100–2

universal self/*Brahman* 78–9, 81–2, 156–8
Unmoved Mover 110, 123 n.8
Upaniṣads 160–1, 173–4, 224
utilitarianism 144
utility 19

virtue 6–7, 24–7, 51–5, 112–14, 150–1, 187, 208
virtue friendship 37–8
virtuous action 15–16, 30 n.8, 105, 106–7

weakness-of-will. *See* incontinence
wealth 68, 181, 228
well-doing 212–13
wish 14, 18–20, 29

yogas. *See* paths/*yogas*

www.ingramcontent.com/pod-product-compliance
Lightning Source LLC
Chambersburg PA
CBHW071823300426
44116CB00009B/1410
* 9 7 8 1 3 5 0 2 1 5 1 3 9 *